First SIGHAN Workshop on Chinese Language Processing 2002

Held at COLING 2002

Taipei, Taiwan
1 September 2002

ISBN: 978-1-62748-370-4

Printed from e-media with permission by:

Curran Associates, Inc.
57 Morehouse Lane
Red Hook, NY 12571

Some format issues inherent in the e-media version may also appear in this print version.

Printed by Curran Associates, Inc. (2013)

Association for Computational Linguistics
209 N. Eighth Street
Stroudsburg, Pennsylvania 18360

Phone: 1-570-476-8006
Fax: 1-570-476-0860

acl@aclweb.org

Additional copies of this publication are available from:

Curran Associates, Inc.
57 Morehouse Lane
Red Hook, NY 12571 USA
Phone: 845-758-0400
Fax: 845-758-2634
Email: curran@proceedings.com
Web: www.proceedings.com

TABLE OF CONTENTS

Extraction of Translation Unit from Chinese-English Parallel Corpora

CHANG Baobao
Institute of Computational Linguistics
Peking University,
Beijing, P.R.China, 100871
chbb@pku.edu.cn

Pernilla DANIELSSON and
Wolfgang TEUBERT
Centre for Corpus Linguistics
Birmingham University,
Birmingham, B15 2TT United Kingdom
pernilla@ccl.bham.ac.uk
teubertw@hhs.bham.ac.uk

Abstract

More and more researchers have recognized the potential value of the parallel corpus in the research on Machine Translation and Machine Aided Translation. This paper examines how Chinese English translation units could be extracted from parallel corpus. An iterative algorithm based on degree of word association is proposed to identify the multiword units for Chinese and English. Then the Chinese-English Translation Equivalent Pairs.are extracted from the parallel corpus. We also made comparison between different statistical association measurement in this paper.

Keywords: Parallel Corpus, Translation Unit , Automatic Extraction of Translation unit

Introduction

The field of machine translation has changed remarkably little since its earliest days in the fifties. So far, useful machine translation could only obtained in very restricted domain. We believe one of the problems of traditional machine translation lies in how it deals with unit of translation. Normally Rule-Based Machine Translation system takes word as basic translation unit. However, word is normally polysemous and therefore ambiguous, which causes many difficulties in selecting proper target equivalent words in machine translation, especially in translation between unrelated language pairs, such as Chinese and English. On the other hand, human translation is rarely word-based. Human translators always translate group of words as a whole, which means human do not view words as the basic translation units, and it seems they view language expressions that can transfer meaning unambiguously as basic translation units instead. Following this observation, we believe translation unit shall be not only words but also words groups (Multi-Word Unit) and a collection of bilingual translation unit will be certainly a very useful resource to machine translation.

Manual compilation of such a database of translation unit is certainly labor intensive. But following the recent progress in Corpus Linguistics, especially in parallel corpus research such as Gale,W. (1991), Tufis,D. (2001), Wu, D., Xia, X.(1994). Automatic identification of translation unit and its target equivalents from existed authentic translation might be a feasible solution; at least it can be used to produce a candidate list of bilingual translation unit.

As a first step towards building a database of bilingual translation units, we selected the Hong Kong Legal Documents Corpus (HKLDC) as the parallel corpus for the feasibility study. This paper elaborates the methods we adopted. We will first give our model of (semi-) automatic acquisition of bilingual translation unit based on parallel corpora in section 1. Then we will show how the corpus could be preprocessed in section 2. In section 3, several statistic measurements will be introduced which will serve as a basis for late steps in extracting of bilingual translation units. Section 4 will focuses on identification of multi-word units. Section 5 will describe how translation equivalents could be extracted. In section 6, we give some evaluation regarding to the performance in extracting the translation equivalent pairs.

1 Framework of automatic acquisition of

bilingual translation unit

The whole process of identification of bilingual translation unit could be further divided into three major steps as depicted in Figure 1.

(1) Preprocessing of the parallel corpora

For the purpose of extracting bilingual translation unit, some prior processing of the corpus is necessary. These include alignment of the bilingual texts at sentence level and unilingual annotation of the Chinese and English texts respectively.

(2)Identification of multi-word unit in the aligned the texts

As we mentioned before, translation unit shall not be only single words, but also multi-word units. In this step, Both the Chinese and English multi-word units are identified separately from the corpus.

(3) Extraction of the bilingual translation units

After identification of the multi-word units for texts of both languages, this step tries to set the correspondence between Chinese and English translation units. The result of this step will be a list of bilingual Translation Equivalent Pairs and every TEP is composed of a Chinese Translation unit and an English Translation unit.

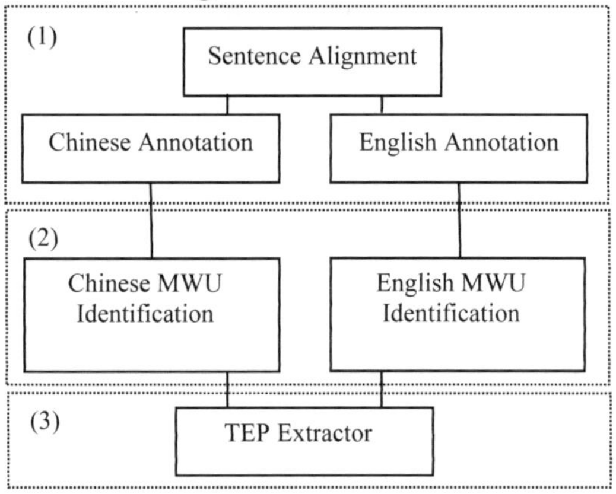

Figure 1. Framework of translation unit acquisition

2 Preprocessing the corpus

The Hong Kong legal documents were collected from Internet. The corpus is composed of laws and amendments issued by the Hong Kong Special Administration Region (HKSAR) during. All the texts in it are in both Chinese and English. We selected about 6 million words of both Chinese texts and English words (6,833,762 Chinese words and 6,391,919 English words).

All the Chinese texts in the corpus are encoded with Big-5 code. Since all our Chinese tools can only deal with Chinese GB code. We firstly converted all the Chinese texts from Big-5 code into GB code. Then the Corpus was aligned with a length-based sentence aligner. For the legal documents have been already well arranged with section by section, which makes the sentence alignment much easier and the precision is high. The Chinese texts were then segmented and pos-tagged with a program developed by the institute of Computational linguistics, Peking University. And all the English Texts were tokenized, lemmatized, and pos-tagged with a freely available tree-based tagger. Two tag sets were used for Chinese and English respectively, ICL/PKU tag set for Chinese texts and UPENN tag set for English texts. Figure 2. shows a sample of the corpus after preprocessing.

```
Chinese texts         English Texts
…                     …
<s id=5>              <s_id=5>
本       r            This       DT    this
条例     n            Ordinance  NN    ordinance
可       d            may        MD    may
…                     …
通则     n            General    JJ    general
条例     n            Clauses    NNS   clause
》       w            Ordinance  NN    ordinance
。       w            .          .     .
<s id=6>              <s_id=6>
附注     n            Remarks    NNS   remark
：       w            :          :     :
…
```

Figure 2. Samples of the corpus after preprocessing

In Figure 2., both corpus was arranged one token per line. The XML-like tag <s> marks the start of the sentence. The single-letter tags right to the Chinese tokens are their part of speech tags. The two columns right to the English tokens are part of speech tags and lemmas.

3 Statistical measurement used

Four statistical measurements were used in identification of unilingual multi-word units and the correspondences of the bilingual translation units. All four statistical formulas measures the degree of association of two random events.

Given two random events, X and Y, they might be two Chinese words appears in the Chinese texts and two translation units appears in an aligned region of the corpus. The distribution of the two events could be depicted by a 2 by 2 contingency table.

	Y	$\neg Y$
X	a	b
$\neg X$	c	d

Figure 3. A 2 by 2 contingency table

The numbers in the four cells of the table has the following meanings:

a : all counts of the cases the two events X and Y co-occur.

b : all counts of the cases that X occurs but Y does not

c : all counts of the cases that X does not occur but Y does

d : all counts of the cases that both X and Y do not occur

Based on the above-mentioned contingency table, different kinds of measurements could be used. We have tried four of them, namely, point-wise mutual information, DICE coefficient, χ^2 score and Log-likelihood score. One other measurement used by Gale(1991) is ϕ^2 score, which is equivalent to the χ^2 score. All the four measurements could be easily calculated using the following formula.

(1) Point-wise mutual information

$$MI(st,tt) = \log_2 \frac{n \times a}{(a+b)\times(a+c)}$$

(2) DICE coefficient

$$DICE(st,tt) = \frac{2a}{(a+b)\times(a+c)}$$

(3) χ^2 score

$$\chi^2(st,tt) = \frac{n\times(a\times d - b\times c)^2}{(a+b)\times(a+c)\times(b+d)\times(c+d)}$$

(4) Log-Likelihood score

$$LL(st,tt) = 2\times(a\times\log\frac{a\times n}{(a+b)\times(a+c)} + b\times\log\frac{b\times n}{(a+b)\times(b+d)}$$

$$+ c\times\log\frac{c\times n}{(c+d)\times(a+c)} + d\times\log\frac{d\times n}{(c+d)\times(b+d)})$$

4. Identification of multi-word units

What might constitute multi-word units is probably a question critical to identification of them. It seems rational to assume Multi-word units are something between phrases and words, which might have the following properties:

1) The component words of a multi-word unit should tend to co-occur frequently. In the significance of statistics, multi-word unit should be word group that co-occur more frequently than expectation.
2) Multi-words units are not arbitrary combinations of arbitrary words; they shall form valid syntactic structure in the meaning of linguistics.

Based on the above-mentioned observations, we used an iterative algorithm using both statistical and linguistics means. The algorithm runs as follows: firstly the algorithm tries to find all word pairs that show strong coherence. This could be done using the measurements listed in section 3. After this step, all the word pairs in both of Chinese texts and English Texts whose association value is greater than a predefined threshold are marked. But this can only list of word groups of length of 2. Word groups of length more than 3 words could not be found by only one run of the algorithm. But apparently they could be found by a series of runs until there are no word groups having greater association value than the threshold anymore. The algorithm is designed as recursive structure, it marks longer word groups by viewing the shorter word group marked in the previous run as one word.

It is no doubt that pure statistics cannot perform very reliable. Some word groups found by the algorithm are awkward to be accepted as multi-word unit. The result of the algorithm shall be viewed as a candidate list of multi-words units. Some kind of refinement of the results might be required. For thinking that multi-word unit shall form valid syntactic pattern, we use a filter module which check all the word groups found and see if they fall into a set of predefined syntactic patterns.

"a+n",	"NN+NN",
"b+n",	"NN+NNS",
"n+n",	……
…	"NN+IN<of>"
"MWU+n",	"JJ+NN",
"n+MWU",	…
"MWU+MWU"	"MWU+MWU"

Figure 4. Syntactic patterns

Figure 4. shows some patterns used by the filter. Patterns in the left side are for Chinese while the right side for English.

5. Extracting of the bilingual translation units

We adopt the same hypothesis-testing approach to set the correspondence between the Chinese-English translation units. It follows the observations that words are translation of each other are more likely to appear in aligned regions(Gale,W. (1991), Tufis,D. (2001)). But we also take the multi-word units into consideration.

The whole procedure could be divided logically into two phases. The first phase could be called a generative phase, which lists all possible translation equivalent pairs from the aligned corpus. And the second phase can be viewed as a testing operation, which selects the Translation Equivalent Correspondences show an association measure higher than expected under the independence assumption as translation equivalence pairs. Again we use DICE coefficient, point-wise mutual information, LL score and χ^2 score to measure the degree of association.

One of problems of above-mentioned approach is its inefficiency in processing large corpus. Because in the generative phase, the above-mentioned approach will list all translation equivalent pairs and can lead to huge search space. To make the approach more efficient, we adopted the following assumption: Source translation units tend to be translated into translation units of the same syntactic categories. For example, English nouns tend to be translated into Chinese nouns, and English pattern "JJ+NN" tend to be translated into Chinese pattern "a+n" or "b+n". Apparently, this assumption is not always true for translation of Chinese into English and vice versa. But it really makes the algorithm much more efficient while the precision does not fall severely.

6. Experiments and Results

We have performed some preliminary experiments to test the performance of different statistic measurements, performance change when the categorial hypothesis is used.

For the experiments, we used a very small portion of the corpus of 500 sentence pairs. Figure 5. show the performance of Chinese MultiWord Unit Identification, we count how many correct MWUs are there in the first hundred of candidate MWUs produced by the program.

	MI	DICE	LL	χ^2
Correct	63	31	76	74
Incorrect	37	69	24	26
Accuracy	63%	31%	76%	74%

Figure 5. Performance variations of different statistical measurements for identification of MWU

Figure 6 shows the performance of the TEP extraction using different statitical means. we count how many correct and partially correct correspondences there are in the first hundred of translation equivalent pairs produced by the algorithm.

	MI	DICE	LL	χ^2
Correct	39	5	70	75
Partially correct	5	1	10	6
Accuracy	44%	6%	80%	81%

Figure 6. Performance variations of different statistical measurements for TEP extraction

Both Figure 5. and Figure 6 shows LL score and χ^2 score achieves better accuracy over mutual information and DICE coefficient.

Experiments also show the categorial hypothesis might lead to fall in accuracy, we did tests on the above-mention 500 sentence pair corpus using the hypothesis, the precision fall by 4% but the efficiency improved by more than 200%.

Figure 7. shows a sample of extracted translation equivalent pair from the test corpus. Some of them are wrong(see no 2), but most of them are correct translation equivalent pairs.The numbers in the right are χ^2 scores

1. 见 see /* 496.471 */
2. 追溯力_的 see /* 496.471 */
3. 款 subsection /* 496.237 */
4. 废除 repeal /* 495.814 */
5. 命令 order /* 493.195 */
7. 豁免 exemption /* 490.829 */
25. 附属_法例 subsidiary_legislation /* 477.173 */
26. 公共_机构 public_body /* 475.711 */
28. 财政司_司长 Financial_Secretary /* 475.711 */
31. 条例 ordinance /* 470.081 */
34. 基本_文书 primary_instrument /* 468.068 */
41. 卫生_主任 health_officer /* 468.068 */
42. 裁判官 magistrate /* 468.068 */
43. 担当 discharge /* 468.068 */
45. 合约 contract /* 468.068 */
46. 终审_法院_首席_法官 Chief_Justice_of_Final Appeal /* 468.068 */
53. 香港_特别_行政区 Hong_Kong_Special_Administrative_region /* 448.576 */
63. 审裁处 tribunal /* 420.579 */
64. 宣布 declare /* 420.579 */

Figure 7. sample of results extracted from the corpus

Conclusion

As we see in the last section, the approach used in this paper does really list many real translation equivalent pairs from the corpus. It seems not all the results could be taken as translation units, but it really offers a candidate list from which useful translation unit could be selected by means of human validation. For a complete evaluation of the approach, large scale experiments are still needed, which are now underway.

Acknowledgements

We would like to give our thanks to Professor Dan Tufis. His help in the lexical alignment and suggestions are very important for our work. We also would like to give thanks to all our colleagues who help us in many kinds of forms.

References

Teubert,W.(1997). Translation and the corpus, proceedings of the second TELRI seminar, 147-164.

Gale,W. (1991). Identifying words correspondences in parallel Texts, DARPA speech and Natural language workshop. Asilomar, CA.

Tufis,D. (2001), Computational bilingual lexicography: automatic extraction of translation dictionaries, In Journal of Information Science and Technology, Romanian Academy, Vol. 4, No. 3

Maynard, D., Term Recognition using Combined Knowledge Sources, PH. D. thesis, Manchester University, United Kingdom.

Yu Shiwen, Specification of Chinese text segmentation and POS tagging, see: http://www.icl.pku.edu.cn/research/corpus/coprus-annotation.htm

Manual of Upenn Tree bank tag set, see: http://www.cis.upenn.edu/~treebank/

Wu, D., Xia, X.(1994), Leaning an English-Chinese Lexicon from a Parallel Corpus, in AMTA-94, Association for MT in the Americas, Columbia, MD

Some Considerations on Guidelines for Bilingual Alignment and Terminology Extraction

Lawrence Cheung, Tom Lai, Robert Luk[§], Oi Yee Kwong, King Kui Sin, Benjamin K. Tsou

Language Information Sciences Research Centre
City University of Hong Kong
Tat Chee Avenue, Kowloon, Hong Kong
{rlylc, cttomlai, rlolivia, ctsinkk, rlbtsou}@cityu.edu.hk

[§]Department of Computing
Hong Kong Polytechnic University
Hung Hom, Kowloon, Hong Kong
csrluk@comp.polyu.edu.hk

Abstract

Despite progress in the development of computational means, human input is still critical in the production of consistent and useable aligned corpora and term banks. This is especially true for specialized corpora and term banks whose end-users are often professionals with very stringent requirements for accuracy, consistency and coverage. In the compilation of a high quality Chinese-English legal glossary for ELDoS project, we have identified a number of issues that make the role human input critical for term alignment and extraction. They include the identification of low frequency terms, paraphrastic expressions, discontinuous units, and maintaining consistent term granularity, etc. Although manual intervention can more satisfactorily address these issues, steps must also be taken to address intra- and inter-annotator inconsistency.

Keyword: legal terminology, bilingual terminology, bilingual alignment, corpus-based linguistics

1. Introduction

Multilingual terminology is an important language resource for a range of natural language processing tasks such as machine translation and cross-lingual information retrieval. The compilation of multilingual terminology is often time-consuming and involves much manual labour to be of practical use. Aligning texts of typologically different languages such as Chinese and English is even more challenging because of the significant differences in lexicon, syntax, semantics and styles. The discussion in the paper is based on issues arising from the extraction of bilingual legal terms from aligned Chinese-English legal corpus in the implementation of a bilingual a text retrieval system for the Judiciary of the Hong Kong Special Administrative Region (HKSAR) Government.

Much attention in computational terminology has been directed to the development of algorithms for extraction from parallel texts. For example, Chinese-English (Wu and Xia 1995), Swedish-English-Polish (Borin 2000), and Chinese-Korean (Huang and Choi 2000). Despite considerable progress, bilingual terminology so generated is often not ready for immediate and practical use. Machine extraction is often the first step of terminology extraction and must be used in conjunction with rigorous and well-managed manual efforts which are critical for the production of consistent and useable multilingual terminology. However, there has been relatively little discussion on the significance of human intervention. The process is far from being straightforward because of the different purposes of alignment, the requirements of target users and the corpus type. Indeed, there remain many problematical issues that will not be easy to be resolved satisfactorily by computational means in the near future, especially when typologically different languages are involved, and must require considerable manual intervention. Unfortunately, such critical manual input has often been treated as an obscure process. As with other human cognitive process (T'sou et al. 1998), manual terminology markup is not a straightforward task and many issues deserve closer investigation.

In this paper, we will present some significant issues for Chinese-English alignment and term extraction for the construction of a bilingual legal glossary. Section 2 describes the background of the associated bilingual alignment project. Section 3 discusses the necessity of manual input in bilingual alignment, and some principles adopted in the project to address these issues. Section 4 provides an outline for further works to improve terminology management, followed by a conclusion in Section 5.

2. High Quality Terminology Alignment and Extraction

2.1 Bilingual Legal Terminology in Hong Kong

The implementation of a bilingual legal system in Hong Kong as a result of the return of sovereignty to China in 1997 has given rise to a need for the creation and standardization of Chinese legal terminology of the Common Law on par with the English one. The standardization of legal terminology will not only facilitate the mandated wider use of Chinese among legal professionals in various legal practices such as trials and production of legal documentation involving bilingual laws and judgments, but also promote greater consistency of semantic reference of terminology to minimize ambiguity and to avoid confusion of interpretation in legal argumentation.

In the early 90's, Hong Kong law drafters and legal translation experts undertook the unprecedented task of translating Hong Kong Laws, which are based on the Common Law system, from English into Chinese. In the process, many new Chinese legal terms for the Common Law were introduced. On this basis, an English-Chinese Glossary of legal terms and a Chinese-English Glossary were published in 1995 and 1999 respectively. The legal terminology was vetted by the high level Bilingual Laws Advisory Committee (BLAC) of Hong Kong. The glossaries which contain about 30,000 basic entries have become an important reference for Chinese legal terms in Hong Kong. The Bilingual Legal Information System (BLIS) developed by the Department of Justice, HKSAR provides simple keyword search for the glossaries and laws that are available in both Chinese and English. Nevertheless, the glossaries are far from being adequate for many different types of legal documentation, e.g. contracts, court judgments, etc. One major limitation of the BLIS glossary is its restricted coverage of legal terminology in the Laws of Hong Kong, within a basically prescriptive context as when the laws were studied at the time of its promulgation. There are other important bilingual references (Li and Poon 1998, Yiu and Au-Yeung 1992, Yiu and Cheung 1996) which focus more on the translation of Common Law concepts. These are almost exclusively nominal expressions.

In 2000, the City University of Hong Kong, in cooperation with the Judiciary, HKSAR, initiated a research project to develop a bilingual text retrieval system, Electronic Legal Documentation/Corpus System (ELDoS), which is supported by a bilingually aligned corpus of judgments. The purpose of the on-going project is twofold. First, the aligned legal corpus enables the retrieval of legal terms used in authentic contexts where the essence and spirit of the laws are tested (and contested) in reality, explicated and elaborated on, as an integral part of the evolving and defining body of important precedent cases unique to the Common Law tradition. Second, the corpus covers judgment texts involving interpretation of different language styles and vocabulary from Hong Kong laws. The alignment markup also serves as the basis for the compilation of a high-quality bilingual legal term bank. To complete the task within the tight timeframe, a team of annotators highly trained in law and language are involved in alignment markup and related editing.

2.2 Need for Human Input

The legal professionals which are the target users of ELDoS have very stringent demands on terminology in terms of *accuracy*, *coverage* and *consistency*. Aligned texts and extracted terms must therefore be carefully and thoroughly verified manually to minimize errors. Furthermore, many studies on terminology alignment and extraction deal predominantly with nominal expressions. Since the project aims to provide comprehensive information on the manifestations of legal vocabulary in Chinese and English texts, the retrieval system should not restrict users to nominal expressions but should also provide reference to many other phenomena such as alternation of part-of-speech (POS) (e.g. noun-verb alternation) inherent in bilingual texts, as will be seen in Section 3.

The availability of bilingual corpora has made it possible to construct representative term banks. Nonetheless, current alignment and term extraction technology are still considered insufficient to meet the requirements for high quality terminology extraction. In ELDoS project, many issues are difficult to be handled satisfactorily by the computer in the foreseeable future. Although human input is essential for high quality term bank construction, the practice of manual intervention is not straightforward. Indeed, the manual efforts to correct the errors can be substantial, and the associated cost should not be underestimated. The annotator must first go through the entire texts to spot the errors and terms left out by the machines. In this process, both the source and target materials have to be consulted. The annotator must also ensure the consistency of the output. As a result, guidelines should be set up to streamline the process.

3. Aspects of Terminology Alignment

The approach adopted for the manual annotation of alignment markup and the maintenance of term bank in the ELDoS project will be described. Additional caution has been taken in the coordination of a team of annotators.

3.1 Term Frequency

An important reason for manual intervention in bilingual term alignment is the relatively poor recall rate for low frequency terms. Many extraction algorithms make use of statistical techniques to identify multi-word strings that frequently co-occur (Wu and Xia 1995; Kwong and Tsou 2001). These methods are less effective for locating low frequency terms. Of the 16,000 terms extracted from ELDoS bilingual corpora, about 62% occur only once in about 80 judgments. For high quality alignment and extraction, failure to include these low frequency terms would be totally unacceptable.

3.2 Correspondence of Aligned Units

Because of the different grammatical requirement and language style, a term in the source language often differs in different ways from the corresponding manifestations in the target language. These differences could be alternation of POS and the use of paraphrastic expressions. Although many term banks avoid such variations and focus primarily on equivalent nominals or verbs, the correspondence of terms between two typologically different languages is often more complicated. For example, the English nominal ("fulfilment") is more naturally translated into Chinese as a verb ("不履行", "拒絕履行", "悔約"). More examples can be found in Table 1.

Alternation of POS

English	Chinese	POS alternation
The accused	被告	det + adj ~ noun
hold	裁決	verb ~ noun
fulfillment	履行	noun ~ verb
administration	承辦	noun ~ verb
repudiation	不履行	noun ~ neg + verb

Table 1. Alternation of POS

In some cases, there are simply no equivalent words in the target language. Paraphrasing or circumlocution may be necessary. Such correspondence is far less consistent and obvious to be identified by the computer.

Paraphrasing/Circumlocution

English	Chinese
The judge **entered judgment in favour of** the respondents in respect of their claim for arrears of wages, and severance payment.	法官**判**答辯人的欠薪及遣散費索償**勝訴**。
In our view,…	**我等認爲**…
…**evidenced** by the Defendant's letter …	…由原告人所簽署確認的函件中**可獲得證據**…

Table 2. Examples of paraphrasing

Because of language differences, legal terms can be contextually realized as anaphors in the target language. Examples of such correspondence would be useful for legal drafting and translation. Again, such anaphoric relations are more accurately handled by humans.

Anaphoric Relation

English	Chinese
He was subsequently charged…	**申請人**後來檢控…
Liu JA dealt with that application on 14 March 1996 and dismissed **it**.	上訴法庭法官廖子明於1996年3月14日聆訊並撤銷**該項申請**。
Enforcement of a Convention award may also be refused if the **award** is in respect of a matter which is not capable of settlement by arbitration.	如**公約裁決**所關乎的事項，是不能藉仲裁解決，…則亦可拒絕強制執行該裁決。

Table 3. Examples of anaphors

3.3 Discontinuous Units

Most term extraction algorithms deal with contiguous units, e.g. *n*-gram. These algorithms would be problematical in handling discontinuous units. They include phrasal verbs (e.g. "strike out"), collocation patterns (e.g. "lodge three complaints", "被判…罪名成立"). These have to be manually added or edited. Interestingly, our preliminary study shows that over 90% of the instances of discontinuous units are found in the Chinese manifestation of English terms. Some examples are listed in Table 4.

English	Chinese
convict …	**被判…罪名成立**
The Court of Appeal **allowed** the tenant's appeal	上訴法庭曾**判決**租客上訴**得直**
The agreement **kept** the company **alive**	協議**使**公司能夠**繼續運作**
If the Defendant **misrepresented** to the Plaintiff that what he was signing was only…	倘若被告人**錯誤向**原告人**表示**他簽署的只是…

Table 4. Examples of discontinuous units

3.4 Selective Markup

To avoid producing "uninteresting" term alignment, restricting markup to only terms of the interested domain would be an attractive alternative to full-text alignment. In the ELDoS project, it is possible to mark up only legal terminology. Other non-legal elements can be omitted in alignment annotation. This approach has been accepted by the ELDoS client. Some examples of legal and non-legal terms are shown in Table 5.

Legal Terms			Non-legal Terms		
1	alibi evidence	不在犯罪現場證據	1	collar	領
2	order nisi	暫准命令	2	finger	手指
3	prima facie	表面	3	question	問題

Table 5. Legal vs. Non-legal Terms

However, many other terms are more ambiguous. There is often no hard and fast rule to set criteria for domain membership. Annotators would have to rely on their own individual judgement to decide whether an expression should be counted as a legal term. For example, the English words listed in Table 6 are not used exclusively in the legal domain. However, taking into account their frequency, legal context and the multiple renditions in Chinese, they are worthy of being considered as "semi-legal." What is interesting about "I" is that though the pronoun is a common pronoun, the corresponding Chinese manifestation "本席" is used exclusively in the judgments and should be regarded as legal. These examples suggest that the decision to classify a phrase as a legal term involves a great deal of complications.

Semi-Legal Terms	
impose	制定, 頒下, 判, 訂下, 訂定
terms	措詞, 措辭, 條文, 條款, 觀點
waive	放棄, 寬免, 豁免
I	本席

Table 6. Semi-legal Terms

Selective markup, however, could give rise to intra- and inter-annotator inconsistency. The vagueness of legal terms could lead to variation in the selection of the same term at different times and among different annotators. In ELDoS project, computer-aided markup tools that can instantly check candidate expressions against the term bank is an effective reference for annotators to maintain consistency. Those terms that are found in term bank should be included in the alignment. In this way, the term bank can serve as a working standard for annotators. As for new terms, our annotators have adopted the principle that whenever they have doubts as to domain membership of a new term, they should include the term in the alignment. In this way, all the candidate terms are guaranteed to be available for the term bank manager for final decision. Inter-annotator differences can also be reduced by fostering more communication among annotators such as regular review of peer work.

3.5 Granularity

Term granularity is another major issue not only for machines but also for humans. The terminology list should be as simple and compact as possible to avoid redundancy of entries. For example, instead of having "allegations", "corruption", "allegations of corruption", "allegations of manslaughter" as separate entries, it is preferable to treat only "allegations", "corruption" and "manslaughter" as glossary entries. The annotators have adopted the principle that a term should be a minimal semantic unit.

Here "semantic unit" refers to single- or multi-word terms that have acquired specialized meaning or usage. For example, the phrase "great and general importance" 重大而廣泛重要性 has been used frequently as a frozen chunk, and should not be further divided into "great", "and", "general" and "importance". Similarly, "oral decision" 口頭判詞 refers to the verbal delivery of judgments in trial as opposed to written judgments. Such decisions involve the support of real-world knowledge and sophisticated semantic/pragmatic interpretation and are not easily modelled by the computer.

4. Further Works

Bilingual terminology extracted directly from the bilingual corpora bear the form as it is in the text corpora. English words with different morphological markers will give rise to multiple entries in the resulting glossary. However, from the user's point of view, verbs with the same root but different inflectional markers (e.g. "hold", "held", "holding") should be combined to form one single entry. Similarly, variants of Chinese expressions that differ simply by an optional markers 的 *de* (see Table 7) may better be treated as the same item to minimize redundancy.

English	Chinese
lawful attorney	1. 合法受權人 2. 合法的受權人
order nisi	1. 暫時命令 2. 暫時的命令
presumption in law	1. 法律上推定 2. 法律上的推定

Table 7. Chinese renditions differed by 的 *de*

Term bank management tools will be developed to process the morphological markers and combine related pairs.

5. Conclusion

In this paper, we have studied the importance of human intervention in the preparation of aligned corpus and bilingual terminology, particularly when the specialized language resource and users are involved. Their demand for high quality alignment and terminology gives rise to a number of issues that are difficult, if not impossible, to be dealt with satisfactorily by the computer. These issues include the extraction of low frequency terms, the identification of equivalent units with different POS or paraphrases, discontinuous units, consistency of term granularity, etc. Though human intervention is far more effective in attaining accurate linguistic processing, if not properly planned, it could also suffer from intra- and inter-annotator inconsistency. Regular peer review and appropriate markup checking tools will be essential to minimize inconsistency.

Acknowledgements

This study is supported through the Hong Kong Judiciary contract (#RCL/0794) and the Research Grants Council of Hong Kong under Competitive Earmarked Research Grant (CERG) No. 9040570. We specially thank the Judiciary of HKSAR for providing authentic judgments for this study. Our thanks also go to the team of alignment annotators who provided interesting examples for this paper.

References

Borin, L. (2000) You 'll Take the High Road and I'll Take the Low Road: Using a Third Language to Improve Bilingual Word Alignment. *Proceedings of COLING 2000*, pp. 97—103.

Huang, J.-X. and K.-S. Choi. (2000) Chinese-Korean Word Alignment Based on Linguistic Comparison. *Proceedings of the 38th Annual Conference of the Association for Computational Linguistics*, pp. 392—399.

Kwong, O. Y. and B. K. Tsou. (2001) Automatic Corpus-Based Extraction of Chinese Legal Terms. *Proceedings of the 6th Natural Language Processing Pacific Rim Symposium (NLPRS 2001)*, pp 669—676, Tokyo, Japan.

Li, Z. E. and E. Poon. (1998) *English-Chinese Dictionary of Law*. Hong Kong: Commercial Press.

T'sou, B. K., H. L. Lin, S. W. K. Chan and T. B. Y. (1998) "Cognitive Variation in Cross Straits Perception of Salient Information", in B. K. T'sou, T. B. Y. Lai, S. W. K. Chan and W. S-Y. Wang (Eds.), *Quantitative and Computational Studies on the Chinese Language*, Language Information Sciences Research Centre, City University of Hong Kong, pp.31-56.

Wu, D. and X. Xia. (1995) Large-scale Automatic Extraction of an English-Chinese Translation Lexicon. *Machine Translation* 9 (3-4): 285—313.

Yiu, T.-W. and Z.-Q. Zhang. (1996) *English-Chinese Dictionary of Commercial Law*. Hong Kong: Commercial Press.

Yiu, T.-W. and P.-K. Au-Yeung. (1992) *A Glossary of Law for Hong Kong*. Hong Kong: Commercial Press.

Developing Guidelines for the Annotation of Anaphors in the Chinese Treebank

Susan Converse
CIS, University of Pennsylvania
spc@linc.cis.upenn.edu

Abstract

This paper describes the *CTB Coreference Annotation Guidelines* for annotating pronominal anaphoric expressions in the Penn Chinese Treebank. The goals of the annotation are: to provide training data for learning-based pronoun resolution tools, and to provide a "gold" standard to be used in the evaluation of pronoun resolution algorithms. The choices that were made concerning the coindexing of pronominal anaphors and their antecedents are discussed, as are some questions that arose in trying to categorize those pronominal expressions that did *not* refer to specific nominal entities in the text.

1 Introduction

This paper describes the *CTB Coreference Annotation Guidelines* for annotating the pronominal anaphoric expressions in the Penn Chinese Treebank (CTB). The purpose of the annotation is twofold: to provide training data for learning-based pronoun resolution tools, and to provide a "gold" standard to use in evaluating the outputs of pronoun resolution algorithms.

There were two annotation tasks: coindexing anaphors with NP antecedents whenever possible, and classifying the non-coindexable anaphors into categories. While the coindexing of pronominal anaphors (including the zero pronoun) with their antecedents (or postcedents) was fairly straightforward, the categorization of those pronominal expressions that did *not* refer to nominal entities in the text raised a some questions which are discussed below.

2 What we are annotating

Annotations were made to the parsed files of the June, 2001 corrected release of the Penn Chinese Treebank (Xia et al., 2000). Example 1 shows a sample of the annotation, with both

```
(IP (NP#2-TPC (ADJP (JJ 国有))
              (NP (NN 企业)))
    (NP-SBJ (NN 负债))
    (VP (VV 高达)
        (QP-OBJ (CD 七千亿)(CLP (M 元)))))
(PU ，)
(IP (NP-SBJ (NP#2 (PN 其))   overt pronoun "their"
            (NP (NN 产品)(NN 质量)))
    (VP (ADVP (AD 也))
        (VP (VV 参差不齐))))
(PU ，)                                  dropped subject
(IP (NP#2-SBJ (-NONE- *pro*))             zero pronoun
    (VP (IP-CND
             (NP#EXT-SBJ (-NONE- *pro*)) zero that
             (VP (ADVP (CS 如))      does not co-refer
                 (VP (VE 无)
                     (NP-OBJ (NN 改进)))))
        (PU ，)
        (ADVP (AD 很))(ADVP (AD 难))
        (PP-LOC (P 在)
                (NP (NN 海外)(NN 市场)))
        (VP (VV 参与)
            (NP-OBJ (NN 竞争)))))
```

The debt of state-owned enterprises has reached as high as 700 billion yuan, and **their** product quality is uneven. If there is no improvement, **they** will will find it very difficult to participate in the competition in overseas markets.

Example 1: Sample of the annotation.

an overt pronoun 其 ("their" in this context), and a zero pronoun "*pro*" referring to a nominal entity. The coindexation (**#2**) will be discussed in Section 4 and the annotation **#EXT** on the second *pro* will be discussed below in Section 5.1.3.

2.1 Which anaphoric expressions

Consistent with work in English (e.g., (Dagan and Itai, 1991; Ge et al., 1998; Lappin and Leass, 1994; Morton, 2000)), only third-person pronouns and demonstratives were chosen to be annotated. The pronouns include reflexives (e.g., 自己/"oneself"), reciprocals (e.g., 彼此/"one another"), and possessives. For the possessives, the only distinct possessive forms are 其 and 之 (both "its/his/hers/theirs"), which are annotated. Ordinary third-person pronouns in possessive constructions are annotated just as they would be in other contexts.

Unlike English, however, Chinese is a pro-drop language, and there are zero pronouns in addition to the overt ones. For pro drop, the *Bracketing Guidelines* for the CTB (Xue and Xia, 2000) specify use of the string "*pro*" (*small pro*) to explicitly denote a zero pronoun in a dropped subject or dropped object position in a parse tree.

Not all empty subject positions in the CTB parses are the result of pro drop, however. The *Bracketing Guidelines* specify use of the string "*PRO*" (*big PRO*) when there is a non-overt subject in a clause that is the complement of a control verb, such as 决定/"decide" (subject control) or 使/"cause" (object control)[1].

The *Guidelines* (Section VI.4) also state that *PRO* is to be used as the non-overt subject in "non-finite clauses," typically clauses that are themselves sentential subjects. Big *PRO* is in complementary distribution with lexicalized constituents[2], while *pro* is not so restricted.

The coreference annotation task only deals with the zero pronouns, or small *pro*, in the CTB parses. The big *PRO*s are ignored, just as they are in a coreference task in English.

2.2 What kind of antecedents

We specify that anaphors are to be coindexed only with entities that are represented in the text by lexicalized noun phrases, or in some cases quantifier phrases, QPs.

Antecedent entities that must be inferred, or antecedents that are events or propositions, for example, cannot be coindexed with any overt NP, and are to be labeled with one of the categories described in Section 5.

[1]Note that *pro* and *PRO* do not represent movement. Movement is denoted using other empty category labels. Refer to the *Bracketing Guidelines*, Section VI: "Null Elements."

[2]This is consistent with Government and Binding Theory. See, for example, (Haegeman, 1994).

3 Two tasks: coindexing and categorizing

As in other languages, pronouns not only are used to refer to explicit nominal phrases in the text, but also are used discourse deictically and in an existential manner. In addition, they can refer to nominal entities that are not explicitly mentioned in the text, but that are available through inference.

The approach taken to annotation was therefore twofold.

The first task was to classify each overt pronoun, demonstrative, and small pro either as a coindexable anaphor that was coreferential with a noun phrase that explicitly appeared in the text, or as an anaphor that belonged to one of a set of categories of non-coindexable anaphors. The second task was to assign indices to the coindexable anaphors and their antecedents.

We will first describe the questions that arose in the coindexation task, then discuss the categorization of the non-coindexable pronouns.

4 Choices in coindexing overt nominal antecedents

4.1 Nesting level

When NPs are nested, such that an embedded NP refers to the same entity as the NP that contains it, there is a choice between annotating the head NP at the lowest level *vs.* annotating the top NP. The choice to annotate high, rather than at the head NP, was made for two reasons. One was that the head may be automatically recovered from the parent. The second was that including the modifying material uniquely identifies entities that are different but that have identical lexical heads.

In Example 2, the overt NPs that are tagged with the indices #3 and #4 have identical head NPs, but one is actually a subset of the other.

4.2 NP apposition

The only exception to annotating high was in a particular kind of construction with NP apposition, namely those NP-APP that had the pattern

```
(NP (NP-APP (title/descriptive phrase))
    (NP (name)))
```

In that case, either the title or full descriptive NP alone referred to the same entity denoted by the name, and the taggers were asked to annotate both the NP-APP and the head NP containing the name.

In more complex appositive constructions, the NP-APP usually was a list, ending in **etc.**, of sample members of a set that was denoted by the head noun. Since the list was exemplary, rather than definitive, NPs containing such lists were to be annotated only at the parent level. That is, the NP-APP constituent was treated as another modifier, rather than as a referent.

4.3 NP-Predicate constructions

When the antecedent of a pronoun, demonstrative, or *pro* is a subject that is followed by the copula 是 or 为 and a predicate NP (NP-PRD) with *definite* reference, then the annotators were instructed to put the entity's index not only on the subject, but also the NP-PRD. Example 3 illustrates this.

Analogous to this, there are verbs that establish identity between their subjects and objects, usually after a change of state. These verbs are words like "become" (成为) or "establish" (建成). When subjects in these constructions were antecedents, the annotators were asked to index any NP-OBJ with definite reference as well.

Example 4 shows one such instance with the verb 成为/"become."

4.4 Quantifier phrases

Although syntactically, quantifier phrases (QPs) occur in the same contexts as NPs in the CTB, they are not necessarily equivalent in their semantic usage. While an NP denotes an entity, a QP usually denotes the value of a quantifiable property or attribute of an entity, rather than the entity itself.

Note that in Example 2 the QP-OBJ "109.82 billion US$" in the first clause was not annotated. Entity #3 is "the value of imports and exports", and the extent of that value is 109.82 billion at one particular time. But the measure does not uniquely denote the entity.

On the other hand, quantifier phrases may sometimes be abbreviated expressions denoting a particular set of entities, in which case the QP constituent is annotated as if it were an NP.

Example 5 illustrates such a case. The QP#1-SBJ is shorthand for 七十家企业/"70 enterprises".

```
(IP(NP#3-SBJ
      (CP(WHNP-1 (-NONE- *OP*))
          (IP (NP#2-SBJ (-NONE- *pro*))
              (VP (NP-TMP (NT 去年))                last year
                  (VP (VV 实现)                      realize
                      (NP-OBJ (-NONE- *T*-1))))))
      (NP (NN 进出口)                        imports+exports
          (NN 总值)))                            total value
   (VP (VV 达)                                         reach
       (QP-OBJ (CD 一千零九十八点二亿)             109.82 B
               (CLP (M 美元)))))                         US$
(PU ，)
(IP(NP-SBJ
      (CP (WHNP-2 (-NONE- *OP*))
          (CP (IP (NP#3-SBJ (-NONE- *pro*))
                  (VP (VV 占)                            stand
                      (NP#4-OBJ (NP (DP (DT 全))
                                    (NP (NN 国)))
                                      entire country
                                (NP (NN 进出口)
                                    (NN 总值)))
                                  imports+exports
                                      total value
                      (NP-EXT (-NONE- *T*-2))))
              (DEC 的)))
      (NP (NN 比重)))                                proportion
   (VP (VRD (VV 提高)(VV 到))                         rise up to
       (QP-OBJ (CD 百分之三十九)))))                      39%
```

NP#2 is 外商投资企业/"foreign-owned enterprises"

The **value of imports and exports** that they realized last year reached 109.82 billion US$. The proportion that this represented in the **value of imports and exports** of the entire country rose to 39%.

Example 2: Annotating parent instead of head NP.

```
(IP (NP#2-PN-SBJ (NR 崇明))
    (VP (VC 是)
        (NP#2-PRD (NP-PN (NR 中国))
                  (QP (OD 第三))
                  (ADJP (JJ 大))
                  (NP (NN 岛))))
```

Chongming is China's third largest island

Example 3: NP-PRD with definite reference.

5 Categorizing non-coindexable anaphors

As mentioned above, not all pronominal expressions are coreferential with overt NP/QP constituents that denote specific nominal entities.

```
(IP(NP#2-SBJ (-NONE- *pro*))
   (VP(VV 成为)
      (NP#2-OBJ (DNP(NP (NP-PN (NR 无锡市))
                        (NP (NN 经济)
                            (NN 发展)))
                    (DEG 的))
                (ADJP (JJ 主))
                (NP (NN 骨架)))))
```

NP#2 is 超亿元产值的大型企业/"large-scale enterprises with production value exceeding 100 M yuan"

They have become the backbone of Wuxi Municipality's economic development

Example 4: Predicative NP-OBJ.

```
(IP (NP-SBJ (ADJP (JJ 入区))
            (NP (NN 企业)))
    (VP (QP-PRD (CD 一百二十二)
                (CLP (M 家)))))
(PU ，)
(IP (NP#EXT-SBJ (-NONE- *pro*))
    (VP (ADVP (AD 已))
        (VP (VE 有)
            (IP-OBJ
                (QP#1-SBJ (CD 七十)
                          (CLP (M 家)))
                (VP (VV 拥有)
                    (NP-OBJ
                        (DNP(NP#1 (PN 自己))
                            (DEG 的))
                        (NP (NN 产品))))))))
```

Enterprises entering the region number 122, and already **there** are **seventy** that have their own products.

Example 5: An annotated quantifier phrase and an existential subject.

An attempt was made to classify these "non-coindexable" anaphors.

We therefore defined a set of categories with which to label those anaphors that could not be coindexed. Table 1 provides a brief summary of the categories. A discussion of each category follows.

5.1 The straightforward cases

5.1.1 AMB: ambiguous

This category is intended to identify cases in which a particular anaphor, whether an overt lexical item or a zero pronoun, could have more than one possible interpretation, depending on the understanding of the reader. The ambiguity may be between two or more possible NP antecedents in the text for example, or it may be between an entity denoted by an NP in the text and an entity that is not lexicalized but can be inferred.

5.1.2 DD: discourse deictic

Pronouns are often used to refer to events or propositions as well as to entities. When an anaphor refers to an event or proposition or to the meaning of an entire span of text, then it is labeled **DD**, for *discourse deictic.* Note that in addition to the demonstratives 这/"this" and 此/"this" that one would expect to be used for this purpose, there were situations in which *pro* was tagged with this label as well.

5.1.3 EXT: existential

Analogous to pleonastic constructions in English, the verbs (没)有/"(not)have" and 无/"without" in Chinese can be used in an "existential" manner. When they are, they have the part-of-speech tag VE[3]. The label **EXT** is used to tag *pro* when it is the subject of one of these verbs (and the verb has the reading "there are" or "there are no"). Examples 1 and 5 contain *pro*'s annotated in this way.

5.1.4 INFR: inferrable

The coindexing task is very restricted in that the only antecedents that can be assigned indices are NP constituents in the same document that denote the same entity that the anaphor refers to. The label **INFR** is to be used when the anaphor refers to an entity that is not itself explicitly lexicalized in the text, but can be inferred from the context or using real-world knowledge. The entity must be a particular nominal entity, not a generic "anyperson" or "anything" with arbitrary reading (see Section 5.2, below).

For example, the pronoun 他们/"they" might be used to refer to the people in charge of some place/institution, but the only overt NP in the text is the place/institution itself. The real antecedent of the pronoun, a reference to the people themselves, is not overtly mentioned in the text, so the anaphor would be labeled INFR.

[3] VE denotes a verb in an existential construction. Refer to the CTB *Bracketing Guidelines*, Section IV.4.1.

Table 1: Categories for pronouns that do not have a specific or clear coreferent

AMB	**ambiguous**: for anaphors that can have more than one possible antecedent, depending on the interpretation of the text
DD	**discourse deictic**: the pronominal expression refers to an event, situation, or proposition rather than to a nominal entity
EXT	**existential**: a *pro* that is the subject of an existential (VE) 有 or 无 or 存在
INFR	**inferrable**: a pronoun or *pro* that refers to a particular nominal entity that is not explicitly lexicalized in the text, but that can be *inferred* from the text
ARB	**arbitrary**: a *pro* that does not refer to a specific entity that can be inferred from or is lexicalized in the text, but instead takes an "arbitrary" reading

5.2 More subtle cases of *pro*

5.2.1 The choice of the category ARB

The above categories describe the manifestations of discourse phenomena that are familiar to English speakers as well as to Chinese speakers. The final category applies only to small *pro*, and is more specific to the phenomena observed in the parses in CTB-I.

In the first version of the guidelines, there were five categories: the four just mentioned, plus an "ANONymous" category that was meant to account for arbitrary dropped subjects in titles or slogans (analogous to the use of "one" in English). During the initial adjudication meetings, however, it became clear that there were occurrences of small *pro* that did not fall neatly into any of the five proposed categories.

Many of these *pro*'s appeared in subordinate constructions that functioned like English infinitives and gerundive clauses, and they frequently could *not* be replaced by any overt NP, even a pronoun. For these reasons, a sixth category, labeled UNTNS for untensed, was added to the guidelines in an attempt to capture a meaningful category of dropped subjects.

Unfortunately, adding this category caused more problems than it solved. First, it was too hard to clearly define. The reason it was difficult to define is the same reason that the question of a finite *vs.* non-finite distinction in Chinese is so problematic: there is no reliable diagnostic of (non-)finiteness in Chinese (and, some would argue, no non-finite/finite distinction at all (Hu et al., 2001)).

In the absence of diagnostic tests, the *Guidelines* described the category using sample syntactic structures. Although there are a few syntactic structures such as sentence-initial purpose clauses that appear to be "prototypical" untensed constructions, there are many more structures that require more subjective judgements.

Second, even if a diagnostic test for UNTNS were available, there were two basic difficulties with adding the UNTNS category. The first problem was that just as big PRO can be coindexed (e.g., in subject or object control contexts), in a similar way the *pro* in the "untensed" syntactic structures could sometimes be coindexed with an NP. This presented a problem with consistently annotating such a *pro*: should it be coindexed or marked UNTNS?

The second difficulty with just adding UNTNS to the coreference *Guidelines* was that both of the categories ANON and UNTNS contained *pro*'s with arbitrary reference, and there was no clean way to differentiate them. A diagnostic that an ANON *pro* could be substituted by an overt NP was not sufficient.

As a result of these two overlaps (UNTNS that could be coindexed, and arbitrary references in both ANON and UNTNS), there was reliably poor inter-annotator agreement in annotating *pro*'s belonging to these categories.

To simplify the categorization, therefore, the decision was made on the one hand to replace the ANON and the UNTNS categories with the single category ARB (for "arbitrary"), and on the other hand to instruct the annotators to always coindex a *pro* when possible. That is, any *pro* that can be coindexed, whether or not it appears in an "infinitival" or "gerundive" construction, and whether or not it can be replaced by an overt NP, should be coindexed. Only those *pro*'s that have arbitrary readings, with no possible specific or inferrable

```
(IP(PP (P 据)                                    according to
      (IP (NP#ARB-SBJ (-NONE- *pro*))
          (VP (VV 认为))))                          understand
  (PU ，)
  (NP-SBJ (DNP (NP (DP (DT 此)                            this
                       (CLP (M 次)))                         M
                   (NP (NN 访问)))                        visit
               (DEG 的))                                    DE
          (NP (NN 目的)))                                 goal
  (VP(VC 是)                                                is
     (PP-PRD
       (P 为了)                                    in order to
       (IP (NP#ARB-SBJ (-NONE- *pro*))
           (VP
             (VP (VV 加强)                          strengthen
                 (NP-OBJ
                   (ADJP (JJ 双边))                 both sides
                   (NP (NN 经贸)                   econ.+trade
                       (NN 合作))))                cooperation
             (PU ，)
             (VP (VV 扩大)                              expand
             ...                                          etc.
```

It is understood that the purpose of this visit is to strengthen bilateral economic and trade cooperation and to expand ...

Example 6: Arbitrary reference and zero subject of untensed clause.

antecedent, will be marked **ARB**.

With respect to training a tool to do automatic coreference resolution of *pro* this annotation decision will overgenerate coindexed *pro*'s in the data, since some of them probably should actually be big *PRO*s. Against that negative are the pluses of easier choices for the annotators and better inter-annotator agreement.

5.2.2 Some examples

There are cases in which a small *pro* does not refer to a single, specific entity, but could be replaced by an overt, generic expression, such as 某人/"someone" or 我们/"we" in the general sense. Example 6 illustrates one such situation in the complement of a sentence-initial PP. The same example illustrates another use of ARB in a clause that could be considered "infinitival".

An example of a *pro* in an untensed construction that *can* be coindexed is shown in Example 7. It is usually possible to coindex a *pro* in these clause-initial modifiers at the sentence level with the matrix subject. The

```
(IP (PP-PRP
      (P 为)                                      in order to
      (IP (NP#4-SBJ (-NONE- *pro*)) (former UNTNS)
          (VP (VV 规范)                            standardize
              (NP-OBJ (NN 建筑)                   construction
                      (NN 行为)))                     behavior
    (PU ，)
    (NP#4-SBJ (NN 新区)                             new region
              (NN 管委会)) management committee
    (VP (VV 出台)(AS 了)                             announced
      ...
```

In order to standardize the construction procedures, the management committee of the new region announced ...

Example 7: Sentence-initial purpose clause.

```
(IP (IP-SBJ (NP#ARB-SBJ (-NONE- *pro*))
            (VP (VV 利用)
                (NP-OBJ (NN 外资))))
    (VP (VV 趋向)
        (NP-OBJ (NN 多元化))))
(PU ，)
(IP (NP-SBJ (QP (CD 大批))
            (NP (NN 特区)(NN 企业)))
    (VP (VV 走向)
        (NP-OBJ (NP (NN 国际)
                    (NN 资本)
                    (NN 市场))
                (ADJP (JJ 直接))
                     (NP (NN 融资)))))
```

The use of foreign capital is showing a trend toward diversification, and a large number of enterprises in the special zone are entering the international capital market for direct financing.

Example 8: An untensed IP-SBJ.

most common clauses with dropped subjects in this position are sentence-initial purpose clauses with 为/"in order to" and adverbial IPs with verbs like 利用/"utilize".

Example 8 illustrates a *pro* subject of an IP that is itself the matrix subject.

Pre-verbal modifier prepositional phrases with IP complements, like the sentence-level adverbials, sometimes act like infinitives and sometimes like gerunds. Some have *pro* subjects that can be coindexed, often with the matrix subject (such as benefactive prepositional phrases headed by 为/"for"). Others, such as manner PPs with 以/"using" appear less likely to be coindexable.

6 Annotation process/status

Initially 40 files were annotated by two native speakers of Mandarin, both from Taipei, Taiwan. One is a trained linguist, the other is a computer science graduate student who has taken a syntax course. In the process of annotating and adjudicating, the *Guidelines* were revised, to broaden the definition of INFR from a more narrow interpretation and to add the UNTNS category and distinguish it from the ANON category.

Those *Guidelines* were used by two annotators to independently annotate all the remaining files in CTB-I for coindexation only. The annotators are two native speakers who are trained linguists. One is from the Peoples Republic of China, the other is the linguist from Taiwan who did the first 40 files.

The *Guidelines* were again recently revised to document the replacement of ANON and UNTNS by ARB and the choice to coindex whenever possible. These changes are currently being integrated into "gold" files as the files that already have been coindexed are adjudicated.

A third native speaker from the PRC is independently annotating a portion of CTB-I using this last revision of the *Guidelines*, and her annotations will be compared to the "gold" files to calculate some inter-annotator agreement numbers for this last version of the *Guidelines*.

7 Future work

The CTB-I is a rather limited corpus, both in size (100K words) and in linguistic structures. It is very declarative and concrete, and thus the range of figurative language and "messy" linguistic phenomena is relatively restricted. For example, there were no examples of object drop in the CTB-I, although there are examples in CTB-II.

The expectation is that when a more balanced corpus is tagged, the *Guidelines* will need to be refined with more specific instructions concerning the handling of such things as more complex plural antecedents, quoted speech, metonymy, and other figurative expressions.

8 Acknowledgements

Many thanks to Fu-dong Chiou, Nianwen Xue, Szu-ting Yi, Jennifer Chia, Betsy Klipple, and Martha Palmer.

References

Ido Dagan and Alon Itai, 1991. *A Statistical Filter for Resolving Pronoun References*, pages 125–135. Elsevier Science Publishers.

Niyu Ge, John Hale, and Eugene Charniak. 1998. A statistical approach to anaphora resolution. In *Proceedings of the Sixth Workshop on Very Large Corpora*, pages 161–170, University of Montreal, August.

Liliane Haegeman. 1994. *Introduction to Government & Binding Theory*. Blackwell, Cambridge, MA, 2nd edition.

Jianhua Hu, Haihua Pan, and Liejiong Xu. 2001. Is there a finite vs. nonfinite distinction in Chinese? *Linguistics*, 39:1117–1148.

Shalom Lappin and Herbert Leass. 1994. An algorithm for pronominal anaphora resolution. *Computational Linguistics*, 20(4):535–561. Lappin and Leass note to test.

Thomas S. Morton. 2000. Coreference for nlp applications. In *Proceedings of the 38th Annual Meeting of the Association for Computational Linguistics*, pages 173–180, Hong Kong, October.

Fei Xia, Martha Palmer, Nianwen Xue, Mary Ellen Okurowski, John Kovarik, Fu-Dong Chiou, Shizhe Huang, Tony Kroch, and Mitch Marcus. 2000. Developing guidelines and ensuring consistency for Chinese text annotation. In *Proceedings of the Second International Conference on Language Resources and Evaluation (LREC-2000)*, Athens, Greece, May 30.

Nianwen Xue and Fei Xia. 2000. *The Bracketing Guidelines for the Penn Chinese Treebank Project*. Number 00-08. Technical Report, Institute for Research in Cognitive Science, University of Pennsylvania. **http://www.ldc.upenn.edu/ctb/**.

Finding the Better Indexing units for Chinese Information Retrieval

Hongzhao He
Department of Computer Science and Engineering, Tianjin University
Weijin Road, Tianjin University
Tianjin, China, 300070
hehongzhao@hotmail.com

Pilian He
Department of Computer Science and Engineering, Tianjin University
Weijin Road, Tianjin University
Tianjin, China, 300070
plhe@tju.edu.cn

Jianfeng Gao
NLC, Microsoft Research Asia
No.49, Zhichun Road, Haidian District
Beijing, China, 100080
jfgao@microsoft.com

Changning Huang
NLC, Microsoft Research Asia
No.49, Zhichun Road, Haidian District
Beijing, China, 100080
cnhuang@microsoft.com

Abstract

In the processing of Chinese documents and queries in information retrieval (IR), one has to identify the units that are used as indexes. Words and n-grams had been used as indexes in several previous studies, which showed that both kinds of indexes lead to comparable IR performances. In this study, we carried out more experiments to find the better way to index Chinese texts. First, we investigated the inpacts on IR performance of the accuracy of word segmentation. Second, fifteen different groups of indexing units, which were the possible combination of words and character n-grams, were discussed detailedly. Experiments showed that better segmentation results in better IR performances, and a combination of words with uni-grams is the better choice to index Chinese texts for IR.

Introduction

It is well known that the major difference between Chinese information retrieval (IR) and IR in European languages lies in the absence of word boundaries in sentences. As Chinese sentences are written as continuous character strings, a preprocessing has to be done to segment sentences into shorter units that may be used as indexes. Those units may be of two kinds: words or character n-grams (simplifed as n-grams hereafter). In the previous studies, several experiments had been carried out using these two kinds of indexing units (Nie et al, 1996) (Kwok et al, 1996) (Chen et al, 1997) (Hsiao, 1997) (Gao et al, 2001a) (Shi et al, 2001). It turns out that these two kinds of units are effective in Chinese IR.

However, several problems have not been fully investigated: Does the accuracy of word segmentation have a significant impact on IR performance? Is it worthwhile to combine words with n-grams in Chinese IR? How should this be done? These are the questions we will examine in this study. A series of tests will be conducted on TREC and NTCIR-2 collection. This is a step forward to find a good way to index Chinese texts.

The remainder of this paper is organized as follows: In Section 1, we provide a brief survey of Chinese word segmentation. In Section 2, we discuss in detail of Chinese IR indexing units. In section 3, experimental results are presented. Finally, we present our conclusion.

1 Chinese Word Segmentation

1.1 Chinese Language

Chinese language is based on characters. There are 6763 frequently used Chinese characters.

Each Chinese word is a semantic concept that is about 1.6 characters on average. But there is no standard lexicon (or dictionary) of words -- linguists may agree on some tens of thousands of words, but they will dispute tens of thousands of others.

Furthermore, sentences are written without spaces between words. So a sequence of characters will have many possible segmentation in the word tokenization stage.

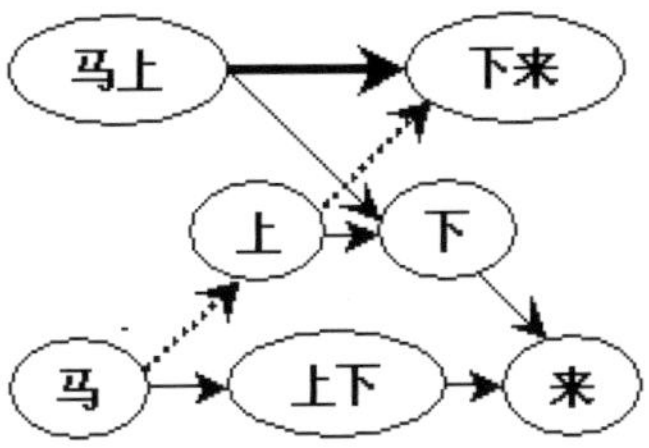

Figure 1: The word graph of Chinese sentence "马上下来"(Gao et al, 2001b)

Figure 1 shows the tokenization of a simple sentence with only four characters. Here, these four characters can be segmented in five ways into words. For example, the dotted path represents "*dismounted a horse*", and the bolded path represents "*immediately coming down*". This figure also shows seven possible "words", some of which (e.g., 上下) might be disputable on whether they should be considered "words".

Large amount of methods of Chinese word segmentation have been proposed to deal with these kinds of difficuties of Chinese.

1.2 Previous Methods for Chinese Word Segmentation

The segmentation of Chinese sentences into words requires linguistic knowledge. Several types of knowledge may be used: manually constructed dictionary which stores a set of known words, heuristic rules on word formation, or some statistical measures based on cooccurrences of characters. These three types of knowledge may be combined in different ways. For example, an approach based on a dictionary often uses also a set of heuristic rules. A statistical approach may also incorporate a set of heuristic rules.

Various experiments have been carried out on different segmentation approaches in the past 16 years. There is no one single approach shown to be clearly superior to the others. Most elaborated approaches can achieve a segmentation accuracy of over 90%. This performance has been believed to be sufficient for IR.

However, does the accuracy of word segmentation have a significant impact on IR performance? In this paper, we will use a special word segmentation system to investigate it.

1.3 Song's Segmentation System

Song's Segmentation System (System S) is a knowledge based system developed by Prof. Song from Beijing University of Language and Culture. The system is one dictionary-based segmentation complemented by a set of heuristic rules (Song, 2001). The basic algorithm is the longest-matching word segmentation algorithm. Several heuristic rules were used to identify such words as proper noun (e.g. 中国移动 – China Mobile)， date expressions (e.g. 一九三四年 – year 1934), suffix structures (e.g. 使用者– user), etc. User can choose different rules they need to get different accuracy word segmentation results by selecting the appropriate switches on the user interface. Thus it is possible for us to investigate the impacts on Chinese IR of those different accuracy word segmentation results.

2 Chinese IR Indexing units

2.1 Different Indexing units for Chinese IR

Generally speaking, there are 2 chategories of Chiense IR indexing units: (1) n-grams and (2) words.

The advantage of n-grams is that it does not require any linguistic knowledge. This is the main reason for using n-grams in Chinese and other Asian languages (Lee and Ahn, 1996) (Ogawa, 1995). A string is simply cut down into units of fixed length. Usually, one uses uni-grams (or characters) and/or bi-grams. For example, a string ABCD (where each letter represents a Chinese character) can be segmented into bi-grams AB BC CD, or uni-grams A B C D.

Words have been the basic units of indexing in traditional IR, which requires linguistic knowledge as mentioned in Section 1.2.

2.2 Possible Indexing units for Chinese IR

There are several kinds of indexing units and their combinations for Chinese IR. In this paper, we divided possible indexing units into three groups of indexing units: (1) basic units; (2) combination of two basic units and (3) combination of more than two basic units.

Four kinds of basic units are investigated in this paper: (1) uni-grams; (2) words; (3) bi-grams and (4) tri-grams. It is also possible to use longer n-grams, e.g. four-grams. However, the cost for indexing in IR would be much higher as there will be a lot more possible units to be considered, thereby increasing the number of indexes. Our experiments show that this additional cost does not seem to be useful for Chinese IR because most meaningful Chinese words are composed of one or two characters (our statistics shows that the average length of words in usage is 1.59). That is to say, these four basic units can cover most of the words sucessfully. Therefore, we do not need to discuss about longer n-grams in this paper.

There are six possible combinatin of two basic units. E.g. the combination of uni-grams and words.

There are five possibe combination of more than two basic units. E.g. the combination of uni-grams, words and bi-grams.

In this paper, we investigate these 15 kinds of indexing units to find the better indexing units of Chinese IR.

3 Experiments and Results

3.1 Test collection

The tests are conducted on the TREC corpus and NTCIR-2 Chinese corpus.

The documents in TREC (Harman and Voorhees, 1996) are articles published in the People's Daily from 1991 to 1993, and a part of the news released by the Xinhua News Agency in 1994 and 1995. A set of 54 queries has been set up and evaluated by people in the NIST (US National Institute of Standards and Technology).

The documents in NTCIR-2 are called CIRB010 (Chinese Information Retrieval Benchmark Version 1). These documents are all news stories downloaded from web sites of Chinatimes, Chinatimes Commercial. Chinatimes Express, Central Daily News, and China Daily News during the period of May 1998 to May 1999 (Chen and Chen, 2001), (Chiang, 1999). A set of 50 queries has been set up and evaluated by people in the NTCIR.

Some characteristics of these corpuses are given in table 1 and table 2.

	Number of doc.	Total Size (megabyte)	Average length per doc.
TREC	164,789	167.4	507 characters
NTCIR-2	132,173	192.1	635 characters

Table 1: Characteristics of the document collection

	Number of queries	Average length per query
TREC	54	119 characters
NTCIR-2	50	167 characters

Table 2: Characteristics of the query collection

3.2 Okapi System

Once Chinese sentences have been segmented in separate items, traditional IR systems may be used to index them. These separate items are called "terms" in IR. For our experiments, We used the Okapi system Windows2000 version for our runs. The system was developed in October 2000. A detailed summary of the contributions to TREC1-9 by the Okapi system is presented in (Robertson and Walker, 1999). In this section, we give a very brief introduction to the system.

In our experiments, the information retrieval evaluation system is called the Okapi Basic Search System (BSS). It is a set-oriented ranked output system designed primarily for probabilistic type retrieval of textual material using inverted indexes. There is a family of built-in weighting scheme functions, known as BM25 and its variants. In this paper, we use BM2500 as the weighting scheme function. In addition to weighting and ranking facilities it has the usual Boolean and quasi-boolean (positional) operations and a number of non-standard set operations. Indexes are of a fairly conventional inverted type. The detailed description can be found in (Gao et al, 2001c)

3.3 Different Accuracy Word Segmentation vs. Chinese IR Performance

As mentioned in Section 1.3, we can use System S to investigate the Chinese IR performance with different accuracy word segmentation results. User can choose different rules they need to get different accuracy word segmentation by selecting the appropriate switches on the user interface.

In order to evaluate the IR performance based on word indexing with different segmentation results, we use a collection (431KB), which have been segmented manually. We call this collection as TT.

Here, we define Accuracy as following:

$$Accuracy = \frac{\#\text{Total Char} - \#\text{Error Char}}{\#\text{Total Char}} \times 100\%$$

where Total Char is the total Chinese characters in the collection and Error Char is the total characters which are segmented incorrectly.

We use TT and TREC collections to do a series of experiments as following:

1. Baseline: we do not choose any switch on the user interface. That is to say, only the longest-matching word segmentation algorithm is used.
2. We only choose the “disambiguity switch” on the user interface. On this condition, several errors of Baseline may be corrected. E.g. 中共/与其/他国/家 (China/rather than/other countries/home) will be corrected as 中共/与/其他/国家 (China/and/other/countries).
3. We only choose the “number switch” on the user interface. On this condition, number expressions will be recgonized. (E.g. 一九三四– 1934).
4. We choose the “propernoun switch” and “number switch” on the user interface. On this condition, propernoun or number experessions will be recgonized. (E.g. 东方红三号– Dong Fang Hong III).
5. We choose the “suffix switch”, “propernoun switch” and “number switch” on the user interface. On this condition, not only propernoun or number experessions but also suffix structures (e.g. 使用**者**– user) will be recgonized.
6. We choose all the switches above. On this condition, we can get the best acurracy segmentation.

Number	Accuracy of TT (%)	Average Precision of TREC (11pt Avg)
1	91.10	0.3729
2	92.48	0.3769
3	92.19	0.3774
4	93.09	0.3719
5	93.09	0.3747
6	94.43	0.3822

Table 3: Different segmentation results vs. Chinese IR performance

In Table 3, the second column showes the accuracy of segmentation and the third column showes the average of 11-points’ precision value, which is the average of precision value on 11 points evenly chosen from 0.0 to 1.0 in the precision-recall curve. Table 3 shows that better segmentation results in better IR performances, but the difference is not significant. The reason is that we can not reach 100% accuracy in word segmentation by now. The segmentation errors may cause noise in some degree, so the improvement of better segmentation may be not significant.

3.4 Different Indexes vs. Chinese IR performance

As we have mentioned in section 2.2, we use NTCIR-2 collection to do a series of experiments [1]. We segment the queries and documents with different indexes as following respectively: (1) uni-grams(U); (2) words(W); (3) bi-grams(B); (4) tri-grams(T); (5) (U+W); (6) (U+B); (7) (U+T); (8) (W+B); (9) (W+T); (10) (BT) ; (11) (U+W+B); (12) (U+W+T); (13) (U+B+T); (14) (W+B+T); (15) (U+W+B+T). Then we use Okapi system to retrieval 15 groups of relevant documents. We use the two kinds of relevance assessment (Relaxed Relevance and Rigid Relevance) to evaluate the results. The standard of Rigid Relevance assessment is stricter than Relaxed Relevance assessment (Chiang, 1999).

No	Units	Relaxed	Rigid
1	U	0.6644	0.6002
2	W	0.7022	0.6485
3	B	0.6837	0.6104
4	T	0.5892	0.4979
5	U+W	0.7296	0.6654
6	U+B	0.7126	0.6369
7	U+T	0.6625	0.5619
8	W+B	0.7064	0.6447
9	W+T	0.6677	0.5837
10	B+T	0.6506	0.5525
11	U+W+B	0.7237	0.6566
12	U+W+T	0.6883	0.5998
13	U+B+T	0.6719	0.5825
14	W+B+T	0.6824	0.5899
15	U+W+B+T	0.6959	0.6099

Table 4: the results of different indexing units

Table 4 shows the average of 11-points' precision value. We can see that almost every kind of indexing units can get satisfied retrieval results in some degree.

[1] Similar experiments were carried out with the TREC collections and got the similar results.

For the four basic units: uni-grams, words, bi-grams and tri-grams, it is clear that the best performance can be obtained when using words as indexing units. Words are the natural indexing units in Chinese IR. Actually, people often use key words to describe the main idea of documents. That is why words is the best one of the four basic indexes.

However, we also noticed that bi-grams may result in a performance comparable to words. It may seem surprising because many bi-grams are meaningless. Notice, however, although many bi-grams are meaningless, if the segmentation results are the same between documents and quries, good retrieval results can still be got. For example, if the word 厄瓜多尔(Ecuador) is in a query, the segmentation result should be 厄瓜/瓜多/多尔 for bi-grams. When the same word appears in a document, the segmentation result should also be 厄瓜/瓜多/多尔, which is the same as the result in the query. Although neither of the bi-grams (e.g. 厄瓜) has actually meaning, the IR system may still retrieval the document successfully for both the document and the query have the same indexing units, which results in the similarity between the document and the query is higher than others.

On the other hand, when use tri-grams as indexing units, the result is not good, which is only 88.68% (Relaxed) and 82.96% (Rigid) of using words. As we mentioned in Section 2.2, the average length of words in usage is 1.59. That is to say, tri-grams do not match the actually words. So its result is not good. Now, we can conclude, that for Chinese IR, it is no worth using tri-grams as indexing units.

However, for uni-grams, the results are not very bad: 94.62% (Relaxed) and 93.52% (Rigid) of using words. It is clear that words are made of characters (or uni-grams). That is to say, we also can use uni-grams to get the needed information in documents. However there are only about 3,000 commonly used Chinese characters. If we only use uni-grams as IR indexes, the search space is quite limited, so the precision may become lower in practical use.

For the combinations of two basic units in column 5 to 10 in table 4, the best indexing units is the combinnation of uni-grams and words.

When we only use the longest-matching word segmentation algorithm to segment Chinese documents and queries for IR, the advantage is that longer words usually describe more precise meanings than shorter words. It could be expected that the retrieval precision (the proportion of relevant documents among those retrieved) may be high. However, as we notice, if a long word contains several short words, then only the long word will be identified as an index. The short words included are ignored. For example, if 操作系统 (operating system) is identified as a word, 操作 (operating) and 系统 (system) will not. In practice, very often, we can also refer to an "operating system" by just "system". Although the word "system" is included in "operating system", it will be considered as a completely independent index from "operating system" by IR systems. The effect of this is the loss in recall, or the phenomenon of silence. That is, some relevant documents will not be retrieved.

When the indexing units are the combination of uni-grams and words, in fact, uni-grams (single characters) may ensure a certain level of recall. Therefore, the combination of uni-grams and words may be a reasonable compromise between precision and recall.

We also noticed that the combination of uni-grams and bi-grams can also get comparable results, which is 97.67% (Relaxed) and 95.72% (Rigid) of the combination of uni-grams and words. As we have mentioned before, bi-grams may result in a performance comparable to words. It is naturally that the combination of uni-grams and bi-grams should result in a performance comparable to the combination of uni-grams and words.

We also investigate other possible combinations of these four basic units. From table 4, we can see that all the results are worse than the combination of uni-grams and words.

We can see clearly that as long as different kinds of indexes are combined, the IR performance increases. Some combinations do not increase much the cost in time and space. This is the case for the combinations of uni-grams and words. There are only about 6 000 Chinese characters in the GB codes. The addition of these characters does not increase much the search vector space, and the cost of indexing and retrieval.

On the other hand, any indexing scheme that involves bi-grams is very costly in both time and space. Virtually, there are 6 000 * 6 000 possible bi-grams in Chinese. Although many of these bi-grams actually do not appear, the number is still much higher than the possible words and characters in Chinese. This will result in a very large vector space, leading to excessive indexing time and space. Compared with the combination of uni-grams and words, there is no advantage for bi-grams, except that it does not require a dictionary. However, it is no longer a problem to acquire a high quality Chinese dictionary nowadays, so the use of bi-grams is not justified.

On the other contrary, user will use query expansion to expand the query to retrieval more related documents. On this condition, words is a convenient choice.

In conclusion, the better indexing units for Chinese IR are combination of uni-grams and words[2].

Conclusion

Many experiments have been done on Chinese IR. However, several problems have not been fully investigated: Does the accuracy of word segmentation have a significant impact on IR performance? Is it worthwhile to combine words with n-grams in Chinese IR? How should this be done?

In this study, we investigated the performance of different accuracy word segmentation results by using System S. The results shows that better segmentation results in better IR performances, but the difference is not significant. The reason is that we can not reach 100% accuracy in word segmentation by now. The segmentation errors may cause noise in some degree, so the

[2] Similar results can be got with the TREC collections.

improvement of better segmentation may be not significant.

In this study, we also made a series of experiments to find the better indexing units for Chinese IR. Our experiments show that words, uni-grams and bi-grams can achieve comparable performances. It is no worth to use tri-grams as indexes in Chinese IR. However, if we consider the time and space factors, then it is preferable to use words (and uni-grams) as indexes.

The previous experiments have tested several indexing methods that turn out to be reasonable for Chinese IR. In this paper, we tested several additional approaches. It turns out that a combination of the longest matching word segmentation algorithm with uni-grams is a good method for Chinese IR. The indexing and retrieval speed is much faster than that with bi-grams.

This series of tests is only the first step of our ongoing research program. In a later stage, Chinese IR will be used as a step in English Chinese cross language IR.

Acknowledgements

Our thanks go to Prof. Song who provide us System S. We also would like to thank Stephen Walker and Stephen Robertson who provide Okapi system to us.

References

Aitao Chen and Jianzhang He (1997) *Chinese Text Retrieval Without Using a Dictionary.* SIGIR 1997.

Chen K.H. and Chen H.H. (2001) *The Chinese Text Retrieval Task of NTCIRII Workshop*. NTCIR Workshop 2 Meeting, pp. 4-15.

Chiang Y.T. (1999) *A study on Design and Implementation for Chinese Information Retrieval Benchmark.* Master Thesis, Department of Library and Information Science, National Taiwan University.

China Times. http://news.chinatimes.com .tw/

Gao J.F., Nie J.Y., Zhang J., Zhou M. and Su Y. (2001a) *TREC-9 CLIR Experiments at MSRCN.* NIST Special Publication.

Gao J.F., Joshua Goodman, Mingjing Li and KaiFu Lee. (2001b) *Toward a unified approach to statistical language modeling for Chinese.* ACM Transactions on Asia Language Information Processing.

Gao J.F., Cao G.H., He Hongzhao, Zhang Min, Nie J.Y., Stephen Walker, Stepen Roberson (2001c) *TREC-10 Web Track Experiment at MSRA.* In TREC10.

Harman, D.K. and Voorhees, E. M. (1996) Eds. *Information Technology: The Fifth Text REtrieval Conference (TREC5),* NIST SP 500-538. Gaithersburg, National Institute of Standards and Technology, 1996.

Kwok, K. L. and Grunfeld, L (1996) TREC-5 English and Chinese Retrieval Experiments using PIRCS, *The Fifth Text REtrieval Conference (TREC5),* 1996.

Lee, J. H. and Ahn, J. S. (1996) *Using n-grams for Korean text retrieval.* Conference on Research and Development in Information Retrieval, ACM SIGIR, Zurich, pp. 216-224.

Nie J.Y., Martin Briseboies and Xiaobo Ren (1996) *On Chinese Text Retrieval.* SIGIR 1996, pp. 225-233.

Ogawa, Y. (1995) *A new characterbased indexing organization using frequency data for Japanese documents.* Conference on Research and Development in Information Retrieval, ACMSIGI*R*, Seattle, pp. 121-129.

Reuy-Lung, Hsiao (1997) *Surveys of Some Critical Issues in Chinese Indexing – Chinese Doument Indexing and Word Segmentation.* SIGIR 1997.

Robertson, S. E., and Walker, S. (1999) *Okapi/Keenbow at TREC8.* In TREC9.

Shi. S.C. et al, (2001) *The Development of Chinese Text Retrieval Technology – from whole Text Retrieval to Knowledge Retrieval Based on Natural Language Processing* (in Chinese), 20th Annual Conference of Chinese Information Association Society, pp. 79-88.

Song Rou, (2001) *Word Segmentation and Its Applications*, Chinese-Japanese Natural Language Processing Joint Research Promotion Conference, Kyoto, 2001

Categorical Ambiguity and Information Content

A Corpus-based Study of Chinese

Chu-Ren Huang, Ru-Yng Chang
Institute of Linguistics, Preparatory Office, Academia Sinica
128 Sec.2 Academy Rd., Nangkang, Taipei, 115, Taiwan, R.O.C.
churen@gate.sinica.edu.tw, ruyng@hp.iis.sinica.edu.tw

1. Introduction

Assignment of grammatical categories is the fundamental step in natural language processing. And ambiguity resolution is one of the most challenging NLP tasks that is currently still beyond the power of machines. When two questions are combined together, the problem of resolution of categorical ambiguity is what a computational linguistic system can do reasonably good, but yet still unable to mimic the excellence of human beings. This task is even more challenging in Chinese language processing because of the poverty of morphological information to mark categories and the lack of convention to mark word boundaries. In this paper, we try to investigate the nature of categorical ambiguity in Chinese based on Sinica Corpus. The study differs crucially from previous studies in that it directly measure information content as the degree of ambiguity. This method not only offers an alternative interpretation of ambiguity, it also allows a different measure of success of categorical disambiguation. Instead of precision or recall, we can also measure by how much the information load has been reduced. This approach also allows us to identify which are the most ambiguous words in terms of information content. The somewhat surprising result actually reinforces the Saussurian view that underlying the systemic linguistic structure, assignment of linguistic content for each linguistic symbol is arbitrary.

2. Previous Work

Assignment of grammatical categories or tagging is a well-tested NLP task that can be reliably preformed with stochastic methodologies (e.g. Manning and Shutz 1999). Depending on the measurement method, over 95% precision can be achieved regularly. But the question remains as to why the last few percentages are so hard for machines and not a problem for humans. In addition, even though over 95% seems to be good scores intuitively, we still need to find out if they are indeed better than the naïve baseline performance. Last but not the least, since natural languages are inherently and universally ambiguous, does this characteristic serve any communicative purpose and can a computational linguistic model take advantage of the same characteristics.

Since previous NLP work on categorical assignment and ambiguity resolution achieved very good results using only distributional information, it seems natural to try to capture the nature of categorical ambiguity in terms of distributional information. This is how the baseline model was set in Meng and Ip (1999), among others. Huang et al. (2002), the most extensive study on categorical ambiguity in

Chinese so far, also uses only distributional information.

Huang et al. (2002) confirmed some expected characteristics of ambiguity with convincing quantitative and qualitative data from the one million word Sinica Corpus 2.0. Their generalizations include that categorical ambiguity correlates with frequency; that verbs tend to be more ambiguous than nouns, and that certain categories (such as prepositions) are inherently more ambiguous.

What is not totally unexpected, and yet runs against certain long-held assumptions is the distribution of ambiguity. It is found that only a small fraction of all words (4.298%) are assigned more than one category. However, in terms of actual use, these words make up 54.59% of the whole corpus. These two facts are consistent with the frequency effect on ambiguity. An interesting fact is that of all the words that can have more than one category, 88.37% of the actual uses are in the default category.

A significant fact regarding Chinese language processing can be derived from the above data. Presupposing lexical knowledge of the lexicon and the default category of each word, a naïve baseline model for category assignment two simple steps: First, if a word has only one category in the lexicon, assign that category to the word. Second, if a word has more than one category in the lexicon, assign the default (i.e. most frequently used) category to that word. Since step 1) is always correct and the precision rate of step 2) depends on the percentage of use of the default category. Huang et al. (2002) estimated the expected precision of such a naïve model to be over 93.65%.

Huang et al.'s (2002) work, however, has its limitation. It takes categorical ambiguity as a lexical attribute. In other words, an attribute is either + or -, and a certain word is either categorically ambiguous or not. For Huang et al. (2002), the degree of ambiguity is actually the distribution of the attribute of being ambiguous among a set of pre-defined (usually by frequency ranking) lexical items. Strictly speaking, this data only shows the tendency of being categorically ambiguous for the set members. In other words, what has been shown is actually:

> Words with higher frequency are more likely to be categorically ambiguous.

The data has noting to say about whether a lexical item or a set of lexical items are more ambiguous than others or not.

A good example of the inadequacy of Huang et al.'s (2002) approach is their measurement of the correlation between number of potential categories and the likelihood of default category to occur.

No. of Categories	Freq. (by type)	Freq. (by token)
2	77.65%	91.21%
3	77.71%	88.39%
4	74.21%	89.50%
5	73.83%	92.43%
6	73.46%	86.09%
7	68.51%	86.09%
Total	77.36%	88.37%

Table 1. Frequency of Default Category

In table one, the number seems to suggest that number of possible categories of a word form is not directly correlated with its degree of ambiguity, since its probability of being assigned the default category is not predictable and remains roughly the same in average. This is somewhat counter-intuitive in the sense that we expect the more complex the information structure (i.e. more possible categories), the less likely that it will be assigned a simple default. Since the methodology is to take distributional information over a large corpus, it is most likely the number shown in table 1 is distorted by the dominance of the most frequent words.

Is there an alternative to pure distributional measurement? Recall that ambiguity is about information content. Hence if the quantity of information content is measured, there will be a more direct characterization of ambiguity.

3. Towards an Informational Description of Categorical Ambiguity

3.1. Degree of Categorical Ambiguity

In this paper, we will adopt Shannon's Information Theory and measure categorical ambiguity by entropy. We define the information content of a sign as its entropy value.

$$H = -(p_0 \log p_0 + p_1 \log p_1 + \ldots + p_n \log p_n)$$

When measuring categorical ambiguity, for a word with n potential categories, the information content of that word in terms of grammatical categories is the sum all the entropy of all its possible categories. We will make the further assumption of that the degree of ambiguity of a word corresponds to the quantity of its information content. The above definition nicely reflects the intuition that the more predictable the category is, the less ambiguous it is. That is, a word that can be 90% predicted by default is less ambiguous than a word that can only be predicted in 70% of the context. And of course the least ambiguous words are those with only one possible category and can be predicted all the time (it information value is actually 0).

3.2. Degree of Ambiguity and Number of Possible Categories Revisited

Armed with a new measurement of the degree of ambiguity for each lexical item, we can now take another look at the purported lack of correlation between number of possible categories and degree of ambiguity. Instead having to choose between type of token as units of frequency counting, we can now calculate the degree of categorical ambiguity for each lexical form in terms of entropy. The entropy of all lexical forms with the same numbers of possible categories can then be averaged. The results is diagramed below:

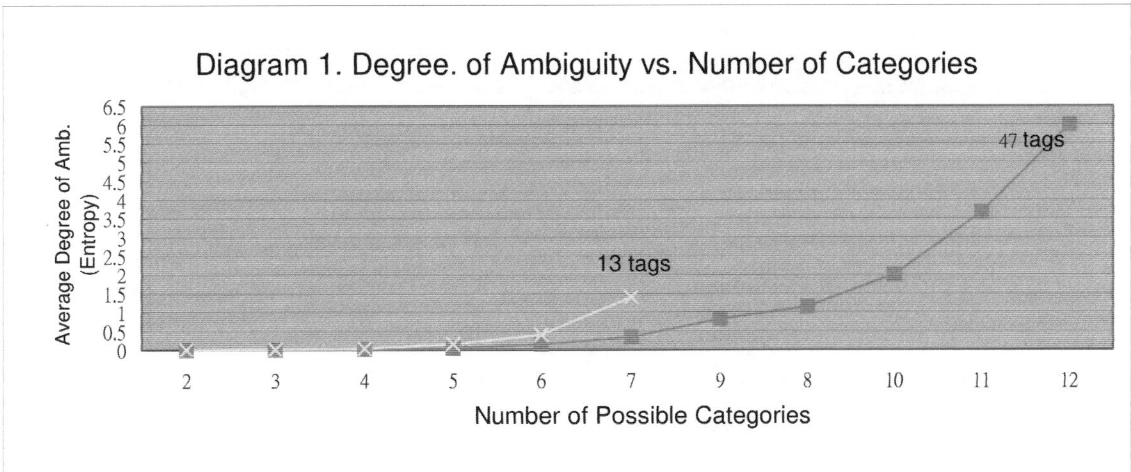

In the above diagram, we can clearly see that whether a 47 tags system or 13 tags system is chosen, the number of potential categories correlates with the degree of ambiguity. The higher number of potential categories a word has, the more ambiguous it is. This correctly reflects previous observational and theoretical predictions.

3.3. Frequency and Degree of Ambiguity

One of the important findings of Huang et al. (2002) was that the likelihood to be ambiguous indeed correlates with frequency. That is, a more frequently used word is more likely to be categorically ambiguous. However, we do not know that, of all the categorically ambiguous words, whether their degree of ambiguity corresponds to frequency or not.

In terms of the number of possible categories, more frequent words are more likely to have larger number of categories. Since we have just showed in last session that larger number of possible categories correlates with degree of ambiguity. This fact seems to favor the prediction that more frequent words are also more ambiguous (i.e. harder to predict their categories.)

Common sense of empirical models, however, suggests that it is easier to predict the behaviors of more familiar elements. Confidence of prediction corresponds to quantity of data. A different manifestation of this feature is that there is a data sparseness problem but never a data abundance problem. In addition, the high precision rate of categorical assignment requires that most frequent words, which take up the majority of the corpus, be assigned correct category at a reasonable precision rate. These two facts seem to suggest that the less frequent words may be harder to predict and hence more ambiguous.

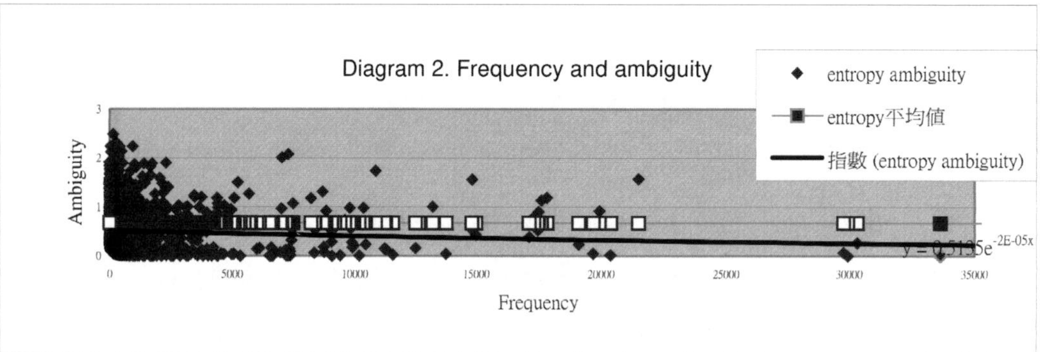

Diagram 2 plots the degree of ambiguity of each ambiguous word in terms of its frequency in the Sinica Corpus (Chen et al. 1996). Not only does the distribution of the degree of ambiguity vary widely, the medium tendency line (thick black line in the diagram) varies barely perceptibly across frequency ranges. As suggested by the two competing tendencies discussed above, our exhaustive study actually shows that there is no correlation between degree of ambiguity and frequency. This generalization can be shown with even more clarity in Diagram 3.

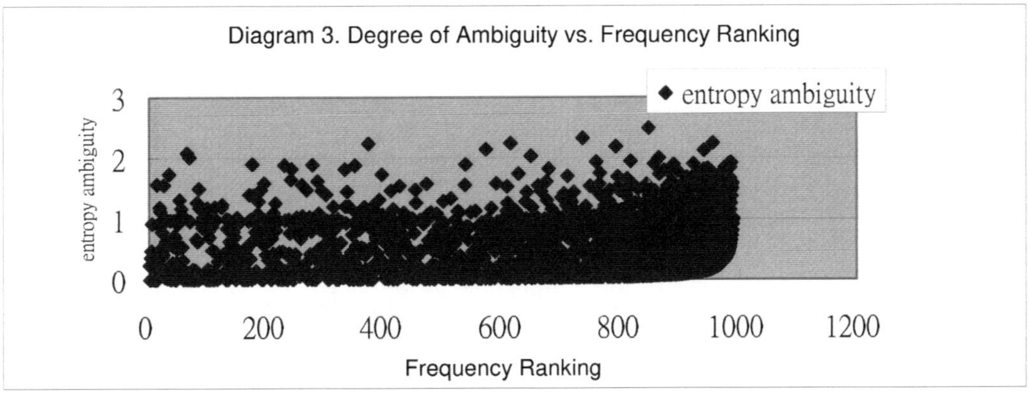

In Diagram 3, entropy value of each word form is plotted against its frequency ranking. When word forms share the same frequency, they are given the same ranking, and no ranking jumps were given after multiple elements sharing the same ranking. Due to the sharing of rankings, the highest rank only goes to 1,000. Diagram 3 shows unequivocally that the range of degree of ambiguity remains the same across different frequency ranges. That is, degree of ambiguity does not correlate to word frequency.

4. Conclusion

In this paper, we propose an information-based measure for ambiguity in Chinese. The measurement compliments the more familiar distributional data and allows us to investigate directly the categorical information content of each lexical word. We showed in this paper that degree of ambiguity indeed correlates with the number of possible categories of that word. However, degree of ambiguity of a word does not correlates with its frequency, although its tendency to be categorically ambiguous is dependent on frequency.

The above findings have very important implications for theories and applications in language processing. In terms of representation of linguistic knowledge, it underlines the arbitrariness of the encoding of lexical information, following Saussure. In terms of processing model and empirical prediction, it suggests a model not unlike the theory of unpredictability in physics. Each word is like an electron. While the behavior of a group of words can be accurately predicted by stochastic model, the behavior of any single word is not predictable. In terms of linguistic theory, this is because there are too many rules that may apply to each lexical item at different time and on different levels, hence we cannot predict exactly how these rules the results without knows exactly which ones applied and in what order. This view is compatible with the Lexical Diffusion (Wang 1969) view on application of linguistic rules.

In NLP, this clearly predicts the performance ceiling of stochastic approaches. As well as that the ceiling can be surpassed by hybriding with specific lexical heuristic rules covering the 'hard' cases for stochastic approaches, as suggested in Huang et al. (2002).

References:

Chen, Keh-jiann, Chu-Ren Huang, Li-ping Chang, and Hui-Li Hsu. 1996. Sinica Corpus: Design Methodology for Balanced Corpora. In. B.-S. Park and J.B. Kim. Eds. Proceeding of the 11th Pacific Asia Conference on Language, Information and Computation. 167-176. http//:www.sinica.edu.tw/SinicaCorpus

Chinese Knowledge Information Processing (CKIP) Group. 1995. An Introduction to Academia Sinica Balanced Corpus for Modern Mandarin Chinese. CKIP Technical Report. 95-01. Nankang: Academia Sinic

Huang, Chu-Ren, Chao-Ran Chen and Claude C.C. Shen. 2002. Quantitative Criteria for Computational Chinese The Nature of Categorical Ambiguity and Its Implications for Language Processing: A Corpus-based Study of Mandarin Chinese. Mineharu Nakayama (Ed.) Sentence Processing in East Asian Languages. 53-83. Stanford: CSLI Publications

Manning Christopher D. and Hinrich Shutze. 1999. Foundations of Statistical Natural Language Processing. Cambridge: MIT Press.

Meng, Helen and Chun Wah Ip. 1999. An Analytical Study of Transformational Tagging for Chinese Text. In Proceedings of ROCLING XII. 101-122. Taipei: Association of Computational Linguistics and Chinese Language Processing.

Schutz, Hinrich. 1997. Ambiguity Resolution in Language Learning: Computational and Cognitive Models. Stanford: CSLI Publications.

Wang, S.-Y. W. 1969. Competing Changes as a Cause of Residue. Language. 45.9-25.

PCFG Parsing for Restricted Classical Chinese Texts

Liang HUANG
Department of Computer Science,
Shanghai Jiaotong University
No. 1954 Huashan Road, Shanghai
P.R. China 200030
lhuang@sjtu.edu.cn

Yinan PENG
Department of Computer Science,
Shanghai Jiaotong University
No. 1954 Huashan Road, Shanghai
P.R. China 200030
ynpeng@sjtu.edu.cn

Huan WANG
Department of Chinese Literature and Linguistics,
East China Normal University
No. 3663 North Zhongshan Road, Shanghai,
P.R. China 200062

Zhenyu WU
Department of Computer Science,
Shanghai Jiaotong University
No. 1954 Huashan Road, Shanghai
P.R. China 200030
neochinese@sjtu.edu.cn

Abstract

The Probabilistic Context-Free Grammar (PCFG) model is widely used for parsing natural languages, including Modern Chinese. But for Classical Chinese, the computer processing is just commencing. Our previous study on the part-of-speech (POS) tagging of Classical Chinese is a pioneering work in this area. Now in this paper, we move on to the PCFG parsing of Classical Chinese texts. We continue to use the same tagset and corpus as our previous study, and apply the bigram-based forward-backward algorithm to obtain the context-dependent probabilities. Then for the PCFG model, we restrict the rewriting rules to be binary/unary rules, which will simplify our programming. A small-sized rule-set was developed that could account for the grammatical phenomena occurred in the corpus. The restriction of texts lies in the limitation on the amount of proper nouns and difficult characters. In our preliminary experiments, the parser gives a promising accuracy of 82.3%.

Introduction

Classical Chinese is an essentially different language from Modern Chinese, especially in syntax and morphology. While there has been a number of works on Modern Chinese Processing over the past decade (Yao and Lua, 1998a), Classical Chinese is largely neglected, mainly because of its obsolete and difficult grammar patterns. In our previous work (2002), however, we have stated that in terms of computer processing, Classical Chinese is even easier as there is no need of word segmentation, an inevitable obstacle in the processing of Modern Chinese texts. Now in this paper, we move on to the parsing of Classical Chinese by PCFG model. In this section, we will first briefly review related works, then provide the background of Classical Chinese processing, and finally give the outline of the rest of the paper.

A number of parsing methods have been developed in the past few decades. They can be roughly classified into two categories: rule-based approaches and statistical approaches. Typical rule-based approaches as described in James (1995) are driven by grammar rules. Statistical approaches such as Yao and Lua (1998a), Klein and Manning (2001) and Johnson, M. (2001), on the other hand, learn the parameters the distributional regularities from a usually large-sized corpus. In recent years, the statistical approaches have been more successful both in part-of-speech tagging and parsing. In this paper, we apply the PCFG parsing with context-dependent probabilities.

A special difficulty lies in the word segmentation for Modern Chinese processing. Unlike Indo-European languages, Modern Chinese words are written without white spaces indicating the gaps between two adjacent words. And different possible segmentations may cause consistently different meanings. In this sense, Modern Chinese is much more ambiguous than those Indo-European Languages and thus more difficult to process automatically (Huang et al., 2002).

For Classical Chinese processing, such segmentation is largely unnecessary, since most Classical Chinese words are single-syllable and single-character formed. To this end, it is easier than Modern Chinese but actually Classical Chinese is even more ambiguous because more than half of the words have two or more possible lexical categories and dynamic shifts of lexical categories are the most common grammatical phenomena in Classical Chinese. Despite of these difficulties, our work (2002) on part-of-speech tagging has shown an encouraging result.

The rest of the paper is organized as follows. In Section 1, a tagset designed specially for Classical Chinese is introduced and the forward-backward algorithm for obtaining the context-dependent probabilities briefly discussed. We will briefly present the traditional two-level PCFG model, the syntactic tagset and CFG rule-set for Classical Chinese in Section 2. Features of the Classical Chinese grammar will also be covered in this section. In Section 3 we will present our experimental results. A summary of the paper is given in the conclusion section.

1 Tagset and Context-Dependent Probabilities

Generally speaking, the design of tagset is very crucial to the accuracy and efficiency of tagging and parsing, and this was commonly neglected in the literature where many researchers use those famous corpora and their tagset as the standard test-beds. Still there should be a tradeoff between accuracy and efficiency. In our previous work (2002), a small-sized tagset for Classical Chinese is presented that is shown to be accurate in their POS tagging experiments. We will continue to use their tagset in this paper. We will also use a forward-backward algorithm to obtain the context-dependent probabilities.

1.1 Tagset

The tagset was designed with special interest not only to the lexical categories, but also the categories of components, namely *subcategories* a word may belong. For example, it discriminates adjectives into 4 subcategories like *Adjective as attributive*, etc. (See table 1). And several grammatical features should be reflected in the tagset. These discriminations and features turn out to be an important contributing factor of the accuracy in our parsing experiments.

Table 1. The tagset for Classical Chinese

n	名词	Noun	楚**人**有直躬
aa	形容词作定语	Adjective as attributive	**楚**人有直躬
aw	形容词作谓语	Adjective as verbal phrase	被甲者**少**也
ab	形容词作表语	Adjective as predicate	仲尼以为**孝**
ad	副词	Adverb	**必**禁无用
vi vt	不跟宾语的动词 跟宾语的动词	Verb without object， Verb with object	知者不**惑** 今**修**文学
conj	连词	Conjunction	君子和**而**不同
yq	语气词	Exclamation	被甲者少**也**
prep	带宾语的介词	Preposition with object	应之**以**乱则凶
prepb	省略宾语的介词	Preposition with object omitted	仲尼**以**[之]为孝
num	数词	Number	虽有**十**黄帝
qpron	疑问代词	Wh-pronoun	则人**孰**不为也?
npron	名词性代词	Noun-pronoun	而人主兼礼**之**。
apron	形容词性代词	Adjective-pronoun	故明主用**其**力。
za	“之”作定语后置标志	*Special for Old Chinese*	乡人**之**善者
zj	“者”作名词性词尾	*Special for Old Chinese*	乡人之善**者**
zd	“之”作“的”	*Special for Old Chinese*	古**之**人不余欺。
fy	发语词	*Special for Old Chinese*	**夫**离法者罪。
conjad	副词性连词	Adverbial conjunction	用之**则**乱法。
Period	终止性标点		。；？！
Comma	停顿性标点		，、：

1.2 Tagging Algorithms

We apply the Hidden Markov Model (HMM) (Viterbi, 1967) and the forward-backward algorithm (James, 1995) to obtain the context-dependent probabilities.

Generally there are 2 types of HMM taggers for parsers, the trigram model and the bigram forward-backward model. Charniak (1996) suggested that the former is better for parsers.

But the former only result in a *deterministic* sequence of most probable POS, in other words, it assigns only *one* POS tag for each word. Although the accuracy of trigram by our previous work (2002) is as high as 97.6%, for a sentence of 10 words long, the possibility of all-correctness is as low as low as $(97.6\%)^{10} = 78.4\%$, and the single-tag scheme does not allow parsers to *re-call* the correct tags, as is often done if we apply the forward-backward model. So in this paper we still apply the traditional bigram forward-backward algorithm. We suggest that a combination of trigram and forward-backward model would be the best choice, although no such attempt exists in the literature.

2 PCFG Model and Classical Chinese Grammar

In this section we will cover the PCFG model and context-sensitive rules designed for Classical Chinese. Features of the rule-set will be also discussed.

2.1 PCFG Model and Rule Restriction

CFG: A context-free grammar (CFG) is a quadruple (V_N, V_T, S, R) where V_T is a set of terminals (POS tags), V_N is a set of non-terminals (syntactic tags), $S \in V_N$ is the start non-terminal, and *R* is the finite set of rules, which are pairs from $V_N \times V^+$, where *V* denotes $V_N \cup V_T$. A rule $< A, \alpha >$ is written in the form $A \to \alpha$, *A* is called the left hand side (LHS) and α the right hand side (RHS).

PCFG: A probabilistic context-free grammar (PCFG) is a quintuple (V_N, V_T, S, R, P), where (V_N, V_T, S, R) is a CFG and $P: R \mapsto (0,1]$ is a probability function such that $\forall N \in V_N : \sum_{\alpha: N \to \alpha \in R} P(N \to \alpha) = 1$

Rule Restriction: We restrict the CFG rules to be binary or unary rules, but ***NOT*** as strict as the Chomsky Normal Form (CNF). Each $R_i \in R$ could be in the following two forms only:

1. $R_i : N_j \to AB$
2. $R_i : N_j \to A$

where $N_j \in V_N$ and $A, B \in V$

The advantage of binary/unary rules lies in the simplicity of parsing algorithm, and will be discussed in Section 4.

The major difference between our model and CNF is that for unary rules, we do not require the right-hand-side to be terminals. And this enables us easier representation of the Classical Chinese language.

2.2 Rule-Set for Classical Chinese

An important advantage of PCFG is that it needs fewer rules and parameters. According to our corpus, which is representative of Classical Chinese classics, only 100-150 rules would be sufficient. This is mainly because our rule set is linguistically sound. A summary of the set of rules is presented as follows.

Table 2. Our non-terminals (also called syntactic tagset, or constituent set)

No.	Tags	Meaning	Examples
1	NP	Noun Phrase	**古之人**不余欺
2	VP	Verb Phrase	古之人**不余欺**
3	S	Sentence	**古之人不余欺。**
4	ADJP	Adjective Phrase	**楚**人有直躬
5	PP	Prepositional Phrase	应之**以乱**则凶
6	PADJP	Post-Adjective Phrase	乡人**之善者**
7	POSTADJP	The main part of PADJP	乡人之**善者**
8	PREDP	Predicate Phrase	仲尼以为**孝。**

A subset of most frequently used rules is shown in the following table.

Table 3. A simple subset of PCFG Rules for Classical Chinese

1.	S ->	NP VP	; simple S/V
2.	S ->	VP	; S omitted
3.	S ->	VP NP	; S/V inversion
4.	S ->	ad S	
5.	VP ->	vi	
6.	VP ->	vt NP	; simple V/O
7.	VP ->	NP vt	; V/O inversion
8.	VP ->	ad VP	
9.	VP ->	PP VP	; prepositioned PP
10.	VP ->	VP PP	; postpositioned PP
11.	VP ->	NP	; NP as VP
12.	VP ->	VP yq	
13.	NP ->	n	
14.	NP ->	npron	
15.	NP ->	ADJP NP	
16.	NP ->	POSTADJP	
17.	NP ->	VP	; V/O as NP
18.	NP ->	fy NP	
19.	ADJP ->	aa	
20.	ADJP ->	apron	
21.	ADJP ->	NP zd	
22.	PP ->	prep NP	; P+NP
23.	PP ->	NP prep	; inversion
24.	PP ->	prepb	; object omitted
25.	PP ->	NP	; prep. omitted
26.	POSTADJP->	VP zj	

Examples of parse trees are shown in the following figure.

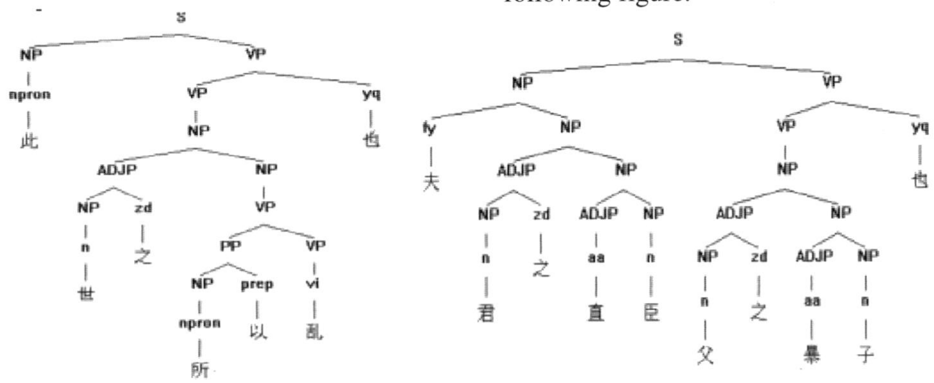

(a) (b)

Fig. 1. the parse trees of 2 sentences (a) 此世之所以乱也。 (b) 夫君之直臣父之暴子也。

2.3 Features of Classical Chinese Grammar Rules

As an aside, it is worthwhile to point out here some peculiarities of the Classical Chinese grammar used in our work. Readers not interested in grammar modeling may simply skip this subsection. As mentioned before, the grammar of Classical Chinese is entirely different from that of English, so a few special features must be studied. Although these features bring many difficulties to the parser, we have developed successful programming techniques to solve them.

From the rule-set, the reader might find that two special grammatical structures is very common in Classical Chinese:

1. Inversion: subject/verb inversion (rule 3), preposition/object inversion (rule 23).
2. Omission: Subject omitted (rule 2), preposition's object omitted (rule 24), preposition omitted (rule 25).

Maybe the strangest feature is the structure of PP. English PP is always P+NP. But here in Classical Chinese, by inversion and omission, the PP may have up to 4 forms, as shown in rule 22-25.

Table 4. The 4 rules from PP. The object of the preposition is in brackets, and [] indicate an omission.

	Rule	Explanation	Example
22	PP -> prep NP	The normal P+NP	儒*以(文)*乱法。
23	PP -> NP prep	Inverted: NP+P (介词宾语前置)	此*(所)以*乱也。
24	PP -> prepb	The object of the preposition is omitted	仲尼*以*(□)为孝。 Omit [之]
25	PP -> NP	The preposition itself is omitted	谒之□*(吏)*。 omit [于]

Another feature that must be pointed out here is the cycle. In our rule-set, there are 2 rules (rule 11 and rule 17) forming a cycle:

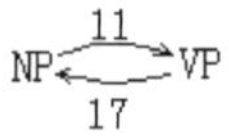

Fig. 2. A cycle in the rule-set. Rule 11: NP-> VP, Rule 17: VP-> NP.

It will ease our parsing because Classical Chinese is lexically and syntactically very ambiguous. An NP can act as a VP (a main verb), while a VP can act as a NP (subject or object). These two features are exemplified in figure 3. There are actually more cycles in the rule-set. Helpful as they are, the cycles bring great difficulty to the memory-based top-down parser. In practice, we develop a closure–based method to solve this problem, as shown in the following pseudo-code:

```
better_results_found=true;
while (better_results_found)
{
        better_results_found=false;
        memory_based_top_down_parse();
        // if better results found, the variable will be set true
}
```

Another point is the use of preferences for ambiguity resolution. While the ambiguities in our rule-set greatly ease our modeling Classical Chinese grammar, it causes the parser to make a lot of ridiculous errors. So we here apply some predefined preferences such as 'an fy must be at the first of an NP' and 'a yq must be at the end of a VP'. This consideration results in a significant increase in the parsing accuracies.

3 Evaluations

In our preliminary experiments, we constructed a treebank of 1000 manually parsed sentences (quite large for Classical Chinese treebank), in which 100 sentences are selected as the test set using the cross-validation scheme, while the others as the learning set. The majority of these sentences are extracted from classics of pre-Tsin Classical Chinese such as *Hanfeizi* and *Xunzi* because in these texts there are fewer proper nouns and difficult words. That is the restriction we put on the selection of Classical Chinese texts. It must be pointed out here that compared from other languages, Classical Chinese sentences are so short that the average length is only about 4-6 words long.

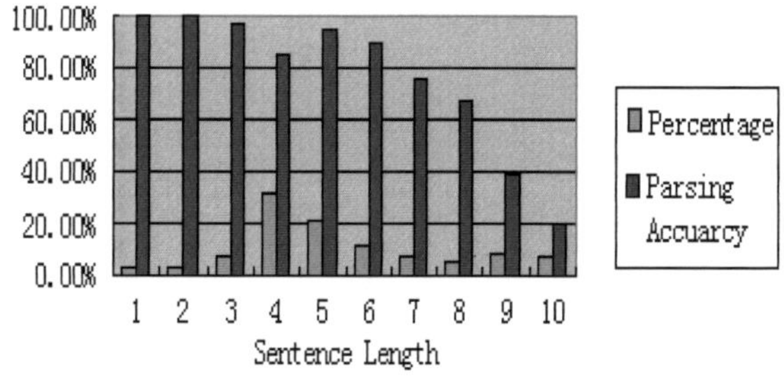

Fig. 3. Sentence Distributions and Parsing Accuracies

Figure 3 shows the distribution of sentences and parsing accuracies for different sentence lengths. For distribution, we can see that those 4-word, 5-word, and 6-word sentences constitute for the majority of the corpus, while those 1-word and 2-word sentences are very few. For accuracy, the parser is more effective for shorter sentences than for longer sentences. And for 1-word and 2-word sentences, there is no error report from the parse results.

Conclusion

Computer processing of Classical Chinese has just been commencing. While Classical Chinese is generally considered too difficult to process, our previous work on part-of-speech tagging has been largely successful because there is almost no need to segment Classical Chinese words. And we continue to use the tagset and corpus into this work. We first apply the forward-backward algorithm to obtain the context-dependent probabilities. The PCFG model is then presented where we restrict the rules into binary/unary rules, which greatly simplifies our parsing programming. According to the model, we developed a CFG rule-set of Classical Chinese. Some special features of the set are also studied. Classical Chinese processing is generally considered too difficult and thus neglected, while our works have shown that by good modelling and proper techniques, we can still get encouraging results. Although Classical Chinese is currently a dead language, our work still has applications in those areas as Classical-Modern Chinese Translation.

For future work of this paper, we expect to incorporate trigram model into the forward-backward algorithm, which will increase the tagging accuracy. And most important of all, it is obvious that the state-of-the-art PCFG model is still two-leveled, we expect to devise a three-level model, just like trigram versus bigram.

Acknowledgements

Our special thanks go to Prof. Lu Ruzhan of Shanghai Jiaotong University for his sincere guidance.

References

Allen, J. (1995) *Natural Language Understanding,* The Benjamin/Cummings Publishing Company, Inc.

Viterbi, A. (1967) *Error bounds for convolution codes and an asymptotically optimal decoding algorithm.* IEEE Trans. on Information Theory 13:260-269.

Yao Y., Lua K. (1998a) *A Probabilistic Context-Free Grammar Parser for Chinese,* Computer Processing of Oriental Languages, Vol. 11, No. 4, pp. 393-407

Huang L., Peng Y., Wang H. (2002) *Statistical Part-of-Speech Tagging for Classical Chinese,* Proceedings of the 5th International Conference on Text, Speech, and Dialog (TSD), Brno, in press

Klein, D., and Manning C. (2001) *Natural Language Grammar Induction using a Constituent-Context Model,* Proceedings of Neural Information Processing Systems, Vancouver.

Yao Y., Lua K. (1998b) *Mutual Information and Trigram Based Merging for Grammar Rule Induction and Sentence Parsing,* Computer Processing of Oriental Languages, Vol. 11, No. 4, pp. 393-407

Johnson, M. (2001) *Joint and conditional estimation of tagging and parsing models,* Proceedings of International computational linguistics conference, Toulouse

Charniak, E. (1996) *Taggers for Parsers,* Artificial Intelligence, Vol. 85, No. 1-2, pp. 45-47.

A Knowledge Based Approach to Identification of Serial Verb Construction in Chinese-to-Korean Machine Translation System

Dong-il Kim*, Zheng-Cui, Jinji-Li**, Jong-Hyeok Lee
Department Computer Science and Engineering, Electrical and Computer Engineering Division,
Pohang University of Science and Technology (POSTECH)
and Advanced Information Technology Research Center (AITrc)
San 31 Hyoja Dong, Pohang, 790-784, Korea
E-mail: {dongil, cuizheng, ljj,jhlee}@postech.ac.kr

Abstraction

In Chinese language processing, the recognition and analysis for serial verb constructions (SVCs) is a fascinating research topic. Chinese language researchers each may have a different definition and interpretation of SVC since the structure of SVC makes Chinese unique to other languages and contains complex semantic and pragmatic information. This paper proposes a formal definition of SVC and a knowledge based approach for the recognition of SVCs, which is adopted in TOTAL-CK, a transfer-based MT system from Chinese to Korean. The recognition process is carried out in two stages: the analysis stage classifies SVCs into general categories, and the transfer stage performs further classification for Korean transfer. Some evaluation result for each stage was also given with statistics of each category of SVCs

Introduction

Many Chinese language researchers have paid special attention to the so-called ‘serial verb constructions (SVCs)’, where two or more semantically or pragmatically related verb phrases or clauses are juxtaposed together without any functional marker. Because of different definitions and interpretations of SVCs among researchers, their categorizations differ according to researchers’ viewpoints.

In a Chinese to Korean machine translation, the hidden relation of the serial verbs should be expressed with some function words from the target language viewpoint. Moreover, the conceptual scope of these function words is different from the scope of SVC categorizations that are classified based on the viewpoint of the Chinese language itself.

In this paper, we proposes a different categorization of SVCs defined by the contrastive analysis of the two languages, and also an SVC identification method that is adopted in a Chinese-to-Korean MT system, TOTAL-CK. The TOTAL (Translator Of Three Asian Languages: Chinese, Korean and Japanese) project has been conducted under a hybrid strategy with transfer-based and example-based engines.

1. Language Characteristics between Chinese and Korean

In this section, some contrastive analyses of the two languages are introduced for better understanding of an SVC sentence. Since Chinese is an isolating language, morphological or syntactic markers rarely appear in a sentence, while in an agglutinative language such as Korean, these functional markers are not an optional unit but an obligatory unit in a sentence.

An example is given in (1). Notice that the Korean alphabets are written with Yale Romanization in this paper.

* Also an assistant professor at Yanbian University of Science & Technology (YUST) Yanji, Jilin, China.

** Also a lecturer at YUST

(1) 他 开门 进去。(*ta kai-men jin-qu*)

Ku-nun mwun-ul yel-ko duleka-nta.

He-NOM door-ACC open-CON get in-PRENT-DEC.

He opens the door and enters (the room).

In the Korean sentence, *ko* is a connective particle, and also *nun*, *ul*, and *nta* denote a topic auxiliary particle, an object case particle and declarative terminative ending, respectively. All these functional markers should be decided in the Korean transfer stage. Specifically, we require a process to select one from the possible conjugational markers when a Chinese SVC sentence is transferred to its Korean counterpart.

2. Related Works

A SVC is studied among several researchers as different names. But the general syntactic form is (NP) V1 (NP) V2 (NP)[1]. The variance of definition for SVC comes from the different scope of interpretation for the sentence pattern.

We will introduce three typical researches to clearly outline our definition of SVC. The narrowest view of scope is suggested in (Lü, 1953). In his interpretation, V1 and V2 have the same subject and should be not coordinative, but it is difficult to decide which one is main or additional. Zhu (Zhu, 1981) includes all cases of Lü's and the possibility of adding an adjective to substitute for the second verb position. He also includes the case where an additional verb and a main verb are used, such as V+着 expression in V1 position, which indicates that V1 is additional and V2 is main. The broadest scope is proposed in (Li & Thompson, 1981). According to his interpretation, an SVC includes not only all the patterns noted above but also a pivot construction, a subject/object clause, and a coordinate clause, but excludes the pattern with an adjective in the V2 position. In this paper, the scope of SVC is almost same as Li's but the classification of SVCs differs slightly, detailing the categorization in chapter 4.

A few computational solutions to identifying SVCs have been proposed by some researchers. A formal description is shown in (Chan, 1998) using time lapse notation and the related definition. However, her method makes it difficult to computationally detect SVCs without the resources containing the deep level of analysis of each lexical, which is not obtainable in the current stage of language processing.

3. Overview of TOTAL-CK System Architecture

As a typical transfer system, TOTAL-CK consists of three parts: Chinese analysis, dependency tree transfer, and Korean generation. The system architecture of TOTAL-CK is shown in figure 1. The design principles and the detail descriptions are given in (Kim *et al.*, 2002).

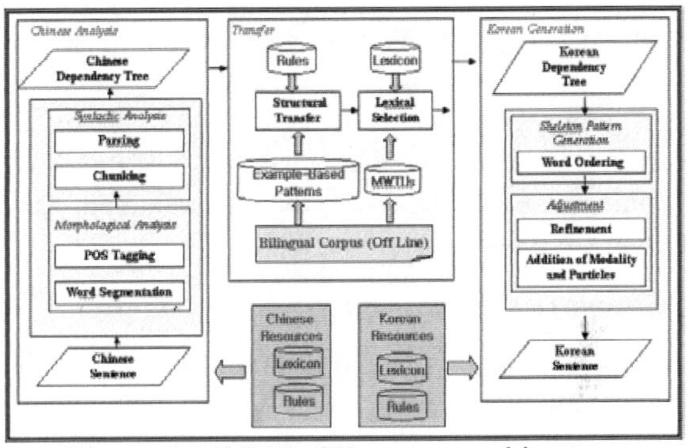

Figure 1: TOTAL-CK system architecture

4. Classification of Serial Verb Construction

In the previous chapter, we mentioned the syntactic format of SVCs which is NP V1 (NP) V2 (NP) and the different scope of definition of SVCs by the Chinese language researches. To outline the scope of SVCs, we define SVCs in terms of dependency relation such that V1 is the head of V2, or V2 is the head of V1. It is formally defined as follows:

Definition 1

Let N represent a set of nodes in a dependency tree, and W a set of words. Further Let V be a set of verbs, and P be a set of all parts of speech in Chinese. Then the functions: head, nw, and npos, are defined as below:

head(n) =hn where n $\in$ *N and hn is the head of n*

nw(n) = w where n $\in$ *N and w* $\in$ *W*

npos(n) = np where n $\in$ *N and np* $\in$ *P*

A definition of SVC is:

Given a node n such that npos(n) $\in$ *V and Head(n) = hn,*

If and only if npos(hn) $\in$ *V and hn is the head of a given sentence then the sentence is a SVC.*

The three sentences from the top of table 1 satisfy the given condition. Also the head of

[1] V1 : first verb, V2 : second verb, NP : noun phrase.

the node is the sentence head, thus these must be SVCs. For the last sentence, nw(n) is 接入, and nw(Head(n)) is 总数 whose the POS is not verb and also whose the node is not the sentence head. Thus it is not an SVC.

Sentence	nw	nwh	SH	SVC
他开门进去。	进	开	Yes	Yes
我没想到你住在北京。	住	想	Yes	Yes
在这里停车犯法。	停	犯	Yes	Yes
各接入网络的总数已经超过1000个。	接入	总数	No	No

Table 1: Example of Testing SVC

Where nw: nw(n); nwh: nw(head(n)); SH :testing if head(n) is the sentence head ; n is a given node.

Our definition is employed to recognize a SVC in the Chinese analysis stage. First we describe the classification that is used in the Chinese analysis stage.

4.1 Categories in Chinese Analysis Stage

All dependency relations, which are detected by the above definition, are classified into five categories: separate events, object, subject, pivotal construction and descriptive clauses, based on the classification of Li (Li & Thompson, 1981).

4.1.1 Separate Events

The serial verb patterns classified by most researchers belong to this group where switching V1 to V2 provides us a different meaning. In addition, we add the case where transposing V1 to V2 provides us the same meaning in this group.

4.1.2 Object

If V2 is the main verb in an object clause or a object phrase then it belongs to this group.

4.1.3 Subject

If V1 is the main verb in the subject clause or subject phrase, it is assigned to this group.

4.1.4 Pivot

If the noun phrase between V1 and V2 is the object of V1 and the subject of V2, then it is a pivot construction.

4.1.5 Descriptive

If V2 describes the noun phrase between V1 and V2, then it is a descriptive SVC.

All categories of SVCs are shown in Table 2

The corresponding Chinese dependency relations to object, subject and pivot constructions also appear in the some research in Chinese language processing (Zhou & Huang, 1994) but the other two are not shown due to their different viewpoints.

The descriptive construction is directly able to be one-to-one mapped to the Korean counterpart. However the separate event SVCs should be further classified for Korean transfer since the separate event SVC is possibly mapped into sentences with several different Korean conjunctional particles. Thus, it is touched in the transfer stage.

Category	Example
Separate Event	我买票进去; 他在饭店吃饭喝茶。
Object	我没想到你住在北京。
Subject	在这里停车犯法。
Pivot	我们让他去北京。
Descriptive	我有一个姐姐喜欢看书。

Table 2: Examples of SVC category

4.2 Subcategories in Transfer Stage

The separate event SVC for each sense of Korean conjunctional particles is classified into the following subcategories: restrictive, quasi-coordinative, simultaneous, transitional, and circumstantial by the Korean language viewpoint.

4.2.1 Restrictive

The action of V2 is performed under the restriction given by V1. There are different types of restriction, such as space, group-related, causal, and instrumental. The examples are presented in table 3.

Sentence	V1	V2	R type
我的妹妹今天离开北京前往汉城[2]。	离开	前往	space
他代表山西省出席了座谈会。	代表	出席	group
我投票赞成第一个人。	投票	赞成	causal
这个图书馆利用计算机进行图书借阅管理。	利用	进行	tool

Table 3: Examples of Restrictive Separate Events

[2] The sentence can also be interpreted as purposive separate events. But it is included into a restrictive separate event SVC because it is impossible to detect the differences between restrictive and purposive, as this requires pragmatic level information

4.2.2 Quasi-Coordinative

In quasi-coordinative, two different cases exist. First, transposing V1 to V2 never causes a meaning shift of the sentence, named alternative. The other is that V1 and V2 are only sequentially related, called consecutive.

4.2.3. Simultaneous

In a simultaneous case, V1 and V2 occur at the same time.

4.2.4 Transitional

If the action of V1 is interrupted by the action V2, then it is transitional.

4.2.5 Circumstantial

When V2 occurs on the condition of the action of V1, then it is classified as a circumstantial case.

The examples for rests of the separate event are given in Table 4.

Type	Example
Q-Coordinative	他在饭店吃饭喝茶。(alternative) 他买票进去。(consecutive)
Simultaneous	他站着唱歌。
Transitional	我的弟弟开车出事了。
Circumstantial	不买别进。

Table 4: Examples of Separate Events

In restrictive, quasi-coordinate, simultaneous, transitional, and circumstantial separate event SVC Chinese sentences, all the above verbs are mapped into the corresponding Korean verb followed by the Korean conjunctional particle 'se', 'ko', 'un-chay-lo', 'taka' and 'myen', respectively.

5. Identification of SVCs

To recognize SVCs, we divide the identifying process into two stages. The general categories of SVCs are able to be found at the analysis stage and the subcategories of a separated event SVC are detected in the transfer stage.

5.1 Analysis Stage

To recognize the five general categories of SVCs, two resources are used: one is the Grammatical Knowledge Base of Contemporary Chinese (GKBCC) and the other is a verb list with valency information (VLVI) (Zhu *et al.*, 1995). Checking a verb in GKBCC allows us to simply detect a pivot SVC. The remainders of the other types of SVCs should be carefully handled. There are two possible ambiguous structures of SVCs

Case 1 : NP V1 V2 (NP2)

Case 2 : NP V1 NP1 V2 (NP2)

Where NP, NP1 and NP2 are noun phrases.

The algorithm for each case is illustrated in figure 2 and figure 3. In Figure 3, the test 'V1 takes NP & VP' means that the verb 偷听 can have a noun phrase or an object clause as an object. The test, 'satisfy valency' denotes that the second verb 喜欢 takes a human subject, and 外国人 can be the subject of the verb 喜欢, thus it is classified as an object case. For the other sentence, since 公园 cannot be the subject of the verb 锻炼, it is determined as a subject case.

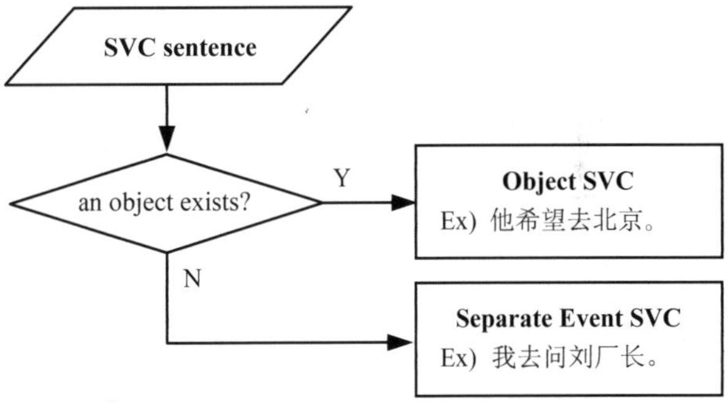

Figure 2: Algorithm of Detecting SVC for Case 1

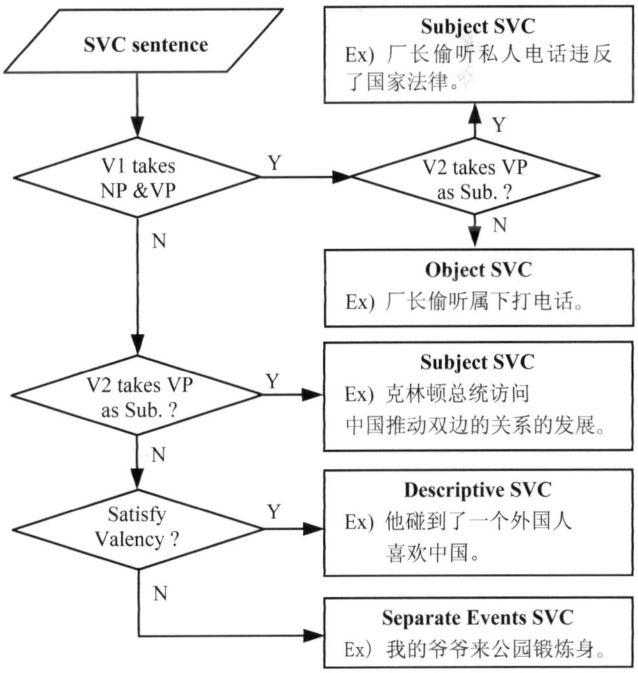

Figure 3: Algorithm of Detecting SVC for Case 2

5.2 Transfer Stage

The simultaneous separate events is easily recognized by the lexical (着) attached to the first verb. Also, we use a simple heuristic to detect the circumstantial separate events with the lexical pattern information.

The resource used in this stage is a Chinese thesaurus called Tongyi-ci-cilin (Mei, 1983). With the thesaurus the remainders of separate event SVCs are processed with great care. If V2 is related to the interrupt concept then the transitional separate events are assigned. The most difficult and frequently occurring cases are the restrictive separate events and quasi-coordinative separate event.

The key idea of using the thesaurus is based on the observation that the verb V2, if restricted by V1 makes it possible that the concept of V2 will also be restricted by the concept of V1. To complete the solution, we first define the relations: RSTV, RSTL and RSTM as follows:

Definition 2

We define the relations: RSTV, RSTL, and RSTM, as follows:

RSTV= {(V1,V2) where V1 and V2 are the first verb and second verb in a given SVC sentence and V2 is semantically restricted by V1 : (V1,V2) ≠ (V2,V1)}

RSTL= {(CL1,CL2) where CL1 and CL2 are the low level concept of the first verb and the low level concept [3] of second verb in the Chinese thesaurus, respectively, and CL2 is semantically restricted by CL1 : (CL1,CL2) ≠ (CL2,CL1)}

RSTM= {(CM1, CM2) where CM1 and CM2 are the middle level concept of the first verb and the middle level concept of second verb in the Chinese thesaurus, respectively, and ML2 is semantically restricted by ML1 : (ML1,ML2) ≠ (ML2, ML1)}

The relations RSTV, RSTL, and RSTM are not symmetric and not reflexive. Based on the definition we derive the following heuristics:

if (V1,V2) ∈ RSRV then (CL1,CL2) ∈ RSTL But if (V1,V2) ∈ RSTV then not always (CM1,CM2) ∈ RSTM.

All three examples from the top of table 5 satisfy the condition that, if (V1, V2) ∈ RSTV then (CL1,CL2) ∈ RSTL and (CM1,CM2) ∈ RSTM. If the condition is always true, then we use the middle-level concept relation for detecting a restrictive separate event in order to increase the applicability of our rules. Also, the data structure of RSTM is easily represented with an adjacent matrix with the size of 21*21 [4] (Sahni, 1998) where the matrix M is a square matrix, whose column and row are the middle-level concept, and if M(i,j) = 1 then concept j is semantically restricted by concept i, otherwise (i,j) ∉ RSTM.

Example	RSTV		RSTL		RSTM	
	V1	V2	CL1	CL2	CM1	CM2
他参加政府会议公开批评了我的谈话。	参加	批评	Hj20	Hi21	Hj	Hi
国家主席江泽民出席讲话。	出席	讲话	Hj20	Hj12	Hj	Hi
他给华大使带来一个大花篮表示祝贺。	带来	表示	Hj36	Hj14	Hj	Hi
他代表山西省出席了座谈会。	代表	出席	Hi17	Hj20	Hi	Hj

Table 5: Example of RSTV, RSTL and RSTM

However, the last example reveals that the condition is not always true since we have the result, both (Hi,Hj) and (Hj,Hi) ∈ RSTM. Thus, it violates the definition of RSTM. Hence, we may not directly use the middle-level concept adjacent matrix and the size of the low-level concept matrix is too large to be used.[5]

We come up with a solution of a frame with multi level concepts. The frame consists of three parts: the middle-level concept adjacent matrix, the low-level concept adjacent lists and the collocation serial verb list for detecting a serial verb that always appears together.

Our solution is that the exceptional cases are covered by either the collocation verb lists or the low-level concept adjacent list. The remaining frequently occurring cases are captured by the middle-level adjacent matrix. This leads to the sparse matrix of the low-level concept which

[3] The thesaurus consists of three levels of hierarchy. For example, H, Hj, and Hj20 correspond to the one of highest concept, the next narrow term called middle-level concept and the narrowest term called low-level concept, respectively.

[4] The number of verbs related middle-level concept in the Chinese thesaurus is 21.

[5] The number of verbs related low-level concepts in the Chinese thesaurus is about 500.

causes the adaptation of adjacent lists rather than an adjacent matrix for the low-level concepts.

The order of searching the frame is the collocation list, the low-level concept list and the middle-level concept matrix. In the collocation list, if V1 and V2 belongs to the collocation list of the restrictive separate events, such as 捉拿归案 or the one of quasi-coordinative, such as 立案侦察 then the sentence is assigned to a restrictive case or a quasi-coordinative case, respectively. In the low-level concept lists and the middle-level concept matrix, if matching succeeds, which means that V2 is semantically restricted by V1, then a restrictive case is assigned; otherwise, a quasi-coordinate case is detected[6]. The detailed process for identifying the subcategories of separate events is shown in figure 4.

6. Evaluation

We randomly selected 1000 SVC sentences from 1998 people's daily newspapers. The number of verbs in the sentence is two since our dependency parser is still being improved to detect the sentences with multiple embedding clauses. In table 6, the distribution of each type of SVC and the precision are shown.

Type	Frequency	Percentage
Separate events	402	40.2
Object	479	47.9
Subject	31	3.1
Pivot	39	3.9
Descriptive	1	0.1
Error	56	5.6 (Presicion:94.4%)
Total	1000	100

Table 6: Distribution of Categories of SVC

The precision is 94.4% and some of the errors occur from the tagger, thus some sentences are not SVCs. The rest of the errors result from missing information in the knowledge bases:

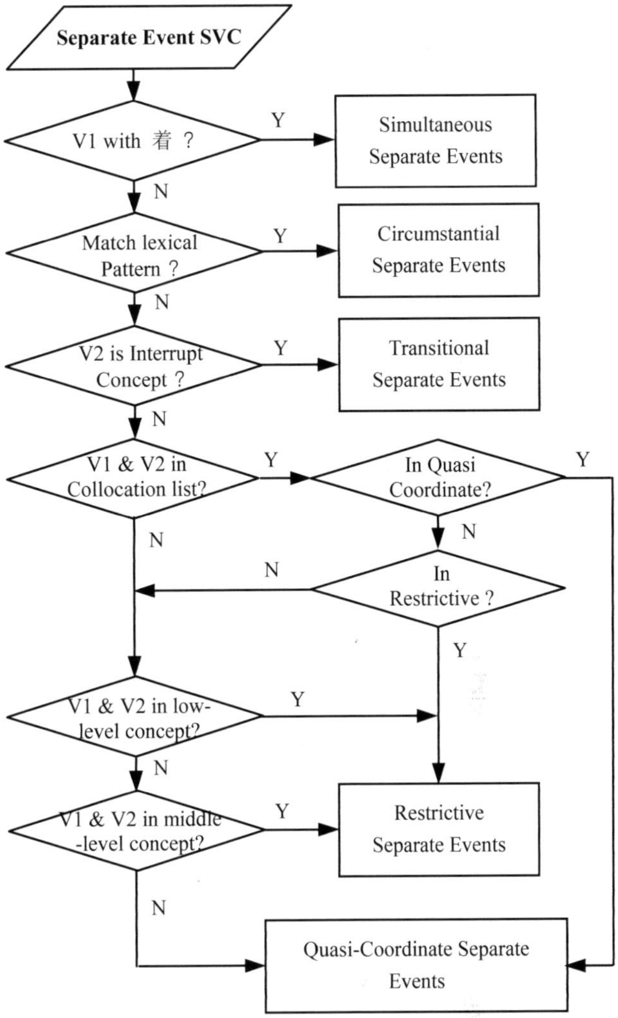

Figure 4: Detection Algorithm of Subcategory of Separate Event SVC.

GKBCC and VLVI. We need the complete list of verbs, which has a clause as a subject. These verbs in the list will be gradually collected in future works.

The evaluation table for the separate event SVCs is provided in Table 7.

Type	Frequency	Percentage
Restrictive	153	38.5
Quasi-coordinative	184	45.7
Simultaneous	33	8.2
Transitional	3	0.7
Circumstantial	12	2.9
Error	19	4.7 (Precision:95.3%)
Total	402	100

Table 7: Result of Separate Event

6 For a sentence 国家主席江泽民出席讲话 where the relation (Hj20,Hj12) is not in the low-level adjacent list, but (Hj,Hi) is 1 in the middle-level matrix, it is assigned to the restrictive case, while for the sentence 他代表山西省出席了座谈会 where (Hi17,Hj20) is in the low-level adjacent list, thus searching is stopped, it is assigned as a restrictive case. A sententence 他在饭店吃饭喝茶 do not satisfy all conditions, thus it is detected as Quasi-Coordinate.

The precision of identifying the category of separate event is 95.3%. The errors resulted from a circumstantial case since our heuristics is too restrictive to detect all cases, thus, it might be revised further, and since the low-level concept lists are not completed. The low-level concept lists will be continuously updated for increasing coverage in the tuning stage of the machine translation system.

Table 8 shows the distribution of the subcategory of restrictive separate events for Korean transfer.

Type	Frequency	Percentage
Space	86	56.2
Group-related	38	24.8
Causal	17	11.1
Instrumental	12	7.9
Total	153	100

Table 8: Category of Restricted Separated Event

In table 9, the frequency for each type of accessed resource is listed. Notice that most restrictive separate event SVCs are recognized in the middle-level matrix. The two cases in collocation are all the case of quasi-coordinative, thus, the total number is greater than 153.

Type of accessed resource	Frequency	Percentage
Middle-level matrix	121	78.0
Low-level list	32	20.6
Collocation list	2	1.29
Total	155	100

Table 9: Access Frequencies for Resource Type

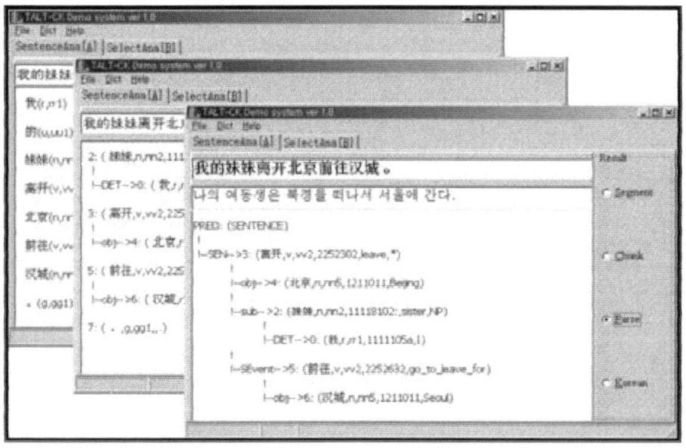

Figure 5: Demo system of TOTAL-CK

In figure 5, a demo system of TOTAL-CK is illustrated. For a given Chinese SVC sentence displayed in the top position of the right-most window, the corresponding Korean sentence is followed in the next row. The tagged results, the segment of chunking, and the Chinese dependency tree with indentation are shown in each window from left to right.

Conclusion and Future work

In this paper, we formally define serial verb constructions, and classified the SVC into several categories. These categories are related to the analysis stage and the transfer stage of TALK-CK. We provided a resolution algorithm detecting SVCs in each step. Finally, at each stage, a promising experimental result is shown.

Further research must help to better resolve the conditional separate event SVC and purposive separate event SVC.

Acknowledgements

This work was supported by the Korea Science and Engineering Foundation (KOSEF) through the Advanced Information Technology Research Center(AITrc).

References

Chan Y. W. (1998) *Formal Criteria for interpreting Chinese Serial Verb Constructions*. Communications of COLIPS 8(1) ,pp.13-29.

Kim D.I., Cui Z, Li J.J. and Lee J.H. (2002). *Resolving Structural Transfer Ambiguity in Chinese-to Korean Machine Translation*. 2002 International Conference on Chinese Language Computing, Taichung, Taiwan.

Li C N. , Thompson S A. (1981), *Mandarin Chinese: A functional reference grammar*. University of California Press, USA.

Lü S. X.(1953) *Yufa Xuexi (The Study of Chinese Grmmar)*. Bejing, Zhungguo Qingnian Press.

Mei J.J.(1983) *Chinese Thesaurus (Tong-Yi-Ci-Ci-lin)*. Shanghai Cishu Press. 1983.

Sahni, S.(1998) *Data structures, algorithms, and applications in C++*. Boston McGraw-Hill, USA.

Zhou M and Huang C. (1994) *Approach to the Chinese Dependency Formalism for the Tagging of Corpus*. Journal of Chinese Information Processing, 8/3, pp. 35-52, 1994

Zhu D.X.(1981), *Yufa Jiangyi (Lectures on Chinese Grammar)*,Bejing, Xiangwu Press.

Zhu X. F, Yu S. W and Wang H. (1995) *The Development of Contemporary Chinese Grammatical Knowledge Base and its Applications*. Communications of COLIPS, 5/1-2

Learning Case-based Knowledge for Disambiguating Chinese Word Segmentation: A preliminary study

Chunyu Kit[†] **Haihua Pan**[†]
Dept. of Chinese, Translation & Linguistics[†]
City University of Hong Kong
{ctckit, cthpan}@cityu.edu.hk

Hongbiao Chen[†‡]
Dept. of Foreign Trade & Economic[‡]
Cooperation of Guangdong Province, China
drhbchen@21cn.com

Abstract

Just like other NLP applications, a serious problem with Chinese word segmentation lies in the ambiguities involved. Disambiguation methods fall into different categories, e.g., rule-based, statistical-based and example-based approaches, each of which may involve a variety of machine learning techniques. In this paper we report our current progress within the example-based approach, including its framework, example representation and collection, example matching and application. Experimental results show that this effective approach resolves more than 90% of ambiguities found. Hence, if it is integrated effectively with a segmentation method of the precision $P > 95\%$, the resulting segmentation accuracy can reach, theoretically, beyond 99.5%.

1 Introduction

It has been nearly two decades since the early work of Chinese word segmentation (Liang, 1984; Liang and Liu, 1985; Liu and Liang, 1986; Liang, 1986) . Tokenization has been recognized as a widespread problem, rather than being unique to Chinese and other oriental languages. It is an initial or prerequisite phase of NLP for all languages, although the obscurity of the problem varies from language to language (Webster and Kit, 1992a; Palmer, 2000). Recent work on tokenization for European languages such as English is reported in (Grefenstette and Tapanainen, 1994; Grefenstette, 1999; Grefenstette et al., 2000), adopting a finite-state approach. However, identification of multi-word units such as proper names and technical terms in these languages is highly comparable to that of multi-character Chinese words: there are no delimiters available.

So far, a great variety of segmentation strategies for Chinese with various linguistic resources have been explored, yielding a large volume of literature on both linguistic and computational sides, as listed in (Liu et al., 1994; Guo, 1997), among many others. In general, these strategies can be divided into two camps, namely, dictionary-based and statistical-based approaches. Nevertheless, the former can be understood as a restricted instance of the latter, with an equi-probability for each word in a given dictionary[1].

Most, if not all, dictionary-based strategies are built upon a few basic "mechanical" segmentation methods based on string matching (Kit et al., 1989), among which the most applicable, thus widely used since the very beginning, are the two *maximum matching* methods (MMs), one scanning *forward* (FMM) and the other *backward* (BMM). Interestingly, their performance, frequently used as the baseline for evaluation, is never too far away from the state-of-the-art approaches in terms of segmentation accuracy. Although performing little statistical computation, the MMs comply, in general, with the essential principle of the statistical-based approaches: select a segmentation as probable as possible among all choices. This *ad hoc* way of choosing the segmentation with fewest words usually leads to, by coincidence, a more probable output than most other choices with more words[2].

[1] A dictionary is actually a restricted form of language model, in this sense.

[2] The coincidence of fewer words with a greater probability can be illustrated as follows: given a string s, the probability of its most probable segmentation seg(s) in terms of a given language model is

$$\text{prob}(\text{seg}(s)) = \max_{s=w_1w_2\cdots w_n} \prod_i^n \text{prob}(w_i|\cdot)$$

where $\text{prob}(w_i|\cdot)$ is some conditional probability in the model. Since all $\text{prob}(w_i|\cdot) < 1.0$, this probability becomes smaller for a greater n. Clearly, it looks more straightforward in an equi-probability setting.

Statistical approaches involve language models, mostly finite-state ones, trained on some large-scale corpora, as showed in Fan and Tsai (1988), Chang et al. (1991), Chiang et al. (1992), Sproat et al. (1996), Pont and Croft (1996) and Ng and Lua (forthcoming). These approaches do not provide any explicit strategy for disambiguation, but they get more ambiguous chunks correctly segmented than MMs by virtue of probability. Other linguistic resources or computational processes can also be integrated for further improvement, e.g., Lai et al. (1991) attempts to integrate POS tagging with word segmentation for the enhancement of accuracy and Gan et al. (1997) integrates word boundary disambiguation into sentence processing within a probabilistic emergent model. There are also other approaches that incorporate various techniques of statistical NLP and machine learning, e.g., transformation-based error-driven learning (Palmer, 1997; Hockenmaier and Brew, 1998) and compression-based algorithm (Teahan et al., 2000).

Recent research shifts its focus onto the following aspects, resorting to a variety of resources and techniques, in particular, machine learning techniques:

1. Lexical resource acquisition, including compilation and automatic detection of high-tech terms and unknown words like names, to complement a never-big-enough dictionary (Chang et al., 1995; Pont and Croft, 1996; Chang and Su, 1997);
2. Investigation into the nature and statistics of ambiguities (Sun and Zhou, 1998);
3. Unsupervised learning of words (Ge et al., 1999; Peng and Schuurmans, 2001)[3];
4. Disambiguation with different approaches (Liang, 1989; Jin, 1994; Sun and T'sou, 1995)

The work reported in this paper belongs to the last category, taking an instance-based learning approach, aimed to examine its prospects of disambiguation.

The rest of the paper is organized as follows. Section 2 briefly introduces the ambiguity problem and existing ambiguity detection strategies. Section 3 defines the notion and representation of examples, and formulates a similarity measure between an ambiguous input and an example. We present our disambiguation algorithm in Section 4 and experimental results and evaluation in Section 5, together with some discussion on the remaining errors, before concluding the paper in Section 6.

2 Ambiguity

Conceptually there are two essential types of ambiguity in Chinese word segmentation, which are conventionally termed as *overlapping* and *combinational* ambiguities. They can be formally defined as follows, given a dictionary $\mathcal{D}$:

Overlapping ambiguity A given string $\alpha\beta\gamma$ involves an overlapping ambiguity, if the set of sub-strings $\{\alpha\beta,\ \beta\gamma\} \subset \mathcal{D}$.

Combinational ambiguity A given string $\alpha\beta$ involves a combinational ambiguity, if the set of sub-strings $\{\alpha,\ \beta,\ \alpha\beta\} \subset \mathcal{D}$.

In practice the first type commonly co-occurs with the second, because almost all Chinese characters can be mono-character words. For the same reason, almost every multi-character word involves a combinational ambiguity. Fortunately, however, most of them are "resolved", characteristically, in a sense, by a MM strategy. Therefore, the focus of disambiguation is unsurprisingly put on the unresolved ones as well as the overlapping ambiguities.

2.1 Ambiguity detection

Conventionally, a straightforward strategy is exploited to detect ambiguities with the aid of FMM and BMM: the discrepancies of their outputs signal ambiguous strings. It appears adequately efficient, because only a forward and a backward scanning of the input will do.

However, its reliability remains a question, although it has been taken for granted for a long time that there would be few ambiguities left out, which is at odds with our observation that there are ambiguous strings for which both MMs output an identical segmentation. E.g.,

[3]Recent research in this direction appears to be closely related to the studies on computational lexical acquisition of other languages such as English (de Marcken, 1996; Brent, 1999; Kit and Wilks, 1999; Kit, 2000; Venkataraman, 2001) and to language modeling technology (Jelinek, 1997), typically involving a version of the EM algorithm (Dempster et al., 1977).

given a string abcde with $\{\texttt{a}, \texttt{ab}, \texttt{bcd}, \texttt{c}, \texttt{de}, \texttt{e}\} \in \mathcal{D}$, it is conceivable that both MMs output $\cdots$ ab c de $\cdots$, and consequently the embedded ambiguity is unseen. So far we haven't seen any report on the incompleteness of ambiguity detection via this strategy.

A more comprehensive strategy would be that we first locate the boundaries of all *possible* words in terms of a given dictionary[4] are first located, and then, the common sub-strings among these words are detected: any common substring indicates an ambiguity.

Since our current work is intended to examine the effectiveness of an example-based learning approach to resolve found ambiguities, its merits do not rely on the completeness of ambiguity detection. The conventional strategy would suffice for the purpose of identifying an adequate number of ambiguities for our experiments.

3 Examples and similarity measure

We intend to disambiguate Chinese word segmentation ambiguities within the framework of *case*-based learning. This supervised learning approach, also labeled as *memory*-based, *instance*-based or *example*-based learning, has been popular for various NLP applications in recent years, e.g., the TiMBL learner (Daelemans et al., 2001). TiMBL is developed as a general memory-based learning environment to integrate a set of learning algorithms. It has been widely applied to disambiguating a variety of NLP tasks, including PP attachment (Zavrel et al., 1998), shallow parsing (Daelemans et al., 1999) and WSD (Veenstra et al., 2000; Stevenson and Wilks, 2001). In this paper, the general principle of case-based learning is followed but the formulation below is nevertheless specific to our problem.

An *example* here is defined as a quadruple $<C^l, e, C^r, S>$, where the strings C^l and C^r are the left and right *contexts* within which the ambiguous string e appears, and S is the correct segmentation of e within the particular context. If denoting the quadruple as E, we also refer to S as seg(E) or seg(e), interchangeably.

The *distance*, or *similarity*, between an example E and a given triple $A = <C^l_a, a, C^r_a>$ with the ambiguous string a is defined as

$$\Delta(A, E) = \delta(a, e)(1 + \sum_i^{\{l,r\}} \delta^i(C^i_a, C^i)) \quad (1)$$

where $\delta(\cdot,\cdot)$ indicates the identity of two ambiguous strings, defined as

$$\delta(a, e) = \begin{cases} 1, & \text{if } a = e \\ 0, & \text{otherwise} \end{cases} \quad (2)$$

and $\delta^i(\cdot,\cdot)$ (for $i \in \{l, r\}$) is the similarity of the corresponding contexts, measured in terms of the length of their common prefix (for the right contexts) or suffix (for the left contexts) in number of words[5]. For two given strings if we denote their common suffix (i.e., affix from the *right*) and prefix (i.e., affix from the *lefty*) respectively as[6] $f^r(\cdot,\cdot)$ and $f^l(\cdot,\cdot)$, we have $\delta^i(\cdot,\cdot) = |f^{\bar{i}}(\cdot,\cdot)|$. Thus, we can rewrite (1) into (3) below.

$$\Delta(A, E) = \delta(a, e)(1 + \sum_i^{\{l,r\}} |f^{\bar{i}}(C^i_a, C^i)|) \quad (3)$$

Actually, the idea behind this equation is more straightforward than it looks. Basically, we measure the similarity of a given triple (i.e., an ambiguous string and its contexts) and an example in terms of the similarity of their contexts. However, this similarity is meaningful if and only if the strings in question are identical. This is why we define $\delta(a, e)$.

Given a triple $A = <C^l_a, a, C^r_a>$ and a collection $\mathcal{E}$ of examples, known as *example base* (EB), the strategy we undertake to determine a segmentation for the ambiguous string a can be formulated as follows, for $\Delta(A, E) \geq 1$:

$$\text{seg}(a \in A) = \text{seg}\left(\arg\max_{E \in \mathcal{E}} \Delta(A, E)\right) \quad (4)$$

where seg$(\cdot)$ denotes the segmentation of a given string or example. Straightforwardly, Equation (4) can be read off as the following: segment a in the same way as its most similar example in the example base.

[4]Notice that ambiguities are dictionary-dependent.

[5]Obviously, measuring the length in number of characters is an alternative to explore in our future research.

[6]For example,

$f^l(\texttt{abc}, \texttt{dbc}) = \texttt{null}$, $f^r(\texttt{abc}, \texttt{dbc}) = \texttt{bc}$
$f^l(\texttt{abc}, \texttt{abd}) = \texttt{ab}$, $f^r(\texttt{abc}, \texttt{abd}) = \texttt{null}$

4 Algorithms

In order to test the effectiveness of the disambiguation strategy formulated above, we need to collect examples from a large-scale unrestricted corpus via a sound ambiguity detection program, and apply the examples to ambiguous strings in a test corpus via an example application program. In this section we present the algorithms for these purposes.

4.1 Ambiguity detection

We take a conventional approach to ambiguity detection, by detecting the discrepancies of the outputs from the FMM and BMM segmentations. Given an input corpus $\mathcal{C}$, it can be realized, plainly, by the following algorithm:

Ambiguity detection algorithm: $\texttt{ambd}(\mathcal{C})$

1. $\mathcal{F} = \texttt{FMM}(\mathcal{C})$ and $\mathcal{B} = \texttt{BMM}(\mathcal{C})$
2. Return $\texttt{diff}(\mathcal{F}, \mathcal{B})$

where $\texttt{FMM}(\cdot)$ and $\texttt{FMM}(\cdot)$ return the FMM and BMM segmentations of $\mathcal{C}$, and $\texttt{diff}(\cdot,\cdot)$ returns the discrepancies of the two segmentations.

The dictionary used to support the MMs is a merger of the word lists from Liu et al. (1994) and Yu (1998), consisting of 53K entries. It is a medium-sized dictionary. With regards to the dictionary size and the weakness of the ambiguity detection algorithm, we keep ourselves alert of the fact that there are a certain number of ambiguities that are not detected by our program. And the resolutions for the ambiguous strings so detected are manually prepared, by selecting an answer from the outputs of the MMs in use.

4.2 Disambiguation

Given an example base $\mathcal{E}$ and a text corpus $\mathcal{C}$ as testing data, the disambiguation algorithm works along the following steps:

Disambiguation algorithm: $\texttt{disamb}(\mathcal{C}, \mathcal{E})$

1. Ambiguity detection: $\mathcal{A} = \texttt{ambd}(\mathcal{C})$
2. For every $\alpha a \beta \in \mathcal{C}$ such that $a \in \mathcal{A}$, let $A = <\alpha, a, \beta>$
   - 2.1 Search for $E = \arg\max_{e \in \mathcal{E}} \Delta(A, e)$
   - 2.2 If $\Delta(A, E) > 1$, $\text{seg}(a) = \text{seg}(E)$
   - 2.3 Else $\text{seg}(a) = \arg\max_{s \in \{\texttt{FMM}(a), \texttt{BMM}(a)\}} q(s)$

where $q(\cdot)$ gives a probability-like score for a segmentation, by which we hope to get a better result than a random or brute-force choice between the FMM and BMM outputs (that we could have made). We refer to $q(\cdot)$ as a *solidness* function that is defined as the following, mainly for the simplicity of implementation:

$$q(w_1 w_2 \cdots w_n) = \prod_i^n p_w(w_i) \tag{5}$$

where $p_w(\cdot)$ is the probability of a given string being a word. It is defined as

$$p_w(w_i) = \frac{f_w(w_i)}{f(w_i)}$$

where $f_w(\cdot)$ and $f(\cdot)$ are, respectively, the frequencies of a given item occurring as a word and as a string in the training corpus. Since it is an approximation, we can count the word frequencies based on the FMM output.

5 Experiment and evaluation

A number of experiments were conducted on unrestricted texts for the purpose of testing the effectiveness of the above disambiguation approach. In this section we present the data for training (i.e., example collection) and testing, experimental results and evaluation.

5.1 Data

The data we used for the experiments are news texts collected from mainland China, Hong Kong and Taiwan. The corpus size is of 778K words and 1.5M characters in total, in 1534 text files. About 3/4 of the data, of 1.16M characters in 1.1K files, are used for training and the remaining 1/4, of 360K characters in about 0.4K files, for testing. The statistics about the ambiguous strings found in the training and testing data is given in Table 1. From the ambiguity-word (EW) ratio, we can see that the ambiguity distribution among the two data sets is approximately even.

5.2 Results and evaluation

Theoretically, disambiguation accuracy on the training data should be 100%, because all found ambiguities are manually resolved. In contrast, the accuracy on the test set is more indicative of the effectiveness of the disambiguation strategy.

Training Data			EW Ratio
Number of cases	Total	5401	0.91%
	Unique	3018	0.51%
Testing Data			EW Ratio
Number of cases	Total	1648	0.90%
	Unique	995	0.54%

Table 1: Ambiguities in training & testing data

Our experimental results show that among 1648 ambiguities found in the test set, 1488 are properly resolved, in terms of our manual checking of the disambiguation outputs. Accordingly, the disambiguation accuracy is 90.29%.

We do not report the overall segmentation accuracy here for a number of reasons. Firstly, almost every paper in recent years reports a segmentation accuracy that nearly reaches the ceiling. This fact suggests that such figures seem to have carried less and less academic significance, in the sense that they do not measure any significant advance in tackling the major remaining problems in Chinese word segmentation, such as unknown words and segmentation ambiguities. Instead, all these figures seem to indicate a similar performance, which is, more interestingly, even similar to the performance reported a decade ago. Secondly, we have not had much ground to compare different systems' performance, not only because they were tested with different sets of data but also because the ways of calculating the segmentation accuracy are observed to be different from one another. On the contrary, the disambiguation accuracy is more specific, revealing exactly the capacity of a disambiguation strategy to resolve particular ambiguities found. It is reasonable to assume that everyone can get the unambiguous part correct in word segmentation, so we need not bother taking this part into account for the evaluation of disambiguation performance. Instead, we choose to concentrate on the problematic part, reporting only the disambiguation accuracy for the purpose of evaluation.

5.3 Discussions

As pointed out before, the conventional strategy for ambiguity detection that we have adopted is known to be incomplete. Many remaining ambiguities in the data are still to be brought to light. It is certainly a research direction that deserves more effort. Discovering more such missing cases can no doubt enlarge the example base significantly, and consequently enhance the strength of this case-based learning approach to disambiguation.

This problem is also related to the intrinsic disambiguation ability of the rudimental MMs: they segment many ambiguous strings correctly because of their own characteristics rather than by chance. Thus, it is worth digging out these uncovered ambiguities as examples so that they can be correctly handled when they show up elsewhere that would puzzle the MMs.

A more detailed analysis of experimental results is also expected, e.g., how many cases are resolved by existing examples and how many others by chance, i.e., by the $q(\cdot)$ function, which was designed to alleviate, rather than resolve, the problem. Also, a careful analysis of unseen cases in the testing data is also critical for a more thorough evaluation of the merits of the case-based learning approach. It will reveal the *coverage* of the EB and severity of the sparse data problem. A conceivable solution for the moment is that we construct all possible ambiguities based on a given dictionary and assign to them proper resolutions, so as to produce an EB with greater coverage.

6 Conclusions

In this paper we have presented a case-based learning approach to resolving Chinese word segmentation ambiguities. We adopted a simple representation for the examples, each consisting of an ambiguous string and its contexts, and also formulated a similarity measure for matching an ambiguity and an example from the example base. The effectiveness of this learning approach was tested on a set of unrestricted news texts of 1.5M characters, and a disambiguation accuracy of 90% was achieved

With this promising result, what we can expect is that if this approach could be effectively integrated with a segmentation algorithm that has a segmentation performance of the accuracy P, the overall segmentation accuracy one can expect would be

$$P' = P + (1 - P)90\% = (90 + 10P)\%$$

From this formula, we can see that if $P > 90\%$,

then $P' > 99\%$, and if $P > 95\%$, then $P' > 99.5\%$. Therefore, a bright future seems to be promised, because most Chinese word segmenters were reported to have achieved an accuracy over 95%, according to the literature.

However, the problems we still have with this case-based learning approach include, mainly, the incompleteness of ambiguity detection and the unknown coverage of the example base collected from unrestricted texts. All these remaining problems, that we will tackle in our future research, would have certain effect on the effectiveness of integrating it into any Chinese word segmenter.

References

M. R. Brent. 1999. An efficient, probabilistically sound algorithm for segmentation and word discovery. *Machine Learning*, 34:71–106.

Jing-Shin Chang and Keh-Yih Su. 1997. An unsupervised iterative method for Chinese new lexicon extraction. *International Journal of Computational Linguistics & Chinese Language Processing*, 1(1):101–157.

Jyun-Sheng Chang, C.-D. Chen, and S.-D. Chen. 1991. Chinese word segmentation through constraint satisfaction and statistical optimization. In *ROCLING-IV*, pages 147–165, National Chiao-Tung University, Hsinchu, Taiwan.

Jing-Shin Chang, Yi-Chung Lin, and Keh-Yih Su. 1995. Automatic construction of a Chinese electronic dictionary. In David Yarovsky and Kenneth Church, editors, *WVLC-3*, pages 107–120, Somerset, New Jersey, June.

Keh-Jiann Chen and Shing-Huan Liu. 1992. Word identification for mandarin Chinese sentences. In *COLING'92*, volume I, pages 101–107, Nantes, France, July 23-28.

Tung-Hui Chiang, Ming-Yu Lin, and Keh-Yih Su. 1992. Statistical models for word segmentation and unknown word resolution. In *ROCLING-V*, pages 121–146, Taiwan.

W. Daelemans, S. Buchholz, and J. Veenstra. 1999. Memory-based shallow parsing. In *CoNLL-99*, pages 53–60, Bergen, Norway.

Walter Daelemans, Jakub Zavrel, Ko van der Sloot, and Antal van den Bosch. 2001. Timbl: Tilburg memory based learner, version 4.0, reference guide. Technical Report ILK Technical Report 01-04, Induction of Linguistic Knowledge, Tilburg University, The Netherlands.

C. de Marcken. 1996. *Unsupervised Language Acquisition*. Ph.D. thesis, MIT, Cambridge, Mass.y.

A. P. Dempster, N. M. Laird, and D. B.Rubin. 1977. Maximum likelihood from incomplete data via the em algorithm. *Journal of the Royal Statistical Society, Series B*, 34:1–38.

Charng-Kang Fan and Wen-Hsiang Tsai. 1988. Automatic word identification in Chinese sentences by the relaxation technique. *Computer Processing of Chinese and Oriental Languages*, 4(1):33–56.

Kok-Wee Gan, Martha Palmer, and Kim-Teng Lua. 1997. A statistically emergent approach for language processing: Application to modeling effects in ambiguous Chinese word boundary perception. *Computational Linguistics*, 22(4):531–553.

Xianping Ge, Wanda Pratt, and Padhraic Smyth. 1999. Discovering Chinese words from unsegmented text (poster abstract). In *SIGIR'99*, pages 271–272, Berkeley, August.

Gregory Grefenstette and P. Tapanainen. 1994. What is a word, what is a sentence? Problems of tokenization. In *3rd Conference on Computational Lexicography and Text Research, COMPLEX'94*, Budapest, July 7-10.

Gregory Grefenstette, Anne Schiller, and Salah Aït-Mokhtar. 2000. Recognizing lexical patterns in text. In F. van Eynde, D. Gibbon, and I. Schuurman, editors, *Lexicon Development for Speech and Language Processing*, pages 141–168. Kluwer, Dordrecht.

Gregory Grefenstette. 1999. Tokenization. In Hans van Halteren, editor, *Syntactic Wordclass Tagging*, pages 117–133. Kluwer, Dordrecht.

Yingchun Guan and Bei Qin. 1986. The design and implementation of a Chinese word statistical system. *Journal of Chinese Information Processing*, 1(1):26–32. (In Chinese).

Jin Guo. 1997. Critical tokenization and its properties. *Computational Linguistics*, 23(4):569–596.

J. Hockenmaier and C. Brew. 1998. Error-driven learning of Chinese word segmentation. In *PACLIC-12*, pages 218–229, Singapore. Chinese and Oriental Languages Processing Society.

F. Jelinek. 1997. *Statistical Methods for Speech Processing*. MIT Press, Cambridge, MA.

Wanying Jin. 1992. A case study: Chinese segmentation and its disambiguation. Technical Report MCCS-92-227, Computing Research Laboratory, New Mexico State University, Las Cruces.

Wanying Jin. 1994. Chinese segmentation disambiguation. In *COLING-94*, pages 1245–1249.

Chunyu Kit and Yorick Wilks. 1999. Unsupervised learning of word boundary with description length gain. In M. Osborne and E. T. K. Sang, editors, *CoNLL-99*, pages 1–6, Bergen, June.

Chunyu Kit, Yuan Liu, and Nanyuan Liang. 1989. On methods of Chinese automatic word segmentation. *Journal of Chinese Information Processing*, 3(1):1–32. (In Chinese).

Chunyu Kit. 2000. *Unsupervised Lexical Learning*

as Inductive Inference. Ph.D. thesis, University of Sheffield, UK.

Tom B. Y. Lai, Sun C. Lin, Chaofen Sun, and Maosong Sun. 1991. A maximal matching automatic Chinese word segmentation algorithm using corpus tagging for ambiguity resolution. In *ROCLING-IV*, pages 17–23.

Nanyuan Liang and Yuan Liu. 1985. The OM method of automatic word segmentation. *Chinese Information*, 1(2). (In Chinese).

Nanyuan Liang. 1984. Automatic word segmentation for written Chinese and the segmentation system CDWS. *Journal of Beijing University of Aeronautics and Astronautics*, ?(4). (In Chinese).

Nanyuan Liang. 1986. CDWS – an automatic word segmentation system for written Chinese. *Journal of Chinese Information Processing*, 1(2):44–52. (In Chinese).

Nanyuan Liang. 1989. Knowledge for Chinese word segmentation. *Journal of Chinese Information Processing*, 4(2):29–33. (In Chinese).

Yuan Liu and Nanyuan Liang. 1986. Basic engineering for Chinese processing – Modern Chinese word frequency counting. *Journal of Chinese Information Processing*, 1(1):17–23. (In Chinese).

Yuan Liu, Qiang Tan, and Xukun Shen. 1994. *Contemporary Chinese Word Segmentation Standard Used for Information Processing, and Automatic Word Segmentation Methods.* Tsinghua University Press, Bejing. (In Chinese).

Hong I Ng and Kim Teng Lua. (forthcoming). A word finding automation for Chinese sentence tokenization. Submitted to ACM Transaction of Asian Languages Processing.

David Palmer and J. Burger. 1997. Chinese word segmentation and information retrieval. In *AAAI Spring Symposium on Cross-Language Text and Speech Retrieval.*

David Palmer. 1997. A trainable rule-based algorithm for word segmentation. In *ACL-97*, pages 321–328, Madrid.

David D. Palmer. 2000. Tokenization and sentence segmentation. In R. Dale, H. Moisl, and H. Somers, editors, *Handbook of Natural Language Processing*, pages 11–35. Marcel Dekker, New York.

Fuchun Peng and Dale Schuurmans. 2001. Self-supervised Chinese word segmentation. In *4th International Symposium of Intelligent Data Analysis*, pages 238–247.

Jay M. Pont and W. Bruce Croft. 1996. USeg: A retargetable word segmentation procedure for information retrieval. In *Symposium on Document Analysis and Information Retrieval' 96 (SDAIR).* UMass Technical Report TR96-2, Univ. of Mass., Amherst, MA.

R. Sproat, C. Shih, W. Gale, and N. Chang. 1996. A stochastic finite-state word-segmentation algorithm for Chinese. *Computational Linguistics*, 22(3):377–404.

Mark Stevenson and Yorick A. Wilks. 2001. The interaction of knowledge sources in word sense disambiguation. *Computational Linguistics*, 27(3):321–349.

Maosong Sun and Benjamin K. T'sou. 1995. Ambiguity resolution in Chinese word segmentation. In Benjamin K. T'sou and Tom B. Y. Lai, editors, *PACLIC-10*, Hong Kong, December 27-28.

Maosong Sun and Zhengping Zhou. 1998. Word segmentation ambiguity in Chinese texts. In Benjiamin K. T'sou, Tom B. Y. Lai, Samuel W. K. Chan, and Williams S-Y. Wang, editors, *Quantitative and Computational Studies on the Chinese Language*, pages 323–338. Language Information Sciences Research Centre, City University of Hong Kong.

W. J. Teahan, Yingying Wen, Rodger J. McNab, and Ian H. Witten. 2000. A compression-based algorithm for Chinese word segmentation. *Computational Linguistics*, 26(3):375–393.

J. Veenstra, A. Van den Bosch, S. Buchholz, W. Daelemans, and J. Zavrel. 2000. Memory-based word sense disambiguation. *Computing and the Humanities*, special issue on SENSEVAL, 34(1-2y).

Anand Venkataraman. 2001. A statistical model for word discovery in transcribed speech. *Computational Linguistics*, 27(3):353–372.

Jonathan J. Webster and Chunyu Kit. 1992a. Tokenization as the initial phase in NLP. In *COLING'92*, pages 1106–1110, Nantes, France, July 23-28.

Jonathan J. Webster and Chunyu Kit. 1992b. Tokenization for machine translation: What can be learned from Chinese word identification. In *Proc. of 3rd International Conference on Chinese Information Processing,*, Beijing.

Zimin Wu and Gwyneth Tseng. 1993. Chinese text segmentation for text retrieval: achievements and problems. *JASIS*, 44(9):532–542.

Shiwen Yu. 1998. *Knowledge Base of Grammatical Information for Contemporary Chinese.* Tsinghua University Press, Bejing. (In Chinese).

Jakub Zavrel, Walter Daelemans, and Jorn Veenstra. 1998. Resolving PP attachment ambiguities with memory-based learning. In T. Mark Ellison, editor, *CoNLL97: Computational Natural Language Learning*, pages 136–144, Somerset, New Jersey.

Guodong Zhou and Kim Teng Lua. (forthcoming). A hybrid approach toward ambiguity resolution in segmenting Chinese sentences. Submitted to Computer Processing of Oriental Languages.

Corpus-Based Pinyin Name Resolution

Kui-Lam KWOK
Computer Science Dept., Queens College,
City University of New York
65-30 Kissena Boulevard,
Flushing, NY 11367, USA
kwok@ir.cs.qc.edu

Peter DENG
Computer Science Dept., Queens College,
City University of New York
65-30 Kissena Boulevard,
Flushing, NY 11367, USA
deng@ntkk.cs.qc.edu

Abstract

For readers of English text who know some Chinese, Pinyin codes that spell out Chinese names are often ambiguous as to their original Chinese character representations if the names are new or not well known. For English-Chinese cross language retrieval, failure to accurately translate Pinyin names in a query to Chinese characters can lead to dismal retrieval effectiveness. This paper presents an approach of extracting Pinyin names from English text, suggesting translations to these Pinyin using a database of names and their characters with usage probabilities, followed with IR techniques with a corpus as a disambiguation tool to resolve the translation candidates.

Introduction

It is important for many applications to be able to identify and extract person names in text. For English, capital letter beginning of a word is an important clue to spot names, in addition to other contextual ones. When an English story refers to a foreign person, it is relatively easy to represent the person's name if the alphabets have approximate correspondences between the languages. When it refers to a Chinese person, this is not possible because Chinese language does not use alphabets. The most popular method for this purpose is Pinyin coding (see, for example, the conversion project at the Library of Congress website (2002)), China's official method of using English to spell out Chinese character pronounciations according to the Beijing Putonghua convention. Chinese characters are monosyllabic, and the large majority of them has one sound (ignoring tones) and hence one code. However, given a Pinyin it usually maps to multiple characters. Such an English Pinyin name raises ambiguity about the original Chinese characters that it refers to and hence the person. If the name is well known, such as Mao ZeDong, this is not an issue; if the name is less frequently seen, one would like to see or confirm the actual Chinese characters.

The situation is similar to many Chinese word processing systems that use Pinyin as one of their input methods. When a Pinyin is typed (sometimes with tonal denotation), many candidate characters will be displayed for the user to select. The character list can be ordered based on a language model, Chen & Lee (2000), or on the user's past habit. When one comes across names as input however, a language model is not as helpful because practically any character combination is possible for names.

Pinyin names also present difficulties in a cross language information retrieval (CLIR) scenario. Here, an English query is given to retrieve Chinese documents, and Pinyin names could be present as part of the query. In general, one can have three approaches to CLIR as discussed in Grefenstette (1998): translate the Chinese documents to English and do retrieval matching in English; translate the English query to Chinese and do matching in Chinese; or translate both to an intermediate representation. With the first approach, one could use standard table lookup to map the characters of a Chinese name to Pinyin after identifying a name for extraction. Chen and Bai (1998), Sun et.al. (1994) have shown that this extraction process is not trivial since Chinese writing has no white space to delimit names or words. A more general difficulty is that the document collection may not be under a user's control, but available for retrieval purposes only. This makes document translation to the query language (or to an intermediate language) not suitable. A more flexible approach is to translate a query to Chinese and do retrieval in Chinese. This has been the more popular method to use for CLIR in TREC experiments: Voorhees and Harman (2001). Whichever translation direction one chooses, a bilingual dictionary is essential. This dictionary however can be expected to be incomplete, especially with person names. Missing their translations can adversely impact on CLIR effectiveness. This raises the question of how to render Pinyin names into Chinese characters for translingual retrieval purposes.

In the recent NTCIR-2 English-Chinese cross language experiments, Eguchi et.al. (2001), quite a few queries have names. Kwok (2001) found that these lead to good monolingual retrieval because the names are quite specific and have good retrieval properties. On the other hand, for CLIR that starts with English queries, not being able to translate Pinyin names correctly leads to substantial deficit in effectiveness. This causes comparisons with monolingual results particularly dismal.

In this paper, we propose an approach to resolve the characters from a Pinyin code. It is based on: 1) a rule-based procedure to extract Pinyin codes for Chinese person names in English text; 2) a database for proposing candidate Chinese character sequences for a Pinyin code based on usage probabilities; and 3) a target collection and IR techniques as a confirmation tool for resolving or narrowing down the proposed candidates. These are described in Sections 1, 2, and 3 respectively. Section 4 presents some CLIR results and a measure of the effectiveness of our procedures.

We like to stress that even if one obtains the correct Chinese characters for a Pinyin, they can still refer to different persons with the same name. We do not address this issue here.

1 Pinyin Name Extraction

Chinese person names in Pinyin have fairly predictable formats such as: first alphabet of the family name (surname) is capitalized, as is the first word (or second word) of a given name. Two-syllable given names may appear as one word or two. The latter may be hyphenated, a practice popular in places such as Taiwan or Hong Kong. Thus, one may find Chairman Mao's name in any of the following formats:

Mao Ze Dong
Mao ZeDong　　Mao Zedong
Mao Ze-Dong　　Mao Ze-dong

Some publications also place the given name in front of the surname to agree with Western name convention. This style is supported but not used in this paper.

While the surname character is pretty much closed, the given name is not. It is well known that the most popular Chinese surnames number to about 100. Including less frequent ones bring the number to about 400 which we use: see Hundred Surname website (2002). Sun, et.al. (1994) reported over 700 surnames in their studies when additional infrequent ones are included. Other than for a few exceptions, this set all have unique Pinyin codes. These surname codes constitute an important clue for spotting a name sequence. The capitalized word(s), and the monosyllabic nature of words immediately after (or before) the surname give further support of its existence. We also loosen name definition to detect entries that have a hyphen but without a surname. Some rare surnames can be two syllables long, and often pair with one syllable given names. A woman may include her own family name in addition to her husband's. For our current study, we limit testing to a sequence of two to three Pinyin syllables only. This seems sufficient for the large majority of names encountered. Fig.1 shows our procedure to identify possible Pinyin names without the need of a training corpus or a name dictionary.

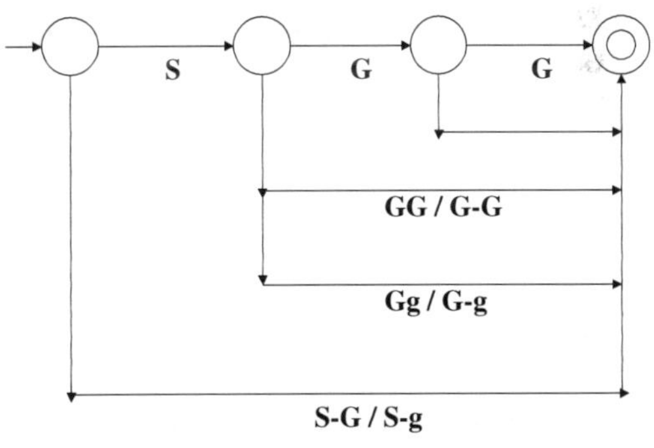

Figure 1: Pinyin Name Detection Algorithm
(S,G = surname & given name syllable with upper-case first character; Gg, G-g = concatenated or hyphenated syllables, second one with lower-case)

2 Mapping Pinyin Name to Chinese

To suggest Chinese characters for the detected Pinyin, we downloaded about 200K Chinese names. This is augmented with another ½ million Chinese name usage isolated from the TREC-6 Chinese collection using BBN's

IdentiFinder (see Section 4). Last name and given name/characters are stored separately to form a database of name usage with frequencies. Two-character given names are stored both ways: as a single entry (observed) and as two separate characters. Observed usage items have their frequencies muliplied by a large factor to separate it from the unobserved type. A potential Pinyin surname is mapped to a set of possible characters. Existence of such characters in this surname database is the first step to decide that one may have a possible name sequence. Otherwise, we assume the Pinyin is not a name.

Knight and Graehl (1997) have proposed to compose a set of weighted finite state transducers to solve the much more complicated problem of back-transliteration from Japanese Katakana to English. Their concern includes all types of source Katakana terms (not just names), corruptions due to OCR, approximations due to modeling of English, Japanese pronunciations, and a language model for English. Proposing Chinese characters for Pinyin is like back-transliteration and can also be viewed probabilistically. Some unique considerations however lead to a much simpler problem.

Given an English Pinyin name E=EsEg (surname Es, given name Eg), our concern is to find the best Chinese name character sequence C=CsCg that maximizes P(C|E), or equivalently P(E|C)*P(C). Since surnames (Es,Eg) and given-names (Cs,Cg) can be considered independent, this probability can be re-written as: P(Es|C)*P(Cs)*P(Eg|C)*P(Cg).The conditioning on C can be replaced by Cs and Cg respectively since Chinese given names Cg should not influence English surname Es, and Cs should not influence Eg. As discussed before, other than a few exceptions Chinese characters have unique Pinyin, and hence P(Es|Cs) and P(Eg|Cg) is deterministic. Maximizing P(C|E) is equivalent to maximizing P(Cs')*P(Cg'), where Cs' and Cg' are sets of characters mapping from Es and Eg respectively. These probabilities are obtainable from frequencies in our database. Given names are limited to one or two syllables. In the latter case, the two characters are also assumed independent, and estimates of P(Cg') are smoothed between character pairs and their corresponding singles.

To illustrate, we use the Pinyin: Jiang ZeMin (correct Chinese name is 江泽民) as an example. This spelling is confirmed as a name because "Jiang" maps to five possible surnames, and "ZeMin" obeys given-name format, and have corresponding characters. Each surname character and all possible combinations of the given name characters are considered and probabilities evaluated based on the database of name usage frequencies. The top 16 candidates and estimated probabilities produced from our procedure are shown below:

.763 江泽民	.119 蒋泽民	.110 姜泽民	.005 江泽敏
.001 强泽民	.001 蒋泽敏	.001 姜泽敏	.000 江泽闽
.000 江则闵	.000 江泽棉	.000 江泽绵	.000 江泽冕
.000 江泽	.000 江泽悯	.000 江泽岷	.000 蒋泽闽

The probabilities are skewed because the first (correct) name has large usage frequency in the training data. However, every candidate is a possible name irrespective of probabilities because of the idiosyncracies of name forming.

Quite often, some places or organizations also sound like names. These will also be translated (see example in Section 4). A couple of notable failures are strings like 'So China', which our procedure decodes as a name 'So Chi-na', 'So' being a legitimate surname in Wade-Giles convention. 'Hong Kong' also passes our test with candidates: 洪孔, 红崆, 鸿空, etc. A 'stoplist' of such string patterns is employed to partially alleviate these errors.

3 Pinyin Name Resolution

Once candidate names for a Pinyin are available, one may output the top n ranked items as answers. However, selecting names based on probability may not be the best strategy. Quite often, people deliberately choose rare characters for naming purpose because they want to be differentiated from the usual run-of-the-mill names. Our strategy is to use IR techniques with a text collection to help in name selection. For cross language retrieval, it is especially helpful to use the target retrieval collection for resolution. This ensures that a translated name exists in the collection for retrieval. For general application, one could employ domain-relevant collections. Moreover, one can also use the occurrence frequency of the names in the collection to help narrow down the candidates: i.e. the higher the frequency, the more probable that the name is the intended one. This has the advantage that selection is tailored more to the application, and less dependent on the name character database of Section 2. When the collection is well chosen, this process can whittle down the candidates to just a few with good accuracy.

4 Experimental Studies

We performed two studies to demonstrate our Pinyin resolution strategy. The first is to repeat retrieval on some queries in NTCIR-2 cross language experiments to see how Pinyin name resolution can affect effectiveness. A second experiment is to use BBN's IdentiFinder as a reference, and to compare how our procedures succeed in extracting Pinyin names and translating them with respect to a reference set.

4.1 CLIR with Pinyin Names

One of the NTCIR-2 cross language retrieval experiments (Eguchi, et.al. 2001) consists of 50 English topics and a Chinese target collection of about 200 MB. The purpose is to retrieve relevant Chinese documents using English text (topics) as queries. The Chinese counterparts to the English topics were also given so that CLIR results can be compared to monolingual. The original topics are lengthy; we limit our queries to a few words from the 'title' section of the topics. Three queries have Pinyin names and two contain non-person Pinyin entities that satisfy our Pinyin name detection format.

On running these 'title' queries through our procedure, the Pinyin codes were identified, candidates suggested, and resolved using the target collection. Listed in Table 1 are the queries. The Pinyin name in each 'Original English' and 'Original Chinese' query is bolded. Under the column 'Selected Names with Occurrence Frequency' are the resolved Pinyin names in Chinese, together with their occurrence frequencies in the retrieval collection. As discussed in Section 3, these selections are narrowed down from a large number of candidates in the intermediate step.

The Pinyin in Query 33 is for a kind of bean, while Query 44 has the name for a well known mountain, but they satisfy our definition of a name pattern. It can be seen that except for Query 46, the name with the largest occurrence agrees with the one intended in the monolingual query. In Query 46, the given name 'Yo-yo' is non-standard Pinyin, with suggested candidates like '唷唷' or '育育', and there are no such entries in the collection. If it were spelt 'You-you', the correct characters '友友' will be among the candidates and selected by the collection. When these Pinyin names with frequency>=5 were added to our MT software concatenated with dictionary translation procedure, Kwok (2001), the initial retrieval results in Table 2 are obtained. Here we follow the TREC convention to evaluate retrieval using the measures RR (relevant documents in top 1000 retrieved), Av.P (average precision), and P@20 (precision at the top 20 documents retrieved).

Substantial improvements were obtained for four of the queries when the names are correctly picked, and come closer to or even surpass the monolingual result. This demonstrates that our approach to Pinyin name resolution can work, but we need more queries of this type to confirm the effect. Query #15 has very high Av.P of .3287 because dictionary translation brought in useful content words not present in the monolingual query like: 绑票 (kidnapping), 杀害, 杀人案件 (murder criminal case). These

Table 1. Pinyin Name Resolution in 5 Queries (* denotes Correct)

Qry#	Original English	Original Chinese	Selected Names with Occurrence Frequency
15	**Bai Xiao-yan** kidnapping murder criminal case.	白晓燕绑架撕票案.	*白晓燕 66
33	**Bai-feng** Bean.	白凤豆.	*白凤 69, 白風 2
44	**Hua-shan** Art Zone.	华山艺术特区.	*华山 41, 華善 2, 花山 2
46	**Ma Yo-yo** cello recital.	马友友演奏会.	马 3792, 麻 234
47	**Jin Yong** kung-fu novels.	金庸武侠小说.	金永 5, 金勇 2, 金泳13, *金庸 186

Table 2: Effect of Pinyin Resolution on Retrieval Results of 5 Queries (Compared to Monolingual and Translation Only)

Qry#	Monolingual			Translation			Translation+ Pinyin		
	RR	Av.P	P@20	RR	Av.P	P@20	RR	Av.P	P@20
15	17	.1594	.15	12	.0611	.10	18	.3287	.30
33	13	.5277	.45	13	.2174	.10	13	.4579	.45
44	7	.3856	.30	5	.0082	.00	6	.1783	.15
46	7	.7543	.35	7	.0078	.00	7	.0077	.00
47	17	.5801	.45	17	.3179	.35	17	.6311	.50

expand the query and combine synergistically with the Pinyin name to provide precision surpassing the monolingual result. As a candidate name, 金庸 in Query #47 has very low probability compared to others because the character 庸 (meaning 'mediocre') is rarely used in names. It was pulled out by high occurrence frequency in the target collection. Thompson & Dozier (1997) have also shown that correctly indexing names in monolingual English retrieval leads to better retrieval.

4.2 Resolving Pinyin Names in Text

In another experiment we intended to test our Pinyin procedure with parallel collections that contain many paired names, but failed to locate one. We intend to evaluate how well our extraction procedure works, and whether candidate suggestion can recover correct Chinese names. A pair of collections was downloaded from the Peoples' Daily website (2001) Year 2001 English version (~17MB) and the Chinese version (~70MB) as our test collections. A sampling shows that they have very different content. Our aim is to isolate Pinyin names from the English collection, and create a list of their Chinese counterparts. We can then compare our Pinyin extraction against the English list. We also like to see how our database suggest Chinese candidates for this fairly recent name set. The evaluation is more approximate compared to doing an evaluation using parallel corpora with lots of names paired.

BBN's Identifinder, described in Weischedel et. al. (1996) was employed to process both collections independently. When given English or Chinese texts, IdentiFinder can bracket enttities of different types such as: PERSON, LOCATION, ORGANIZATION, etc. for later extraction. PERSON entities were isolated and two unique person name lists were produced: 4840 in English and 47621 in Chinese. They include Pinyin, non-Chinese and Chinese person names. The Chinese list contains many entries with one character (such as a surname 陈), translitered foreign names, and some with symbols. These we want to avoid. By capturing entries of length >=2 characters, without symbols, and having legitimate surnames, a filtered list of 23,863 Chinese entries were obtained. They were mapped into Pinyin and intersected with the English list. A total of 897 COMMON entries resulted, forming our reference set (Fig. 2). These are Chinese names obtainable by translating from the 4840-entry English list and which occur on the filtered list.

The original English collection was next processed through our Pinyin identification procedure, and 1769 unique entries were detected to satisfy our criteria. Comparison with IdentiFinder's English list shows that 1467 (83%) are the same, and 302 (17%) different. The non-overlap can be due to: i) non-person entities that sound like names on our list; ii) non-Chinese names on the IdentiFinder list; iii) legitimate Chinese names detected by one and not the other; or iv) errors on either procedures. Candidate Chinese names were suggested for our 1769-entry Pinyin list, and afterwards resolved with the Chinese COMMON list. This tests how well our database suggests names for Pinyin. The result is shown in Table 3. We show suggestions of 1, 5, up to 50 candidates, and recall of the reference set improves steadily from 35.3% to 93.9% (missing 55 of those 897 in COMMON) at 50 suggested. This shows the

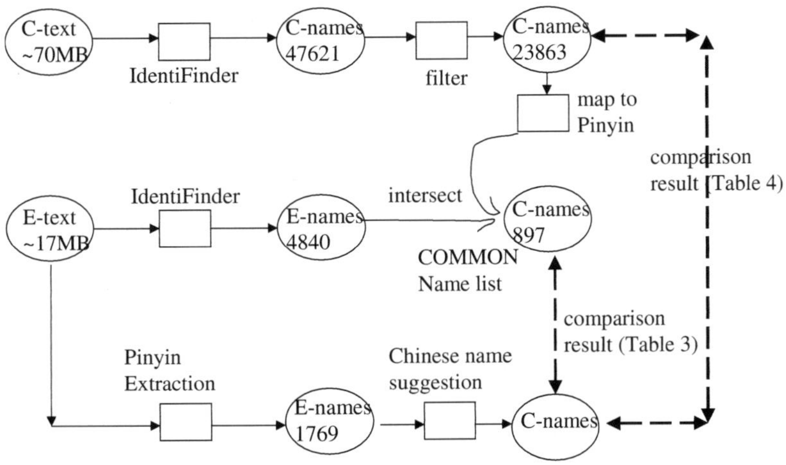

Fig.2 Pinyin Name Extraction & Suggestion: Comparison with IdentiFinder (BBN)

Table3 : 1769 Pinyin Names Resolved Against COMMON Name List (Size=897)

# of Candidates	Breakdown of 1769 Pinyin Names	Recall
1	1452 + **317 in COMMON**	**35.3% of 897**
5	1155 + **614** "	**68.5%** "
10	1041 + **728** "	**81.2%** "
30	949 + **820** "	**91.4%** "
50	927 + **842** "	**93.9%** "

Table 4: 1769 Pinyin Name Resolved Against Filtered Chinese List (Size=23863)

# of Candidates	Breakdown of 1769 Pinyin Names	NewNames Recovered
1	1422 + **347 in Filtered Chinese List**	**347-317=30**
5	1052 + **717** "	**717-614=103**
10	912 + **857** "	**857-718=129**
30	783 + **986** "	**986-820=166**
50	753 + **1016** "	**1016-842=174**

difficulty of suggesting a correct name: only ~35% recall at top 1, ~68% at top 5. In general, small 'top n' is not sufficient to recover a correct name translation, while using too many lead to noise. Hence there is a need to resolve candidates on a relevant collection.

We further compare the suggested Chinese names for the 1769 Pinyin against the filtered Chinese list (23863 entries) to see whether our Pinyin extraction can recover additional Chinese names not obtained by IdentiFinder (from the same English text). We found that at each suggestion level (Tables 4 & 3), more names were found by our Pinyin procedure that were missing in IdentiFinder: 30 at suggestion level 1, up to 174 (~19%) more names at the level of 50. These 174 are names in the filtered portion of the Chinese list but not included in COMMON because the English list from IdentiFinder does not have their corresponding Pinyin. The rest (1769-1016=) 753 on our list could be non-person entities that sounded like names, wrongly identified entries, or person names that do not exist in IdentiFinder's Chinese list. IdentiFinder may fail to extract some Chinese names as well. For example, some Pinyin names with 'An' as surname were missed. This study demonstrates the ability of our approach to locate Pinyin names in English text and translate them.

Conclusion and Discussion

A procedure to translate any Pinyin name into possible Chinese characters with probabilities based on usage frequencies is proposed. Candidates can further be resolved against a text collection to narrow down the possibilities. This leads to better CLIR results. For a recent English news collection, 83% of Pinyin names identified agrees with names found by BBN's IdentiFinder. Chinese name candidates for these Pinyin cover between 35.3 to 93.9% of a COMMON name set for the IdentiFinder names when suggestions varies between 1 to 50. But additional Chinese names not extracted by IdentiFinder can be located using our procedure. Pinyin is an official coding used in China and getting popular elsewhere. Names from other places such as Taiwan use different Pinyin conventions like Wade-Giles. We had some provision for them, but plan to expand our coverage for these names more completely in the future.

Some web search engines offer advanced techniques that allow users to input English key terms and display results from Chinese documents, selecting items that have the English term and Chinese counterpart. These engines serve like giant bilingual dictionaries providing for entity translation. However, web pages usually contain current data and popular names only (like Ma Yo-yo). Lesser known names (like Bai Xiao-yan) are not available. Our approach can suggest Chinese names for Pinyin even if web search fails, or the relevant collection employed does not further resolve the suggested translations. For CLIR, our procedure ties translated names to the retrieval collection. We envisage each of these approaches has its own advantages, and that employing both together may help provide more accuracy for the issue of how to translate Pinyin names.

Acknowledgements

This work was partially sponsored by the Space and Naval Warfare Systems Center San Diego, under Grant No. N66001-00-1-8912. We thank BBN for the use of their IdentiFinder software.

References

Chen, K-J. & Bai, M-H. (1998) *Unknown word detection for Chinese by a corpus-based learning method.* Intl. J. of Computatinoal Linguistics & Chinese Language Processing. 3:27-44.

Chen, Z. & Lee, K-F. (2000) A new statistical approach to Chinese Pinyin input. (available at http://www.microsoft.com/china/research/dload_files/g-nlps/NLPSP/n8.pdf)

Eguchi, K., Kando, N. and Adachi, J. (eds.) (2001) *Proc. of Second NTCIR Workshop on Research in Chinese & Japanese Text Retrieval, and Text Summarization.* NII: Tokyo. (available at http://research.nii.ac.jp/ntcir/)

Grefenstette, G. (1998) *Cross language Information Retrieval.* Kluwer Academic Publishers, Boston.

Hundred Surname website. (2002) (available at http://www.geocities.com/Tokyo/3919/hundred.html)

Knight, K. and Graehl, J. (1997) *Machine transliteration.* Proc.of 35th Annual Meeting of ACL, pp. 128-135.

Kwok, K.L. (2001) *NTCIR-2 Chinese, cross language retrieval experiments using PIRCS.* In: Proc. of Second NTCIR Workshop on Research in Chinese & Japanese Text Retrieval, and Text Summarization. pp. 111-118. NII: Tokyo. (available at http://research.nii.ac.jp/ntcir/).

Library of Congress Website. (2002) (available at http:// www.loc.gov/catdir/pinyin/outline.html)

People's Daily Website. (2001) (available at http://www. peopledaily.com.cn)

Sun, M.S., Huang, C.N., Gao, H.Y. and Fang, J. (1994) *Identifying Chinese names in unrestricted texts.* Comm. COLIPS, 4, pp. 113-122.

Thompson, P. and Dozier, C.C. (1997) *Name searching and information retrieval.* Proc. 2nd Conf. on Empirical Methods in NLP, pp. 134-140.

Voorhees, E. and Harman, D.K. (eds). (1998) *The Sixth Text Retrieval Conference (TREC-6).* NIST Special Publication 500-249. (available at http://trec.nist.gov/)

Voorhees, E. and Harman, D.K. (eds) (2001) *The Ninth Text Retrieval Conference (TREC-9).* NIST Special Publication 500-249. (available at http://trec.nist.gov/)

Weischedel, R. Boisen, S., Bikel, D., Bobrow, R., Crystal, M., Ferguson, W., Wechsler, A. & the PLUM Research Group. (1996) *Progress in Information Extraction.* Proceedings of Tipster Text Program (Phase II). pp. 127-142.

An Indexing Method Based on Sentences*

Li Li [1], Chunfa Yuan[1] , K.F. Wong[2], and Wenjie Li[3]
[1]State Key Laboratory of Intelligent Technology and System
[1]Dept. of Computer Science & Technology, Tsinghua University, Beijing 100084
Email: lili97@mails.tsinghua.edu.cn; cfyuan@tsinghua.edu.cn
[2]Dept. of System Engineering & Engineering Management, The Chinese University of Hong Kong, Hong Kong.
Email: kfwong@se.cuhk.edu.hk
[3] Department of Computing, The Hong Kong Polytechnic University, Hung Hom, Hong Kong.
Email: cswjli@comp.polyu.edu.hk

Abstract

Traditional indexing methods often record physical positions for the specified words, thus fail to recognize context information. We suggest that Chinese text index should work on the layer of sentences. This paper presents an indexing method based on sentences and demonstrates how to use this method to help compute the mutual information of word pairs in a running text. It brings many conveniences to work of natural language processing.

Keywords: natural language processing, index file, mutual information

1. Introduction

Natural Language Processing often needs to analyze the relationships between words within the same sentences or the syntax of the sentences by considering the specific words. To obtain such information, sentences are usually considered as the basic processing units [4]. The fixed window approach is often used in previous studies to observe the contexts of the specific words and extract them from corpora to form a sub corpus for some purposes [5,6]. To observe the other words, corpora have to be scanned again and again. Therefore, creating an index file in advance will help locate the specified words fast and could extend the ability to cope with the large-scale problems.

Although the traditional indexing methods can locate the specific words fast, it needs extra work to provide the context information. Traditional computer indexing methods record the physical position of the words in the corpus. The position information is stored in the index file. To find out where the specified word is, the index file can provide physical position directly. Then the word in the corpus can be quickly located [3]. However, if we want to extract the sentences containing the words, the traditional processing methods have to search forward and backward to find the boundary of these sentences.

The indexing method presented in this paper creates the index file based on sentences. Unlike traditional indexing methods that record the physical position of the word in the corpus, this new method records the logical positions of the words. Not only can the index file give the numbers of the sentences in which the specified word occurs, but also locate these sentences in the corpus instantly. Since the indexing method based on sentences records the information of the contexts of the words, we are able to conveniently study some problems with the words in the sentences concerned, which could be called the logical layer. That makes it feasible to solve some natural language processing problems in a large-scale corpus.

The rest of this paper is organized as follows. The second section describes the principle of the method proposed in this paper. Then the third section summarizes its advantages. And an example applying the method is given in the fourth section. The fifth section closes this paper with conclusion.

2. Description of the method

As mentioned above, the difference between the indexing method presented in this paper and

*Supported by Natural Science Foundation of China(69975008) and 973 project (G1998030507)

the traditional ones is: the method presented here records the logical positions (sentence number), which can be mapped to physical positions (file pointer), while traditional ones only record the physical positions. By using the method presented here, when we want to get where the concerned word is, what we need to know first is not the physical positions, but the logic ones. Then we extract the sentences including the word from the corpus with the logic positions mapping to physical positions.

The indexing method presented in this paper deals with the following five kinds of files:

(1) Corpus File: a large-scale text file.

(2) Separation File: a binary file, recording the positions of the delimiter of each sentence in the corpus.

(3) Word List File: a text file, which consists of a sorted list of words.

(4) Frequency File: a binary file, which records the frequencies and the starting positions of the corresponding blocks in the Index File.

(5) Index File: a binary file, which consists of a series of blocks, the logical positions of the words in the corpus.

Corpus File and Word List File are provided by users. The other three kinds of files, Separation File, Frequency File and Index File, are created in indexing process. With the method presented here, we deal with one large-scale text file as our corpus. Thus we avoid the problem of coding the multiple documents and subdirectories. It is generally believed that Chinese information retrieval should be based on words, not characters [1,2]. So we process the corpus with segmentation.

Before creating an index file, we must have a Word List File that we want to create an index for. Generally, the word list is a sorted list. Thus we can fast locate any specified word in the list.

The Separation File is created according to the Corpus File. So the Separation File needs to be updated if the Corpus File is changed. The Frequency File and the Index File correspond to the Word List File. These three files are bound together. We may have many groups of these three kinds of files built on the same Corpus File and the corresponding Separation File. If the Word List File changes, the corresponding Frequency File and Index File will be updated as well.

The procedure of creating index files is divided into two steps, which are described respectively in the following two parts.

2.1 Create the Separation File

Five delimiters are defined as the separation punctuations of Chinese sentences: Comma (，), Period (。), Interrogation (？), Semicolon (；), and Interjection (！). We scan the corpus for these five delimiters and record the physical positions into the separation file. The Separation File is composed of a series of records; each record consists of two parts:

(1) The code of the delimiters, which distinguishes the different kinds of the delimiters;

(2) The physical position of each delimiter found in the corpus.

The following table shows the structure of the Separation File (one row represents one record):

Code of the 1st delimiter	Physical position 1
Code of the 2nd delimiter	Physical position 2
Code of the 3rd delimiter	Physical position 3
…	…

Table-1 The structure of the Separation File

From the Separation File, the sentence with the specified number from the corpus can be extracted quickly. For instance, the i_th sentence in the corpus is obviously between the physical position stored in record i-1 and the one in record i.

2.2 Create the Frequency File and Index File

From the Separation File, we can retrieve each sentence from the Corpus File in ascending order of the sentence number. Then we record the logical position of every word in the sentence, that is, the sentence number, into the index file. The index file is composed of a series of the blocks. Each word in the Word File corresponds to some consecutive blocks stored in the Index File. The number of the blocks each word associates equals the frequency of the word in the Corpus File. So we need to create the Frequency File to record the frequency of the word and to store the position of the starting block in the Index File.

Each record of the Frequency File consists of two parts:

(1) The frequency of the word occurring in the Corpus, which is equal to the number of the blocks the word associates in the Index File.

(2) The starting position in the Index File, which is the starting position of a series of corresponding blocks in the index file.

The following table shows the structure of the Frequency File (one row represents one record):

Frequency of the 1st word	Starting position 1
Frequency of the 2nd word	Starting position 2
Frequency of the 3rd word	Starting position 3
…	…

Table-2 The structure of the Frequency File

A word may appear several times in one sentence. We record the sentence number for each occurrence of the word, in the Index File. That is, the Index File will have some sequential blocks recording the identical sentence number for the word.

2.3 Search

When a user input the word, the program will search that word in the word file first and get the word number, such as No.i. Then the No.i record in the Frequency File will be obtained. The No.i record includes the information of word frequency and the starting position of its blocks in the Index File. From these blocks the logical positions (sentence numbers) are obtained and will be transformed into physical positions by Separation File. Then, we can extract all the sentences containing the word if necessary.

The following is the data-flow map, which illustrates the procedures described above.

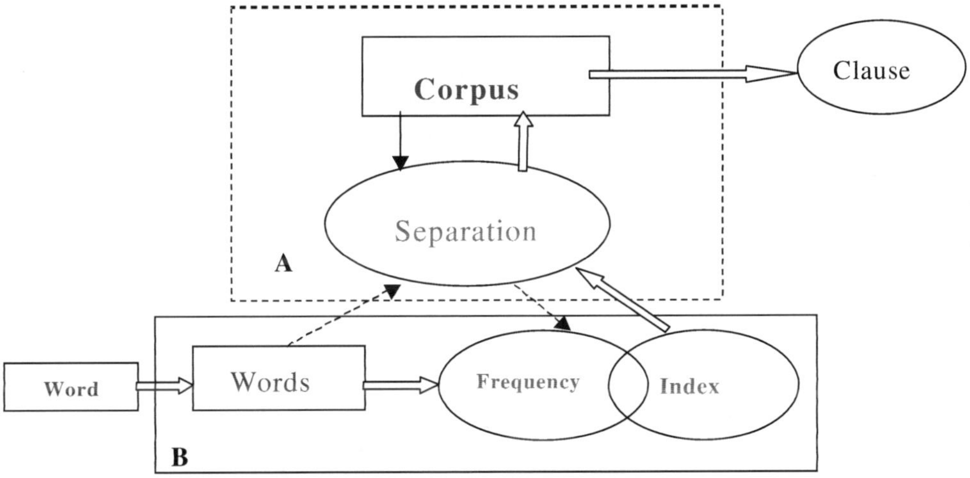

Fig-1 The data flowing map

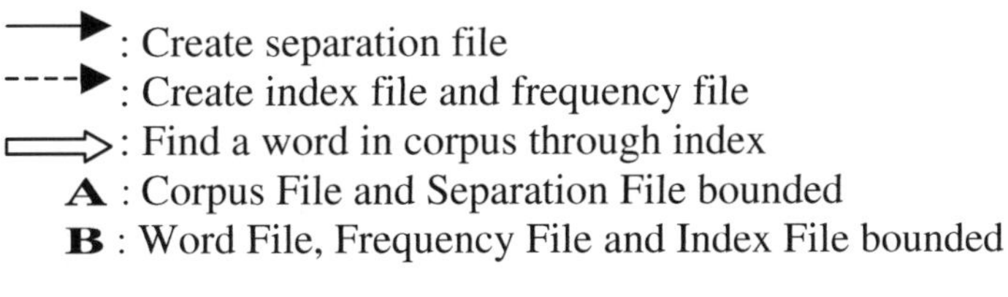

3. The advantages of the method

Text files include many control characters, such as carriage-return and new-line characters. So the natural language content is separated by these control characters. The meaningful separations should be some punctuations in natural languages. Our indexing method screens the effects of the control characters and brings more convenience for natural language processing than traditional ones.

The method can be applied on both raw corpora and processed corpora, quickly supplying the sentences containing keywords. Traditional indexing method can only give the physical positions of the keywords, lacking context information. It has to search forward and backward to find out sentence boundaries if needed. Actually, our method has done the portion of sentence locating work, recorded the information already in the procedure of creating Separation File and saved the time of searching.

When we study the relationship of some words in a large corpus, the method allows preprocessing on the sentences, which make viable some kinds of real-time computing in large-scale corpora. Traditional methods often use fixed-size window to observe the contexts of specified words and thus limit the ability to solve large-scale problems. The sentences, however, are the natural observing windows. The indexing method based on sentences reduces much time consumed for matching words in the corpus and concentrates on the concerned ranges directly. The next section demonstrates an example that applies the method to compute the mutual information of an adjective-noun word pair in a large-scale corpus.

4. An Example applying the method

In some natural language processing tasks, we may need to compute the mutual information of word pairs. In this example, it is assumed that the objective is to compute the mutual information of an adjective-noun pair. The adjective is "美丽" ("beautiful"), and the noun is "草原" ("grassland"). Firstly, we create the Separation File for the corpus, the Frequency File and Index File for the Word List File. Secondly, we get the sentences containing the adjective and the noun. Finally, we select the proper sentences and compute the mutual information.

4.1 Source Files

The initial sources are a corpus file and a word list file. The program runs in a personal computer with Pentium II 466 processor and 128 MB RAM. It costs one hour and two minutes to create the Separation File, three hours and fifteen minutes to create the Frequency File and Index File. Table-3 shows the size and content of these files.

FILE NAME	SIZE	CONTENT
Corpus	240,000KB	120 million tokens
Word List	385KB	62,467 word items
Separation	27,7000KB	5,816,952 sentences in Corpus
Frequency	488KB	62,467 records
Index	100,000KB	26,351,631 word occurrences in Corpus

Table-3 The source files

4.2 Search the adjective and noun pairs

When we search the adjective and the noun in the corpus, we can obtain the adjective's sentence numbers and the noun's sentence numbers from the Frequency File and Index File. By comparing the two series of sentence numbers in order and finding the common ones. We get the sentences in which the adjective and the noun both appear. In fact, we do not see these sentences now, but only get the sentence numbers in the corpus. However, we can extract these sentences from the corpus according to the separation file if necessary. If we are only concerned about the frequency that the adjective-noun pair co-occurrences and don't care about the contexts, there's no need to use the separation file and the corpus file.

We describe the algorithm of obtaining the sentences including the adjective-noun pair in the following procedure:

(1)Get the sentence numbers of the adjective: $a1 \leqslant a2 \leqslant a3 \leqslant \ldots \leqslant am$ according to the frequency file and the index file;

(2)Similarly, get the sentence numbers of the noun:b1⩽b2⩽b3⩽…⩽bn;
(3)Initialize i=1, j=1, count=0;
(4)If ai=bj, then memorize the integer i, and i++, j++, count++
else if ai<bj then i++
else j++;
(5)Repeat (4) until i=m or j=n;
(6)If observing another adjective-noun pair, repeat (1)-(5)

Actually, we've got the intersection of the adjective's sentence number set and the noun's. The sentence numbers are naturally in ascending order, since we scan the corpus sentences one by one to create the index file. This reduces the complexity of the algorithm to be O(m+n), as is shown in Step (3) – Step (5). If they are not in order, the complexity of obtaining the intersection has to be O(m*n); if they are ordered in running programs, the complexity of algorithm has to be O(m*log(m)) or O(n*log(n)).

4.3 Compute mutual information

Mutual information is widely used to measure the association strength of the two events [1,6]. The following equation is used to compute the mutual information of the adjective-noun pair:

$$MI(\text{美丽},\text{草原}) = \log_2 \frac{p(\text{美丽},\text{草原})}{p(\text{美丽})p(\text{草原})}$$

$$p(\text{美丽}) \approx \frac{\mathrm{N}(\text{美丽})}{\mathrm{N}_c}, \qquad p(\text{草原}) \approx \frac{\mathrm{N}(\text{草原})}{\mathrm{N}_c}$$

$$p(\text{美丽},\text{草原}) \approx \frac{\mathrm{N}(\text{美丽},\text{草原})}{\mathrm{N}_c}$$

N_c is the total number of sentences in the corpus, so $N_c = 5{,}816{,}952$. It is observed that $\mathrm{N}(\text{美丽}) = 1884$, $\mathrm{N}(\text{草原}) = 1984$ and $\mathrm{N}'(\text{美丽},\text{草原}) = 18$ which is the number that two words appear in the same sentences. If the observing window size is assumed to be one sentence and the goal is to compute the distributional joint probability of the two words, $\mathrm{N}(\text{美丽},\text{草原}) = \mathrm{N}'(\text{美丽},\text{草原}) = 18$, then $MI(\text{美丽},\text{草原}) = 4.807976$.

If only selecting the sentences in which the adjective "美丽" modifies the noun "草原", we need to extract the 18 sentences and parse them or perform semantic analysis, then $\mathrm{N}(\text{美丽},\text{草原}) \le \mathrm{N}'(\text{美丽},\text{草原}) = 18$. Consequently, the result is $\mathrm{N}(\text{美丽},\text{草原}) = 10$, that means in the other 8 sentences the adjective doesn't modify the noun, but some other word. So $MI(\text{美丽},\text{草原}) = 3.959981$.

5. Conclusion

This paper demonstrates how the method creates the index file and gives the sentences including keywords. It then shows an example that employs the method to discover the sentences containing the adjective-noun pairs and compute their mutual information. As it is shown, the method can effectively extract the sentences including specific words and make the real-time probabilistic computation possible. It is also easy to extend the algorithm to search for three or more specific words appearing in the same sentences or to obtain the intersection, union and difference of their sentence number sets.

The method can be widely applied for many applications in Chinese information processing, such as information extraction, segmentation, tagging, parsing, semantic analysis, dictionary compilation and information retrieval. It is particularly fit for the situation of dealing with specific words and sentences in large-scale corpora and is a supporting tool for the researches of natural language processing.

References

[1] Aitao Chen, Jianzhang He, Liangjie Xu, Fredric C. Gey and Jason Meggs, Chinese Text Retrieval Without Using a Dictionary, In SIGIR, pages 42-49, 1997.
[2] Jian-yun Nie, Martin Brisebois and Xiaobo Ren, On Chinese Text Retrieval, In SIGIR, pages 225-233, 1996.
[3] Gerard Salton and Michael J. McGill, Introduction to Modern Information Retrieval, McGraw-Hill, Inc., 1983.
[4] R.Rosenfeld, A Whole Sentence Maximum Entropy Language Model, In Proceedings of the IEEE Workshop on Automatic Speech Recognition and Understanding, 1997.
[5] 孙宏林, 词语搭配在文本中的分布特征, 中文信息处理国际会议论文集, 1998.
[6] 孙茂松, 黄昌宁, 方捷, 汉语搭配定量分析初探, 中国语文, 1997 年第 1 期, 29-38 页.

Design of Chinese Morphological Analyzer

Huihsin Tseng
Institute of Information Science
Academia Sinica, Taipei
kaori@hp.iis.sinica.edu.tw

Keh-Jiann Chen
Institute of Information Science
Academia Sinica, Taipei
kchen@iis.sinica.edu.tw

Abstract

This is a pilot study which aims at the design of a Chinese morphological analyzer which is in state to predict the syntactic and semantic properties of nominal, verbal and adjectival compounds. Morphological structures of compound words contain the essential information of knowing their syntactic and semantic characteristics. In particular, morphological analysis is a primary step for predicting the syntactic and semantic categories of out-of-vocabulary (unknown) words. The designed Chinese morphological analyzer contains three major functions, 1) to segment a word into a sequence of morphemes, 2) to tag the part-of-speech of those morphemes, and 3) to identify the morpho-syntactic relation between morphemes. We propose a method of using associative strength among morphemes, morpho-syntactic patterns, and syntactic categories to solve the ambiguities of segmentation and part-of-speech. In our evaluation report, it is found that the accuracy of our analyzer is 81%. 5% errors are caused by the segmentation and 14% errors are due to part-of-speech. Once the internal information of a compound is known, it would be beneficial for the further researches of the prediction of a word meaning and its function.

1. Introduction

This is the first attempt to design a morphological analyzer to automatically analyze the morphological structures of Chinese compound words[1]. Morphological structures of compound words contain the essential information of knowing their syntactic and semantic characteristics. In particular, morphological analysis is a primary step for predicting the syntactic and semantic categories of out-of-vocabulary (unknown) words. The existence of unknown words is a major obstacle in Chinese natural language processing. Due to the fact that new words are easily coined by morphemes in Chinese text, the number of unknown words is increasingly large. As a result, we cannot collect all the unknown words and manually mark their syntactic categories and meanings. Our hypothesis to predict the category and the meaning of a word is basically based on Frege's principle: "The meaning of the whole is a function of the meanings of the parts". The meanings of morphemes are supposed to make up the meanings of the words. However, some words like idioms and proper nouns cannot be included in the principle. In general, unknown words could be divided into two different types: the type that has the property of semantic transparency, i.e. the words whose meanings can be derived from their morphemes and the type without meaning transparency, such as proper nouns. In this paper we are dealing with the compound words with semantic transparency only. For the type of compounds without semantic transparency, such as proper nouns, their morphemes and morphological structures do not provide useful information for predicting their syntactic and semantic categories. Therefore they are processed differently and independently. In addition, some regular types of compounds, such as numbers, dates, and determinant-measure compounds, are easily analyzed by matching their morphological structures with their regular expression grammars and the result can be used to predict their syntactic and semantic properties, so they will be handled by matching regular expressions at the stage of word segmentation. According to our observation, most Chinese compounds have semantic transparency except proper nouns, which means the meaning of an unknown word can be interpreted by their own morpheme components. The design of our morphological analyzer will focus on processing these compounds, but words without semantic transparency are excluded. It takes a compound word as input and produces the morphological structure of the word. The major functions are 1) to segment a word into a sequence of morphemes, 2) to tag the part-of-speech of those morphemes, and 3) to identify the

[1] Compound words here include compounds in traditional Chinese linguistics and morphological complex words.

morpho-syntactic relation between morphemes. Once the morpho-syntactic structure of a compound is known, the head morpheme provides the major clue for determining its syntactic and semantic category.

It seems that a Chinese morphological analyzer is similar to a tagging program. Indeed both systems have to resolve the segmentation and tagging ambiguities. However the major difference is that the morphological analyzer does not have contextual information of each target word. In other words, morphological structures of compounds are context independent. We cannot apply the same methods, such as n-gram language models, to resolve the ambiguities. We proposed a method of using the associative strength among morphemes, morpho-syntactic patterns, and syntactic categories to solve the ambiguities. Detail algorithms for morpheme segmentation, part-of-speech, and morpho-syntactic relation assignment are discussed in Section 2. In the final section, we will evaluate the morphological analyzer by comparing its results with those obtained from the analyses of 5 linguists and discussing the categorization of errors found.

2. The Morphological Analyzer

The morphological analyzer contains three functions: to segment a word, to tag the part-of-speech (POS) of morphemes, and to identify the relation between them.

2.1 Segmentation

The goal of this process is to segment a compound word into a sequence of morphemes. Since there are ambiguous segmentations, simple dictionary look-up methods may not work well. For instance, the compound of *meiguoren* (美國人) could be ambiguously segmented into either *mei-guoren* ([美[國人]] beautiful countryman) or *meiguo-ren* ([[美國]人] American people), but only *meiguo-ren* ([[美國]人] American-people) is the proper segmentation. The left-to-right longest matching method is commonly applied to segment either words or text. It works well, but there are still some small percent of compound words that cannot be properly segmented by such a simple algorithm. For instance, the word *xin-shenghuo* ([新[生活]] new life) will be segmented wrongly into *xinsheng-huo* ([[新生]活] the life of a new student) without considering the priority of segmenting the affix *xin* (新 new) first. In particular, words with multi-syllabic suffixes and words with reduplication constructions commonly cause segmentation errors. Those special types of words should be analyzed with other methods.

2.1.1 Affixes and reduplication

In order to remedy the segmentation error caused by the left-to-right longest matching, we observe the results of the algorithm and find that there are two useful clues to avoid segmentation errors, i.e. the information of affix and reduplication.

A word of a reduplication pattern cannot and need not be segmented by the longest left-to-right method, since it has special morphological structures and the reduplication patterns bring enough clues of knowing the syntactic functions of the word. Therefore we try to identify words that belong to reduplication patterns first. In general they fall into the following two types of patterns: reduplications and parallel words. Words, which do not conform to these patterns, will be segmented later.

Table 1 Special types of patterns and their examples

Patterns	Pattern Maker	Note and examples
Reduplication word	AA, AAA, ABB, AAB, AxA, ABAB AABB, AxAy, xByB,	*liang-liang* (亮亮), *dui-dui-dui* (對對對), *song-kua-kua* (鬆垮垮), *chi-chi-kan* (吃吃看), *xiang-yi-xiang* (想一想). *yan-jiu-yan-jiu*(研究研究), *chi-chi-he-he*(吃吃喝喝), *pao-shang-pao-xia*(跑上跑下), *yi-nian-zai-nian*(一唸再唸)
Parallel word	A-BC (AC, BC)	zhong-xiao-xue (中小學)

Reduplication means to duplicate the one or two character words into multi-character words. All reduplication patterns we used are listed in Table 1. If a word belongs to a reduplication pattern, the meaning of the word doesn't change too much. The reduplication word's category can be predicted by their patterns. For example, when B is not a noun, a word which belongs to the pattern AAB is intransitive verb. The category of a word that belongs to the pattern of "parallel word" is always a noun. The characteristic of parallel words is that both AC and BC are words with shared head word C.

At the next step of the morpheme segmentation, we will consider the compounds with affixes. The most productive compound construction is the structure of a morpheme plus an affix. Hence after the affix is identified, it would be easier to segment a word into two parts. The segmentation algorithm works as follows. A word is segmented immediately only if a prefix, infix or suffix morpheme is found. The affix table contains 186 prefixes, 2 infixes and 648 suffixes. Some affixes of the table are multi-syllabic. To segment an affix with higher priority will resolve most of the errors caused by the left-to-right longest matching algorithm. For instance, if *tiaoshangqu* (跳上去 to jump up) is segmented by the left-to-right longest matching method, and the result of the segmentation is *tiaoshang-qu*. The left-to-right longest matching method might cause error segmentation here. However, *shangqu* is one of the suffixes in the affix table, so in our morphological analyzer it would be segmented as *tiao-shangqu*. A word containing an infix is also not suitable for the general segmentation and it would be segmented into single character. There are some affixes examples in Table 2:

Table2 Types of affixes and their examples

Types of affix	Morpheme	Examples
Prefix	*xin*(新)	*xinsheng-huo* (新生活)
Infix	*de*(得)	*suan-de-shang*(算得上)
Suffix	*ju*(劇) *shangqu* (上去)	*feizao-ju*(肥皂劇) *tiao-shangqu* (跳上去)

2.1.2 Left-to-right longest matching

If a word is neither reduplication nor a compound with an affix, it should be segmented from left to right with longest matching. This general method can segment words into morphemes and also provide a possible part-of-speech of each morpheme by looking it up in the morpheme dictionary.

2.2 Tagging

The work here is to provide the part-of-speech for each morpheme and identify a morpho-syntactic relation between two morphemes based on the information of segmentation and their pos. This is the most difficult part of morphological analysis. In achieving the goal, we face two obstacles: the information insufficiency of morpheme categories and morphemes with the multiple categories. Since morpheme categories are not the same as word categories, it is necessary to assign each morpheme with appropriate categories and to compile a morpheme dictionary. Once the morpheme dictionary is built, the remaining job is to resolve the part-of-speech ambiguities of each morpheme. Since the part-of-speech of the morpheme is independent of its word level context, we cannot apply n-gram like language models to resolve part-of-speech ambiguity of morphemes. Even worse, there is no structure tagging training data available either. An EM-like unsupervised training on part-of-speech morphological structures is also not a sensible solution, since morpho-syntactic structure is more sensitive to the semantic combination than the syntactic combination of morphemes. Therefore we propose a method of using morphemes to predict the possible syntactic categories of the target compound word and selecting the most probable consistent result among the candidates of part-of-speech structures and the predicted categories.

2.2.1 Preparation of the morpheme dictionary

Before we start to tag morphemes, two steps are carried out to resolve the obstacles. That is the lack for a morpheme dictionary and morpheme ambiguity. First, in order to resolve the lack for morpheme categories, it is necessary to edit an affix table, as mentioned in Section 2.1, which contains prefixes, infixes, suffixes and their categories. Most frequently encountered 186 prefixes and 648 suffixes are listed in this table. Basically, if its morpheme has more than 2 characters, we adopt its categories in the CKIP Dictionary. Conversely, if it has fewer than 2 characters and it functions as a prefix or a suffix, we use the categories in the affix table.

Below we illustrate two examples to explain the need of morpheme categories. Both words *yu* (語 to speak) and *wu* (舞 to dance) are verbs. However they could also function as morphemes. When they function as morphemes, they are listed as nouns in their category. It is worth noticing that the categories of a morpheme are not the same as those of a word, even if they are in the same form. Therefore, it is important to assign morphemes categories properly.

Table 3 The categories of –*yu* and –*wu* as a suffix and as a word and their examples

Suffix	Category[2] as a suffix	Category as a word	Example
-*yu*(語)	Na	VE	*ying-yu*(英語), *de-yu*(德語)
-*wu*(舞)	Na	VC, Na	*jueshi-wu*(爵士舞)

[2] The category symbols here are based on CKIP(1993). The meaning of each category we adopt here is as following: A(non-predicative adjective), Na(common noun), Nb(proper noun), Nc(location noun), Nd(time noun), VA(active intransitive verb), VB(semi-transitive verb), VC(active transitive verb), VCL(active transitive verb with locative object), VD(ditransitive verb), VE(active transitive verb with sentential object), VG(classificatory verb), VH(stative intransitive verb), VHC(stative causative verb), VJ(stative transitive verb) and so on.

Second, in order to resolve the problem of morpheme ambiguity, we need a list of probabilities which contains all the possible combinations of categorical rules and their probabilities. For instance, in the list the probability P(Na+Na|Na) = 0.4692 means that the categorical rule of combining two common nouns (Na+Na) to form a common noun (Na) has the probability 0.4692. The probability values of each categorical rule were estimated from the set of 11,322 unknown words extracted from Sinica Corpus 3.0. The syntactic category of each extracted word is known but its structure annotation is unknown. Therefore the probability of each categorical rule is roughly estimated by assuming that every ambiguous categorical combination of a word have equal probability.

The process of computing the possibility of a combination is as follows:

1) We assign morphemes in a word with all their possible categories found in the dictionary and the affix table; for example, *sheyingzhan* ([[攝影]展] photography exhibition), which belongs to Na category means "photography exhibition". *Sheyingzhan* could be segmented as *sheying* (攝影 photography) and *zhan* (展 exhibition). After segmentation, we found *sheying* with the categories Na and VA, and *zhan* with the category Na. The possible combinations of *sheying-zhan* are "Na+Na->Na" and "VA+Na->Na". However, we don't know which one is correct, so we presumably assign a frequency of 0.5 to each combination.

2) After we assign morphemes their categories and frequencies, we add up the frequencies of identical combinations. A list containing possible categorical rules and their probabilities is then established. Table 4 shows a part of the categorical rules of VHC.

Table 4 A partial list of categorical rules and their probabilities

Rule	Category	Probabilities
Na+VHC	VHC	0.4494
VH+VHC	VHC	0.2303
Nc+VHC	VHC	0.0674
VHC+VHC	VHC	0.0449
VA+VH	VHC	0.0280
VC+VHC	VHC	0.0224
VJ+VH	VHC	0.0224
Nd+VHC	VHC	0.0112
VC+Na	VHC	0.0112
VC+VC	VHC	0.0112
VC+VHC	VHC	0.0112

2.2.2 Part-of-speech

Once the affix table and the list of categorical rules are prepared, we can tackle the problems of the obstacles we mentioned in the beginning. After morpheme segmentation, each morpheme is assigned with their proper categories according to the morpheme dictionary and the affix table. However, morphemes might be ambiguous, so if the category of the target word is known, the most probable part-of-speech combination is chosen based on the list of categorical rules. However in the real implementation, it is assumed that the syntactic category of a target word is not known. The method mentioned above would not work, unless its syntactic category can be predicted. In our implementation, we adopted the method proposed by Chen, Bai and Chen (1997), by using the association strength between morphemes and categories to predict the syntactic categories of target words. By using the mutual information between affixes and categories, the top one prediction has the accuracy of 67.00% and the top three accuracy of the prediction can reach about 94.02%. We will then check the consistency between predicted the categories and their morpho-syntactic structures to make the final judgments on both the word category prediction and the morpheme category disambiguation. The final prediction is based on the maximal value of the combined probabilities of the category prediction and the categorical rule prediction.

Since P(Rule|compound) = P(Cat|compound) * P(Rule|Cat, compound) ≅ P(Cat|compound) * P(Rule|Cat), we try to find Cat and Rule which maximizes $P(Cat_i|compound) * P(Rule_j|Cat_i)$, for all Cat_i and $Rule_j$. The following is an example of *.she-ying-zhan.*

==

sheying-zhan (攝影展 photography exhibition)

P(Na|*sheying-zhan*) *P(Na+Na|Na)= 0.6324*0.4692=0.2967
---max
P(Na|*sheying-zhan*) * P(VA+Na|Na)=0.6324 *0.0865=0.0547
P(VC|*sheying-zhan*)* P(Na+Na|VC)=0.3675* 0.0069=0.0025
P(VC|*sheying-zhan*)*P(VA+Na|VC)= 0.3675* 0.001=0.0003

sheying-zhan=(Na+Na)->Na

==

The top1 accuracy of the original category prediction for unknown words is 67% by mutual information, but after the combination of the morphological analyzer, the accuracy of the word category prediction is raised to 71%. This is because the morphological analyzer will check if the categorical combination in a word is in its proper category. Therefore, when the original unknown word prediction system predicts a word in a category which the morphological analyzer finds the probability of its categorical combination in the category low, the morphological analyzer might reject the category and suggest the unknown word prediction system to choose the next highest-scoring category in which the categorical combination has higher probability.

In the case that the syntactic category of the compound word is known, we will let P(Cat|compound) = 1 and the most probable part-of-speech combination will simply be the categorical rule $Rule_j$ such that $P(Rule_j|Cat)$ is maximized.

2.2.3 Morpho-syntactic relation between morphemes

Once the information of segmentation and part-of-speech is ready, the morpho-syntactic relation between morphemes can be identified. According to Chao (1968) and Li&Thompson (1981), there are relations between morphemes in compounds such as "modifier-hear", "predicate object" and so on. The purpose of knowing morpho-syntactic relation between morphemes is to help decide the meaning of the target word. The morpho-syntactic relation between morphemes is grouped into the types listed in Table 5. Generally, the relation between morphemes is highly related to the category of an unknown word. So the relation we assign to morphemes must be based on the category of the word. When the unknown word is a noun, the relation between its morphemes is "modifier-head". If it's a verb, it will be more complicated. There are five relation types in verbs. The first one is "verb-object", such as *chifan* (吃飯 to eat rice). The first morpheme must be a transitive one and the second one should be a noun. The second type of the relation is "modifier-head", and it means the second morpheme is the semantic head of the word. The third type is "resultative verb". The second morpheme in this type's word always expresses the result of the action. The forth type is "head-suffix". The appearance of the suffix changes the augment structure of the head verb, but the representing event remains the same. These suffixes are *ru* (如 to be similar to), *yu* (於 by), *wei* (為 to become), *gei* (給 to give), *chu* (出 to exit) and *cheng* (成 to become). The fifth type of the relation is "modifier-head", and there is only a morpheme *hua* (化 to transform) which belongs to this type. *Hua* is the head of a word. If a non-predicative adjective is an adjective, there are two kinds of structure. First, a non-predicative adjective has the same structure as a noun. The relation between its morphemes is also called "modifier-head". Second, the relation between morphemes for a non-predicative adjective which cannot be in the predicate position but has verbs structures can be "predicate-object" or "modifier head". This information will be helpful for predicting the core meaning of a new word.

Table 5 The morpho-syntactic relation between morphemes

	The morpho-syntactic relation between morphemes
Noun	Modifier-head
Verb	Verb-object Modifier-head Resultative Verb (RVC) Head-suffix Modifier-head(suffix)
Adjective	An: Modifier-head Av: verb-object, and modifier-head
Other	directional RVC and reduplication

Once the morpho-syntactic structure of a compound is identified, the head morpheme provides the major clue for determining its syntactic and semantic category. The compound word will inherit from the semantic and syntactic property of its head and the information will be beneficial for the semantic and syntactic categorization of new compound words in the future.

3. Evaluation and Discussion

The major functions of the morphological analyzer are to segment a word into a sequence of morphemes, to tag the part-of-speech of the morphemes, and to identify the morpho-syntactic relation between morphemes. The work in this section is to evaluate the quality of the word information which is processed by each function of the morphological analyzer. However, it is hard to evaluate the accuracy of the morphological analyzer automatically, so we compare the results generated by the morphological analyzer with results generated by human experts, which are made out of their language intuition. The answers agreed by the majority of the human experts are assumed to be the right answers. The closer the results of the morphological analyzer are to the human experts, the more accurate the morphological analyzer is.

The testing data is the set of unknown words extracted from the recently collected text by the system of Ma, Hsieh, Yang and Chen (2001). There is total 4,566 unknown words in our testing data. However, the validity of the morphological information is still uncertain; therefore five linguistic specialists have to manually verify the morphological structure of unknown words by filling out the survey. First, we randomly select 100 words as a testing set and the following three questions are answered by these five specialists.

1) What's the category of the unknown word?
2) What are the morpheme segmentations of the testing words?
3) What is the syntactic tag of each morpheme?

The definition of our "standard answer" is the answer the majority of the subjects give. For example, if three out of the five subjects consider the category of an unknown word X as VG, the standard answer of X would be VG. If five subjects think unknown word X belongs to five different categories, we would ask one more language specialist for opinions to determine the category of this unknown word. The standard answer we obtained from this survey will be the standard answer of the morphological analyzer.
The morphological analyzer contains three functions: to segment a word into morphemes, to tag pos, and to identify the relation between morphemes. The accuracy we mention here is the result from comparing the morphological result with the majority answer.

==

T=the total number of test set
R=the total number of being the same with the "Standard answer" of X
X=Subject1, Subject2, Subject3, Subject4, Subject5, Morphological Analyzer
Accuracy(X)= R(X)/T

==

Table 6 The accuracy of five subjects and morphological analyzer (MA)

	S 1	S 2	S 3	S 4	S 5	Average of 5 Ss	MA
Accuracy	89%	94%	94%	86%	83%	89.2%	81%

After comparing the result of the morphological analyzer with the standard answers obtained from the five linguists, we come to the conclusion that the accuracy of the morphological analyzer is 81%. Out of all the errors, 5% is caused by segmentation on proper nouns and loanwords, such as *bilinshan* (比林山 a name of a mountain), *dingwan* (鼎灣 a name of a place), *yanyou* (延祐 a name of a dynasty), *maniuda* (馬紐大 a name of a place), and *hongburang* (紅不讓 home run). These words cannot be segmented because they only make sense when they are treated as a unit. The remaining 14% is caused in the tagging process produced by a morpheme table which lacks in accuracy. For example, in some cases the suffix *zhou* (週 week) is supposed to be listed as Nd but is instead listed as Nc. Next, there are no proper categories for certain morphemes, such as the morpheme *lie* (列 to list as a verb, a row as a noun) in the word *qinglie* (清列). In the suffix table, the category of *lie* is only Na, but the morpheme *lie* should have a VC category when the meaning of *qinglie* "to list completely" is adopted. Another possible error-causing factor would be the choice made by following the combination rule. When there is more than one possible combination, errors might appear. For example, there are two possible combination for *waizhan* (外展 to stretch out), "Ng+Na" and "Ng+VC". Comparing the score of the two combinations, the combination of "Ng+Na" is chosen. However, it is not the correct category of *zhan* (展 to stretch).
The best way to resolve these problems mentioned above is to revise the morpheme table more often. Since the category of the suffix and prefix is fixed, it might cause a reduction in morpheme ambiguity. We are also interested in the similarity (or the range of agreement with language intuition of each individual) between those subjects. Since the standard answers are the answer of the majority, we can compare the standard answer with each individual. The average rate of the similarity rate is 89.2%. The ten-percentage puzzle might be due to the ambiguity of the word and can be interpreted that there are indeed some words that are not only difficult for a machine to analyze but also difficult for human beings to categorize.

Table 7 The error rate and examples

	Percent-age	Examples
Segmentation Error	5%	*hongburang*(紅不讓), *maniuda*(馬紐大)
		yanyou(延祐), *dingwan*(鼎灣), *bilinshan* (比林山)
Tagging Error	14%	*mihou*(獼猴) ***tao*(桃)(Nc)**, *zixun*(資訊) ***zhou*(週)(Nc)**, *wai*(外) ***zhan*(展)(Na,VC)**

The evaluation of the identification of the morpho-syntactic relation is separated from the evaluation of segmentation and tagging, because the relation between morphemes is identified based on previous information, such as the category of a word, segmentation, and the pos. Once the essential information is clear, the morpho-syntactic relation is known. Nine out of a hundred examples are marked by linguists as errors of the morpho-syntactic identifier.

Furthermore, the reasons causing the error of relation identification are 1) the category predication's error, 2) the part-of-speech error, and 3) the lack of the relation type. Firstly, since the relation identifier is based on the result of the segmentation and pos, it is understandable that the error here is caused by previous functions. The category of *qipai-jia* ([[起拍]價] initial bidding price) is Na, but the system predicts it as an intransitive verb VA. So the identifier guesses the relation between *qipai and jia* as "verb-object" based on the previous information. The error of the category prediction system might result in errors of the relation identifier. Secondly, the relation of *qing-lie* (清列 to clearly list) should be "modifier-head", but the identifier marks it as "verb-object" relation because *lie*(列) is tagged as Na. When the suffix is a Na, the prefix is a verb, and since the category of *qing-lie* is predicted as a verb, the identifier can only predict the relation of *qing-lie* as "Verb-object". Therefore, the error of part-of-speech might cause the identifier errors. Thirdly, the linguists suggest the relation between morphemes in *nian-song* (念誦 to read) is "conjunction relation". That means that both the semantic meaning and syntactic function of *nian* (念 to read) and *song* (誦 to read) are the same. However, we don't have the "conjunction relation", because we think the number of words which belong to the kind of the relation is very limited, and since both morphemes the bring same information, there is no difference that enables us to mark both of them as heads or only one of them as a head for the application of predicating the semantic and syntactic property of a word. Therefore, in the morphological analyzer the words which belong to the "conjunction" relation are identified as "head-final" relations.

4. Conclusion and future work

This is a pilot study to design a morphological analyzer to analyze the morphological structures of Chinese compound words automatically. The major functions are 1) to segment a word into a sequence of morphemes, 2) to tag the part-of-speech of those morphemes, and 3) to identify the morpho-syntactic relation between morphemes. We evaluate the morphological analyzer by comparing 5 linguists' research results and discuss the type of errors we find. The more similar the results of the morphological analyzer compared with the human results, the better the morphological analyzer is. It is found that the accuracy of our analyzer is 81%. In comparison with the performance of human experts resulting in an accuracy of 89%, the performance of the current morphological analyzer is not bad, but still has room for improvement. More, the types and the identification of relations of morphemes still have much room to be improved. It is also worth noticing that the syntactic category prediction for general compounds can also be improved by the morphological analyzer. Once the internal information of a compound is known, it can provide clues for prediction of a word meaning and its function. The prediction of a word's meaning is very hard and will be one of the main themes in our future researches.

5 Reference

Bosch, Antal van den, Walter Daelemans and Ton Weijters. (1996) Morphological Analysis Classification: an Inductive-Learning Approach. *NeMLaP*.

Chao, Yuen Ren. (1968) *A grammar of spoken Chinese*. Berkeley:University of California Press.

Chen, Chao-jan, Ming-hung Bai and Keh-jiann Chen. (1997) Category Guessing for Chinese Unknown Words. *Proceedings of the Natural Language Processing Pacific Rim Symposium 1997*, 35-40.

Chen Yun-chai. (2001) *Corpus Analysis of Reduplication in Mandarin Chinese*. National Kaohsiung Normal University: English Department.

CKIP. (1993) *Technical Report no. 93-05: The analysis of Chinese category*. [中文詞類分析] CKIP:Nankang

Creutz, Mathias and Krista Lagus. (2002) Unsupervised Discovery of Morphemes. *Proceedings of Morphological and Phonological Learning Workshop of ACL'02*.

Beaney, Michael.(editor) (1997) *The Frege Reader*. Oxfort: Blackwell.

Li, Charles and Sandra A. Thompson. (1981) *Mandarin Chinese*. Berkeley: University of California Press.

Ma, Weiyun, Youming Hsieh, Changhua Yang, and Keh-jiann Chen. (2001) "Chinese Corpus Development and Management System " [中文語料庫構建及管理系統設計]. *Proceedings of Research on Computational Linguistics Conference XIV*, 175-191.

A Word Segmentation Method With Dynamic Adapting To Text Using Inductive Learning

Zhongjian Wang
Hokuto System Co.,LTD
Oyachi Higashi1-3-23, Atubetuku, Sapporo, 004-0041 Japan
wang@hscnet.co.jp

Kenji Araki
Graduate School of Engineering, Hokkaido University
N13-W8, Kita-ku, Sapporo, 060-8628 Japan
araki@media.eng.hokudai.ac.jp

Koji Tochinai
Graduate School of Business Administration, Hokkai-Gakuen University,
Asahimachi 4-1-40, Toyohira-ku, Sapporo, 062-8605 Japan

Abstract

We have proposed a method of word segmentation for non-segmented language using Inductive Learning. This method uses only surface information of a text, so that it has an advantage that is entirely not dependent on any specific language. In this method, we consider that a character string of appearing frequently in a text has a high possibility as a word. The method predicts unknown words by recursively extracting common character strings. With the proposed method, the segmentation results can adapt to different users and fields. To evaluate effectivety for Chinese word segmentation and adaptability for different fields, we have done the evaluation experiment with Chinese text of the two fields.

1 Instruction

In NLP applications, word segmentation of non-segmented language is a very necessary initial stage(Sun et al., 1998). In the other hands, with the development of the Internet and popularization of computers, a large amount of text information in different languages on the Internet are increasing explosively, so it is necessary to develop a common method to deal with multi-language(Yamasita and Matsumoto, 2000). Furthermore, the standard of word segmentation is dependent on a user and destination of use(Sproat et al., 1996), so that it is necessary that word segmentation can adapt users, can deal with multi languages.

In our method, we extract recursively a common character string that occur frequently in text and call it a common part. When some common parts contain still same character strings, furthermore we extract the same character string as high dimensional common parts and the remain parts is called different parts. The high dimensional common parts maybe have higher possibility as words because it is extracted by multi steps. Those extracted common parts and different parts are called WS(Word Segment), and classified into some ranks according to extracting condition. The proposed method segments a non-segmented sentence into words using the ranks of WS in order of the higher value of the certainty degrees as words. When there are multiple segmentation candidates, the system gets a list of segmentable candidates, and picks a correct segmentation candidate from the list by using a value of LEF (Likelihood Evaluation Function, Section **2.1**) and so on. In addition, it is not necessary to prepare a dictionary and any word segmentation rules beforehand. A dictionary of adapting to the user or the field is generated with increasing of processed text. Because only surface information of a text is used, it is possible the method is used to deal with general non-segmented language. Here Inductive Learning is the procedure to extract recursively WS by multi steps(Araki et al., 1995).

2 Algrithm

Fig. 1 shows the outline of the proposed method.

(1) Input sentences are segmented by word candidates that were acquired in the dictionary so far.

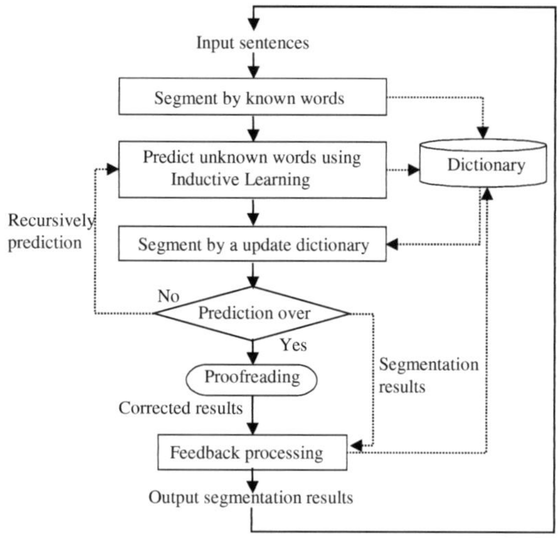

Figure 1: Outline

(2) For the remaining part of the character strings that are unsegmented by the known words, the system predicts unknown words by extracting WS using Inductive Learning.

The system extracts WS as word candidates. This process is based on the supposition that a common character string of appearing repeatedly in text has high probability as a word.

(3) The user judges whether the results of the word segmentation is correct or not. If there are errors in the result, the user will correct errors.

(4) The system compares the proofread results with the segmentation result to update the information in the dictionary. Through this procedure, the certainty of WS as a word is confirmed and increased.

Here, the WS those are used in correct segmentation are called CW (Correct Word).

2.1 Segmentation by Known Words

Input sentence and then the system segments it into words by registered CW and WS that the system has got by using Inductive Learning until that time.

(1) In the first step, the system compares the registered CW or WS in the dictionary with the character string in the input sentence from the beginning of the sentence, and finds out the same character strings with the registered words. The system repeats this comparison process until the end of the sentence is reached. A list of segmentation candidate is established. Then the system segments the sentence into words.

(2) In the second step, however, for the character strings of multiple segmentations, we use the registered candidates in order of their ranks in the dictionary(Section **2.3**). When there are more than one word candidate with the same rank, we decide the correct segmentation from the list of segmentation candidates by the value of LEF. We define LEF as follows:

$$LEF = \frac{FR + \alpha CS - \beta ES + \gamma LE}{FR + CS - ES + LE} \quad (1)$$

Where: FR, CS, ES and LE are the frequency of CW or WS appearing in the text, the frequency of the correct segmentation, the frequency of the erroneous segmentation and the length of CW or WS respectively. α, β and γ are coefficients. The optimum coefficients of LEF are decided by the preliminary experiments using Greedy method, α=10, β=1 and γ=5.

The word that has the maximum value of LEF is decided as the correct segmentation candidate.

(3) When LEF value of the set of possible segmentations is equal to each other, the correct segmentation candidate is decided by the word candidate that the value of ES is minimum, the value of CS is maximum, the value of FR is maximum, the value of LE is the longest or the location of segmentation is the leftmost in a sentence in turn.

2.2 Prediction for Unknown Words

Fig. 2 shows an example of a non-segmented sentence. In this example, every character represents a Chinese character, so we use this example to express a general sentence of non-segmented language to present the proposed method. Those words that are not registered in the dictionary are predicted by using Inductive Learning. After the sentences were segmented by known words, which have been registered in the dictionary, the unsegmented part of character string will be used to extract WS. The prediction method is to find the common character string in text. The extraction procedure is carried out as Fig. 3 shows: the extraction of common parts, sift out the common part of the most possibility as a word, the re-extraction of common parts and the extraction of different parts.

$$\alpha\beta\chi\delta\kappa\varphi\epsilon\phi\gamma\Theta\pi\mu\tau\gamma\beta\pi\alpha\beta\chi\delta$$
$$\Theta\pi\mu\tau\gamma\beta\eta\Psi\epsilon\phi\gamma\tau\gamma\beta\alpha\zeta\theta.$$

Figure 2: An example of non-segmented sentence.

2.2.1 Extraction of a Common Part

A common part in non-segmented text is extracted by two steps:

(1) When a character string appears in text frequently, we call it a common character string. If the common character string consists of more than two characters, we extract it as a word candidate and call it common part and represent it by S1(Segment one). Here, we use length, frequency and location of S1 in the sentence to sift out it, to get the S1 of the most possible as a word. At this step, we acquired S1 from the sentence that is shown in Fig. 2: "$\alpha\beta\chi\delta$","$\epsilon\phi\gamma$" and "$\Theta\pi\mu\tau\gamma\beta$".

(2) When the character string appears in the sentence only one times but meanwhile it is included in other extracted common part and made up by more than two characters, we also extract it as a word candidate. For example in Fig. 2: "$\tau\gamma\beta$" is included in "$\Theta\pi\mu\tau\gamma\beta$". Therefore "$\tau\gamma\beta$" is extracted and belongs to S1.

2.2.2 Extraction of a High Dimensional Common Part and a Different Part

The extracted S1 at **2.2.1** may still include a common character string. At this situation, the common character string can be re-extracted moreover from the extracted S1. We consider it has a higher probability as a word that re-extracted common parts at this procedure. The conditions of re-extraction are presented as follows:

(1) The common part can be re-extracted from the extracted S1 when it includes a common character string that is more than two characters. For example, "$\Theta\pi\mu\tau\gamma\beta$" contains "$\tau\gamma\beta$" which can be extracted from "$\Theta\pi\mu\tau\gamma\beta$", so "$\Theta\pi\mu\tau\gamma\beta$(S1)" is equal to "$\Theta\pi\mu$(S2)" + "$\tau\gamma\beta$(S3)".

The part of re-extraction is called high dimensional common part and represented by S2 (Segment two). The part of remain is called different part and represented by S3 (Segment three). The S1 is deleted from the dictionary

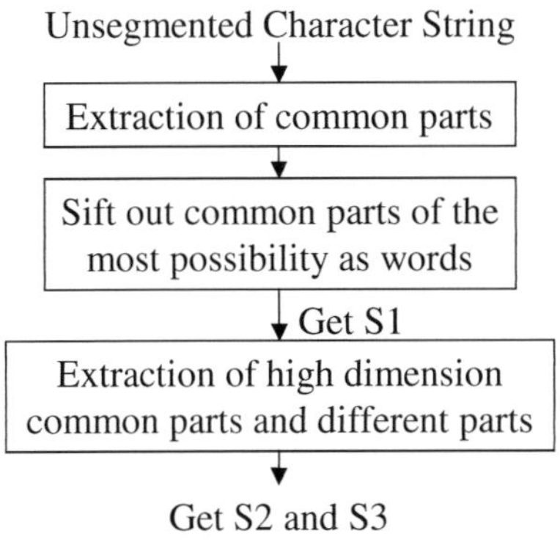

Figure 3: WS extraction procedure

when it is divided into S2 and S3.

(2) Furthermore one character can also be extracted as a word candidate when both sides of it are extracted as a word candidate or both sides were segmented by known words. Like "π" in "$\Theta\pi\mu\tau\gamma\beta\pi\alpha\beta\chi\delta$" is surrounded by "$\Theta\pi\mu\tau\gamma\beta$" and "$\alpha\beta\chi\delta$", and "$\pi$" is extracted as a word candidate belonging to S2.

The extraction procedure is carried out repeatedly until the new WS can not be extracted and the input can not be segmented.

2.3 Segmentation by a Update Dictionary

The extracted WS are classified to "S1", "S2", and "S3". Those WS that are confirmed as a word by proofreading process are called "CW" (Correct Word). Furthermore, the FR(appearing FRequency), CS(Correct Segmentation frequency), ES(Erroneous Segmentation frequency), LE(LEength) and rank of a word candidate are rigestered simultaneously. Word Segmentation is carried out by the update dictionary as **2.1**.

2.4 Feedback Process

After the system segments the sentence into words, the results are judged whether they are correct or not by the user. Then the user corrects the errors if there are errors in the results. The system updates the rank of the registered CW and WS in the dictionary by comparing the corrected results with the segmentation results. And the system increases the priority degree of the words that were used in correct segmentation and decreases the priority degree of words that were used in erroneous segmentations. The

Table 1: Experimental results

Fields	Economics	Engineering	Average
words	92,085	70,017	162,102
CSR[%]	87.50	90.80	89.44
ESR[%]	5.40	5.60	5.45
USR[%]	7.10	3.60	5.11

feedback process is described in detail as follows:

(1) For the Correct Segmentation Results:

- When the result of segmentation is correct, the value of FR and CS of a word that is used to segment are added one.
- If the rank of the words does not belong to CW, it is changed to CW.

(2) For the Erroneous Segmentation Results:

- If the dictionary does not has the correct words, the system registers the words in the dictionary. In this case, their FRs are 1, their ranks are CW.
- If the dictionary has the correct words, the system adds one to the value of FR for a word and changes the value of CL to CW if it does not belong to CW.
- If the reason of erroneous segmentation is that the erroneous word was used, then the ES of erroneous word is added one.

(3) For the Unsegmented Parts:

- The system registers the words in the dictionary, as FR of the words equal 1 and rank equal CW.

3 Evaluation Experiments

3.1 Experimental Data And Procedure

To evaluate the adaptability of the proposed method for different fields and the effectivity for Chinese word segmentation. We use the Chinese text of two specialized fields from Sinica Corpus[1]: the economics contains 92,085 words and the engineering contains 70,017 words. Total words is 162,102. The economics consists of the text of economic system, economic policy and economic theory. The engineering consists of the text of electronics, communication engineering, machine engineering and nuclear industry.

[1] *http://www.sinica.edu.tw/ftms-bin/kiwi.sh*

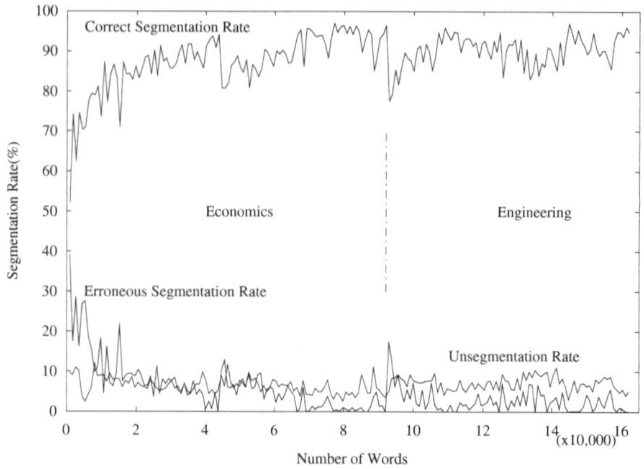

Figure 4: The changes of segmentation rates

In order to confirm the adaptability of proposed method to user, we let the initial dictionary empty. We input a paragraph about hundred words one times and two fields text in turns.

3.2 Experimental Results

The results of experiment are shown in Table 1. Fig. 4 shows the change of CSR, ESR and USR. In our method, the correct segmentation number is the number of correct segmentation that is judged by a user. The unsegmentation number is the number when all unsegmented strings are segmented correctly. The erroneous segmentation number is the number that subtracts the number of correct segmentation and unsegmentation from the number of all words in the input text. To evaluate the experiment result, we use these formulas of CSR (Correct Segmentation Rate), ESR (Erroneous Segmentation Rate) and USR (Unsegmented Rate) as follows:

$$CSR[\%] = \frac{Correct\ segmentation\ number}{Total\ number\ of\ words} \times 100 \quad (2)$$

$$ESR[\%] = \frac{Erroneous\ segmentation\ number}{Total\ number\ of\ words} \times 100 \quad (3)$$

$$USR[\%] = \frac{Unsegmentation\ number}{Total\ number\ of\ words} \times 100 \quad (4)$$

4 Discussion

4.1 Adaptability To Different Fields

Fig. 4 shows the experimental results of two fields. When the text is changed to different domain, because appearance of some new words of different fields, the correct segmentation rate

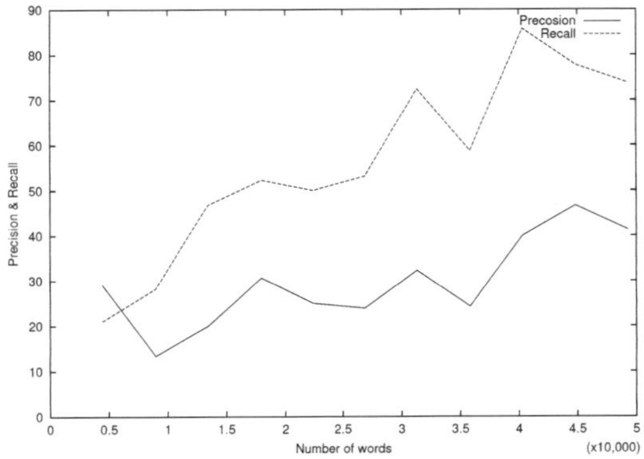

Figure 5: The ability to predict unknown words

is fall down temporary. However with increasing of processed sentence, the correct segmentation rate goes on increasing quickly.

We may consider that the proposed method has adaptability for different fields. Sometimes the correct segmentation rate is a little lower because the domain of text is a little difference, for example: the economics consists of the text of economic system, economic policy and economic theory and so on.

4.2 Evaluation of Ability for Predicting Unknown Words

We use 50,000 words to discuss the predicting ability of proposed method for unknown words.

$$Precision[\%] = \frac{CWN}{TWN} \times 100 \quad (5)$$

$$Recall[\%] = \frac{CWN}{TUN} \times 100 \quad (6)$$

Where, CWN is the number of words that are predicted correctly. TWN is the total number of words that are predicted. TUN is the total number of unknown words.

The precision and recall are shown in Fig. 5. The average precision is 26.0%. The average recall is 31.0%. With increasing of registered words in the dictionary, prediction effect for unknown words is becoming well, after 40,000 words are processed the precision and the recall are 85.0%, 40.0% respectively.

4.3 Analysis of Erroneous Segmentation

We select 1,000 words from the beginning of the experimental date and the end of the experimental date respectively, to analysis the reason of an erroneous segmentation. At the beginning, ESR that is because of unregistered words is 18.0%, but after 16,000 words are processed, ESR that is because of unregistered words is 0.9%. However ESR that is caused by ambiguity goes on increasing from 1.6% to 7.0%. ESR caused by ambiguity is increasing with increasing of registered word in the dictionary. Ambiguous segmentation is still a difficult problem, so that it is necessary to improve the ability to deal with ambiguity.

5 Conclusion

The experiment results show the prediction ability for unknown words by using Inductive Learning. The experiment results of two fields shown the proposed method can adapt to different fields text. In this paper, the emphasis is to evaluate the adaptivity of the method to different user and fields. About comparison with other existed methods will be done in the future.

The proposed method may be used to computer-aided acquisition of language resource. The experimental results show our proposed method has ability of learning, predictability for unknown words and effectivity for Chinese word segmentation. For the future works, we plan to improve the ability of dealing with segmentation ambiguity, and use this proposed method for Chinese morphological analysis.

References

Kenji Araki, Yoshio Momouchi, and Koji Tochinai. 1995. Evaluation for adaptability of kana-kanji translation of non-segmentation japanese kana sentences using inductive learning. *PACLING-II*, pages 1–7.

Richard Sproat, Chilin Shih, William Gale, and Nancy Chang. 1996. A stochastic finite-state word-segmentation algorithm for Chinese. *Association for Computational Linguistics*, 22(3):377–404.

Maosong Sun, Dayang Shen, and Benjamin K Tsou. 1998. Chinese word segmentation without using lexicon and hand-crafted training data. *17th International Conference on Computational Linguistics*, pages 1265–1271.

T. Yamasita and Y. Matsumoto. 2000. Journal of natural language processing(in japanese). *Framework for Language Independent Morphological Analysis*, 7(3):39–56.

Using the Segmentation Corpus to define an inventory of concatenative units for Cantonese speech synthesis

Wai Yi Peggy WONG
Chris BREW
Mary E. BECKMAN
Linguistics Dept., Ohio State University
222 Oxley Hall, 1712 Neil Ave.
Columbus, OH, 43210-1298 USA
{pwong, cbrew, mbeckman}@ling.osu.edu

Shui-duen CHAN
Chinese Language Centre,
Hong Kong Polytechnic University
Yuk Choi Road, Hung Hom, Kowloon,
HONG KONG
chsdchan@polyu.edu.hk

Abstract

The problem of word segmentation affects all aspects of Chinese language processing, including the development of text-to-speech synthesis systems. In synthesizing a Hong Kong Cantonese text, for example, words must be identified in order to model fusion of coda [p] with initial [h], and other similar effects that differentiate word-internal syllable boundaries from syllable edges that begin or end words. Accurate segmentation is necessary also for developing any list of words large enough to identify the word-internal cross-syllable sequences that must be recorded to model such effects using concatenated synthesis units. This paper describes our use of the Segmentation Corpus to constrain such units.

Introduction

What are the best units to use in building a fixed inventory of concatenative units for an unlimited vocabulary text-to-speech (TTS) synthesis system for a language? Given a particular choice of unit type, how large is the inventory of such units for the language, and what is the best way to design materials to cover all or most of these units in one recording session? Are there effects such as prosodically conditioned allophony that cannot be modeled well by the basic unit type? These are questions that can only be answered language by language, and answering them for Cantonese[1] poses several interesting challenges.

One major challenge involves the definition of the "word" in Cantonese. As in other varieties of Chinese, morphemes in Cantonese are typically monosyllabic and syllable structure is extremely simple, which might suggest the demi-syllable or even the syllable (Chu & Ching, 1997) as an obvious basic unit. At the same time, however, there are segmental "sandhi" effects that conjoin syllables within a word. For example, when the morpheme 集 `zaap6`[2] stands as a word alone (meaning 'to collect'), the [p] is a glottalized and unreleased coda stop, but when the morpheme occurs in the longer word 集合 `zaap6hap6` ('to assemble'), the coda [p] often resyllabifies and fuses with the following [h] to make an initial aspirated stop. Accurate word segmentation at the text analysis level is essential for identifying the domain of such sandhi effects in any full-fledged TTS system, whatever method is used for generating the waveform from the specified pronunciation of the word. A further challenge is to find a way to capture such sandhi effects in systems that use concatenative methods for waveform generation.

This paper reports on research aimed at defining an inventory of concatenative units for Cantonese using the Segmentation Corpus, a lexicon of 33k words extracted from a large corpus of Cantonese newspaper texts. The corpus is described further in Section 2 after an excursus (in Section 1) on the problems posed

[1] We use "Cantonese" to mean the newer Hong Kong standard, and not the older Canton City one.

[2] We use the Jyutping romanization developed by the Linguistics Society of Hong Kong in 1993. See `http://www.cpct92.cityu.edu.hk/lshk`.

by the Cantonese writing system. Section 3 outlines facts about Cantonese phonology relevant to choosing the concatenative unit, and Section 4 calculates the number of units that would be necessary to cover all theoretically possible syllables and sequences of syllables. The calculation is done for three models: (1) syllables, as in Chu & Ching (1997), (2) Law & Lee's (2000) mixed model of onsets, rhymes, and cross-syllabic rhyme-onset units, and (3) a positionally sensitive diphone model. This section closes by reporting how the number of units in the last model is reduced by exploiting the sporadic and systematic phonotactic gaps discovered by looking for words exemplifying each possible unit in the Segmentation Corpus.

1 The Cantonese writing system

The Cantonese writing system poses unique challenges for developing online lexicons, not all of which are related to the "foremost problem" of word segmentation. These problems stem from the long and rich socio-political history of the dialect, which makes the writing system even less regular than the Mandarin one, even though Cantonese is written primarily with the same logographs ("Chinese characters").

The main problem is that each character has several readings, and the reading cannot always be determined based on the immediate context of the other characters in a multisyllabic word. For some orthographic forms, the variation is stylistic. For example, the word 支援 'support' can be pronounced `zi1jyun4` or `zi1wun4`. But for other orthographic forms, the variation in pronunciation corresponds to different words, with different meanings. For example, the character sequence 正當 writes both the function word `zing3dong1` 'while' and the content word `zing3dong3` 'proper'. Moreover, some words, such as `ko1` 'to page, telephone', `ge3` (genitive particle), and `laa3` (aspect marker), have no standard written form. In colloquial styles of writing, these forms may be rendered in non-standard ways, such as using the English source word *call* to write `ko1`, or writing the particles with special characters unique to Cantonese. In more formal writing, however, such forms must be left to the reader to interpolate from a character "borrowed" from some other morpheme. For example, `ge3` (genitive particle) might be written 的, a character which more typically writes the morpheme `dik1` in `muk6dik1` 目的 'aim', but which suggests `ge3` because it also writes a genitive particle in Mandarin (`de` in the Pinyin romanization). Thus, 的 has a reading `dik1` that is etymologically related to the Mandarin morpheme, but it also has the etymologically independent reading `ge3` because Cantonese readers can read texts written in Mandarin as if they were Cantonese. Such ambiguities of reading make the task of developing online wordlists from text corpora doubly difficult, since word segmentation is only half the task.

2 The Segmentation Corpus

The Segmentation Corpus is an electronic database of around 33,000 Cantonese word types extracted from a 1.7 million character corpus of Hong Kong newspapers, along with a tokenized record of the text. It is described in more detail in Chan & Tang (1999). The Cantonese corpus is part of a larger database of segmented Chinese texts, including Mandarin newspapers from both the PRC and Taiwan. The three databases were created using word-segmentation criteria developed by researchers at the Chinese Language Centre and Department of Chinese and Bilingual Studies, Hong Kong Polytechnic University. Since these criteria were intended to be applicable to texts in all three varieties, they do not refer to the phonology.

For our current purpose, the most useful part of the Segmentation Corpus is the wordlist proper, a file containing a separate entry for each word type identified by the segmentation criteria. Each entry has three fields: the orthographic form(s), the pronunciation(s) in Jyutping, and the token frequency in the segmented newspaper corpus. In the original corpus, the first field could have multiple entries. For example, there are two character strings, 泛濫 and 氾濫, in the entry for the word faan6laam6 'to flood'. However, the two readings of 支援 were not listed separately in the pronunciation field for that orthographic form (and there was only one entry for the two words written with 正當).

Before we could use the wordlist, therefore, we had to check the pronunciation field for each entry. The first author, a native speaker of Hong Kong Cantonese, examined each entry in order to add variant readings not originally listed (as in the entry for 支援 'support') and to correct readings that did not correspond to the modern Hong Kong pronunciation (as in the entry for 盒 'box'). In addition, when the added variant pronunciation corresponded to an identifiably different word (as in `zing3dong3` 'proper' versus `zing3dong1` 'while' for 正當), the entry was split in two, and all tokens of that character string in the larger corpus were examined, in order to allocate the total token count for the orthographic form to the two separate frequencies for the two different words. Approximately 90 original entries were split into separate entries by this processing. In this way, the 32,840 entries in the original word list became 33,037 entries. Once this task was completed, we could use the wordlist to count all of the distinct units that would be needed to synthesize all of the words in the Segmentation Corpus. To explain what these units are, we need to describe the phonology of Cantonese words and longer utterances.

3 Cantonese phonology

The smallest possible word is a nasal ([m] or [ŋ]) or vowel as a bare tone-bearing syllable nucleus, as in 五 `ng5` 'five' and 啞 `aa2` 'dumb'. A syllable with a vowel as nucleus can also have an onset consonant, and it can have a more complex rhyme which combines the vowel with any of the three coda nasals [m], [n], and [ŋ], the two glides [j] and [w], or the three coda stops [p], [t], and [k], as in 將 `zoeng1` 'will', 胃 `wai6` 'stomach', and 率 `leot2` 'rate'. Tables 1 and 2 show the 11 vowels and 19 consonants of Cantonese, and Figure 1 plots representative F0 contours for each of the tones that contrast on a syllable with an all-sonorant rhyme.

If there were no phonotactic restrictions on combinations of vowels and consonants, there would be 101 distinct rhymes in each of the six tones. However, not all combinations are possible. For example, tone 5 does not occur on syllables with coda stops (and tone 4 on such checked syllables is limited to onomatopoeia). Also, the mid short vowel [e] does not occur in open syllables, and in closed syllables it occurs only before [k], [ŋ], and [j], whereas [i:] occurs in closed syllables only before [p], [t], [m], [n], and [w]. The Jyutping transliteration system takes advantage of this kind of complementary distribution to limit the number of vowel symbols. Thus "`i`" is used to transcribe both the short mid vowel [e] in the rhymes [ek] and [eŋ], and the high vowel [i:] in the rhymes [i:], [i:t], [i:p], [i:m], [i:n], and [i:w]. Ignoring tone, there are 54 rhyme types in standard usage of Jyutping. Canonical forms of longer words can be described to a very rough first approximation as strings of syllables. However, fluent synthesis cannot be achieved simply by stringing syllables together without taking into account the effects of position in the word or phrase.

front	round	central	back round	
i:	y:		u:	high
e		ɵ	o	mid (short)
ɛ:	œ:		ɔ:	mid (long)
		ɐ	a:	low vowels

Table 1. Vowels of Cantonese.

labial	dental	palatal	velar	labio velar	
p^h	t^h, ts^h		k^h	k^{hw}	
p	t, ts		k	k^w	
f	s				h
m	n, l	j	ŋ	w	

Table 2. Consonants of Cantonese.

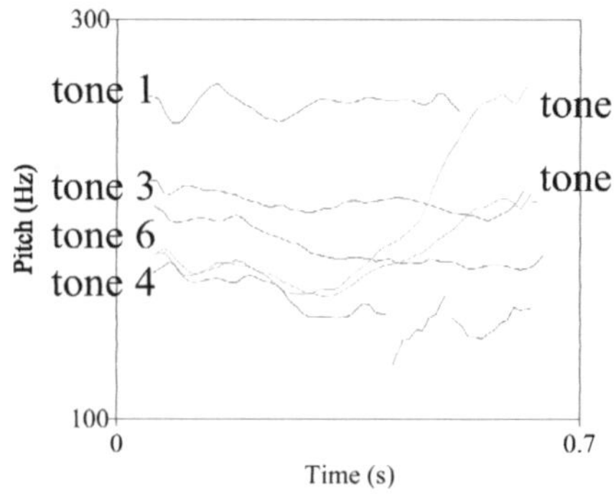

Figure 1. F0 contours for six words [wɐj] with different tones. Numbers to the right identify the endpoints of the two rising tones (in grey) and numbers to the left identify starting points of the other four tones (in black). The discontinuities in `wai4` are where the speaker breaks into creak.

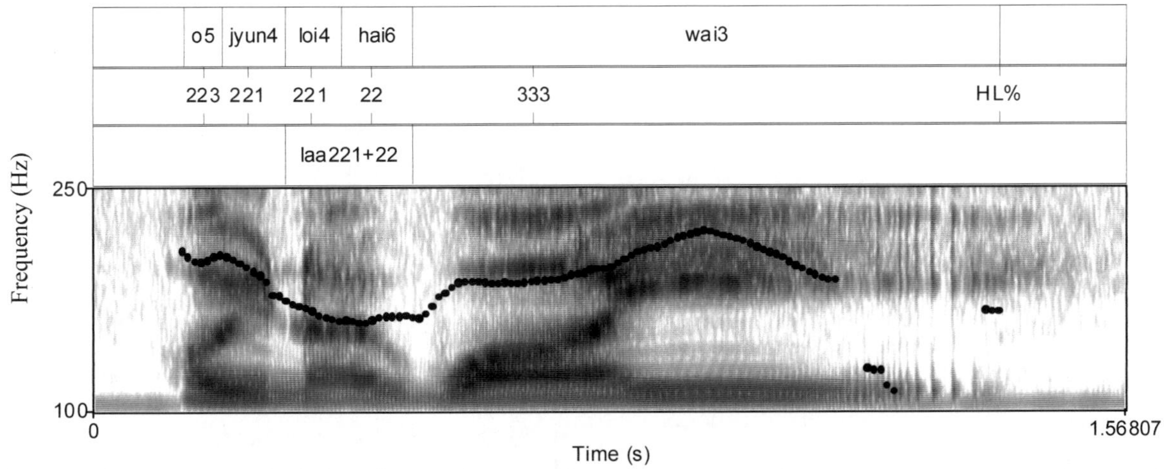

Figure 2. Spectrogram with F0 track superimposed for an utterance of the sentence `o5 jyun4loi4 hai6 wai3` 'Oh, I get it. It was the character 慰!' (The context is a dictation task.) The labelling window above the signal view shows a partial transcription in the annotation conventions proposed by Wong, Chan & Beckman (in press), with a syllable-by-syllable Jyutping transliteration (top tier), a transcription of the (canonical) lexical tones and boundary tone, and a phonetic transcription of fused forms (lowest tier). The HL% boundary tone is a pragmatic morpheme, which we have translated with the 'Oh, I get it.' phrase.

		經		濟			學		家	basic units
Jyutping		ging1		zai3			hok6		gaa1	(added units)
Chu & Ching	keŋ			tsɐj			hɔ:k		<u>ka:#</u>	1042 (1042)
Law & Lee	#k		eŋ$ts			ɐj$h	ɔ:k$k		a:#	1801
diphones	#ke	eŋ	ŋ$ts	tsɐj	ɐj	j$hɔ:	ɔ:k	ka:	a:#	1097

Table 3. The string of basic units and exceptional units (underlined) that would be needed to synthesize an utterance of the word 'economist' in each of the three models.

One of these effects is the fusion of coda [p] with initial [h] in words such as 集合 `zaap6 hap6`. In fluent connected speech, such effects can be extreme. Consonants can be reduced or deleted, with the abutting vowels fused together, as in the pronunciation [jy:n^{21}la:^{212}] for the phrase 原來係 `jyun4loi4 hai6` 'was' (with the verb cliticized onto the preceding tense adverb) as in Figure 2. Eventually, we plan to use the larger Segmentation Corpus to look for likely targets of fusion. For now, however, we focus on positional effects that can be modeled just by recording word lists. Figure 2 illustrates one such effect. The final syllable in this utterance is sustained, to be longer than the other four syllables combined. It also bears two extra tone targets for the HL% boundary tone. (See Wong, Chan & Beckman, in press, for a discussion of these utterance-level effects.) Phrase-final lengthening is not usually so extreme in read speech, and the inventory of boundary tones is more limited. However, there will be sufficient final lengthening to warrant the recording of separate units for (the rhymes of) final syllables. These two positional effects increase the inventory of units, albeit in different ways depending on the choice of "basic" unit.

4 Counting different unit types

Table 3 illustrates three synthesis models using the word 經濟學家 `ging1zai3hok6gaa1` 'economist'. The last column in Table 3 lists the theoretically possible number of basic units. The first model concatenates syllables. If each onset could be combined with each rhyme, there would be 1042 syllable types. A second set of syllables can be recorded to capture final lengthening. However, there is no comparably obvious way to capture the cross-syllabic effects with this concatenative unit. The second model uses cross-syllabic units which combine the rhyme of one syllable with the following initial.

This automatically captures the sandhi effects. The model also captures final lengthening, because separate units are recorded for onsets with no preceding rhyme and rhymes with no following onset. With 54 final rhymes, 1728 combinations of rhyme followed by medial onset, and 19 initial onsets, there are 1801 theoretically possible units. The last model is our diphone model, which differentiates codas from onset consonants. That is, the rhyme `aak$` is distinct from the cross-syllabic diphone `aa$k`. This model has the advantage over Law & Lee's cross-syllable final-initial combination model in that spectral continuity between the initial and rhyme is captured in the CV diphones (such as `#gi` and `zai`). Similarly, the diphones capture the dependency between the quality of the [h] and that of the following vowel (i.e., one records separate cross-syllable diphones for `i$ho`, `i$hi`, `i$haa`, and so on). However, the number of theoretically possible units is smaller, because we do not record consonant sequences that abut silence with silence — e.g., `aak$` can be combined directly with `$ka` or `$ta`, so no cross-syllabic units need be recorded for `k$k` and `k$t`.

Note that none of these counts takes tone into consideration. However, since every syllable bears a (full) tone, and since tones are rarely deleted in running speech, recording different units for rhymes with different tones should improve naturalness, particularly for cases where voice quality is part of the tonal specification (as suggested by the contour for tone 4 in Figure 1). Naturalness may also require different cross-syllabic units for different tone sequences when sonorant segments abut at syllable edges (so as to insure tonal continuity).

Of course, when tone specification is taken into account, the number of necessary units grows substantially. For example, there are 12,120 distinct syllables, and even more units in the other two models. However, when we count only those types that are attested in the words of the Segmentation Corpus, there are many fewer units. For example, the total number of attested units taking tone into account in the diphone model is 2292. If each diphone were recorded in a disyllabic carrier word, a Cantonese speaker could speak all of the words to make a new voice in a single recording session. (For comparison, the number of attested diphones ignoring tone is 634.)

Conclusion

We have shown one way of using a segmented database to inform the design of a unit inventory for TTS. We augmented the Segmentation Corpus with transliterations that would let us predict more accurately the pronunciation that a Cantonese speaker adopting a careful speaking style would be likely to produce for a character sequence. Judgements about the phonology of Cantonese, in combination with the augmented wordlist, and the associated word frequency data, can be used to assess the costs and likely benefits of different strategies for unit selection in Cantonese TTS. In particular, we present data indicating the feasibility of a new diphone selection strategy that finesses some of the problems in modelling the interactions between tone and segmental identity. It remains to be demonstrated that this strategy can actually deliver the results which it appears to promise. This is our future work.

Acknowledgements

This work was supported by a grant from the University Grants Committee of Hong Kong to Y. S. Cheung and an SBC/Ameritech Faculty Research Award to C. Brew and M. Beckman.

References

Chan S. D. and Tang Z. X. (1999) *Quantitative Analysis of Lexical Distribution in Different Chinese Communities in the 1990's*. Yuyan Wenzi Yingyong [Applied Linguistics], No.3, 10-18.

Chu M. and Ching P. C. (1997) *A Cantonese synthesizer based on TD-PSOLA method.* Proceedings of the 1997 International Symposium on Multimedia Information Processing. Academia Sinica, Taipei, Taiwan, Dec. 1997.

Law K. M. and Lee Tan (2000) *Using cross-syllable units for Cantonese speech synthesis*. Proceedings of the 2000 International Conference on Spoken Language Processing, Beijing, China, Oct. 2000.

Wong W. Y. P., Chan M. K-M., and Beckman M. E. (in press) *An Autosegmental-Metrical analysis and prosodic conventions for Cantonese*. To appear in S-A. Jun, ed. Prosodic Models and Transcription: Towards Prosodic Typology. Oxford University Press.

Extracting Pronunciation-translated Names from Chinese Texts using Bootstrapping Approach

Jing Xiao
School of Computing,
National University of Singapore
xiaojing@comp.nus.edu.sg

Jimin Liu
School of Computing,
National University of Singapore
liujm@comp.nus.edu.sg

Tat-Seng Chua
School of Computing,
National University of Singapore
chuats@comp.nus.edu.sg

Abstract

Pronunciation-translated names (P-Names) bring more ambiguities to Chinese word segmentation and generic named entity recognition. As there are few annotated resources that can be used to develop a good P-Name extraction system, this paper presents a bootstrapping algorithm, called PN-Finder, to tackle this problem. Starting from a small set of P-Name characters and context cue-words, the algorithm iteratively locates more P-Names from the Internet. The algorithm uses a combination of P-Name and context word probabilities to identify new P-Names. Experiments show that our PN-Finder is able to locate a large number of P-Names (over 100,000) from the Internet with a high recognition accuracy of over 85%. Further tests on the MET-2 test set show that our PN-Finder can achieve a performance of over 90% in F_1 value in locating P-Names. The results demonstrate that our PN-Finder is effective.

1 Introduction

Pronunciation-translated names (P-Names) are those foreign names that are translated to Chinese characters according to their pronunciations. A P-Name sometimes forms part of but not a complete named entity. For instance, in the place name "贝克利大学" (Berkeley University), only the term "贝克利" (Berkeley) is a P-Name, while "大学" (University) is not since it is translated semantically.

The ability to recognize P-Names helps to reduce ambiguities in word segmentation and improve the performance of Chinese information retrieval since many unknown words are P-Names, especially for international Chinese news. Unlike English, there is no blank between words in Chinese, in which a word is a linguistic token consisting of one or more characters. In addition, the same characters may appear in multiple context with different meanings (Chua and Liu, 2002). The presence of P-Names brings more ambiguities to Chinese word segmentation since every character in a P-Name can be used as a common character.

Intuitively, we can extract the P-Names based on the distinctive sequence of characters that they are used as compared to common words. In addition, we can use local context around the P-Names to confirm and classify them into person or part of location and organization names. One way to perform these tasks effectively is to rely on statistics derived from a large corpus in which the P-Names are annotated. While some annotated corpuses with general named entities are available such as the PKUC (Yu, 1999) and MET-2 (Chinchor, 2001), there is no such annotated corpus for P-Names. While annotated data is difficult to obtain, un-annotated data is readily available and plentiful, especially on the Internet. To take advantage of that, we need to tackle two major problems. The first is how to gather sufficient distinct P-Names from the Internet, and the second is how to use the available resources to derive reliable statistical information to characterize the P-Names.

The problem of gathering sufficient reliable information from a small initial set of seed resources has been tackled in bootstrapping research for information extraction (Agichtein and Gravano, 2000; Brin, 1998; Collins and Singer, 1999; Mihalcea and Moldovan, 2001; Riloff and Jones, 1999). Bootstrapping approach aims to perform unsupervised text processing to extract information from open resources such as the Internet using minimum manual labor. Given the lack of annotated training samples for P-Name extraction, this paper introduces a bootstrapping algorithm, called PN-Finder. It starts from a small set of seed samples, and iteratively locates, extracts and classifies the new and more P-Names. It works in conjunction with a general Chinese named entity recognizer (Chua and Liu, 2002) to extract general named entities.

In the remaining parts of this paper, we describe the details of PN-Finder in Section 2 and its application in locating P-Names from new documents in Section 3. Section 4 presents the experimental results using the MET-2 test corpus. Section 5 contains our conclusion and outline for future work.

2 Bootstrapping Algorithm for Locating P-Names

Currently, there is no standard corpus that annotates all P-Names. Since annotating thousands of P-Names is more difficult than collecting thousands of P-Names from the Internet, we recur to using the Internet search engine to collect a large set of P-Names. Figure 1 illustrates our main components in bootstrapping process.

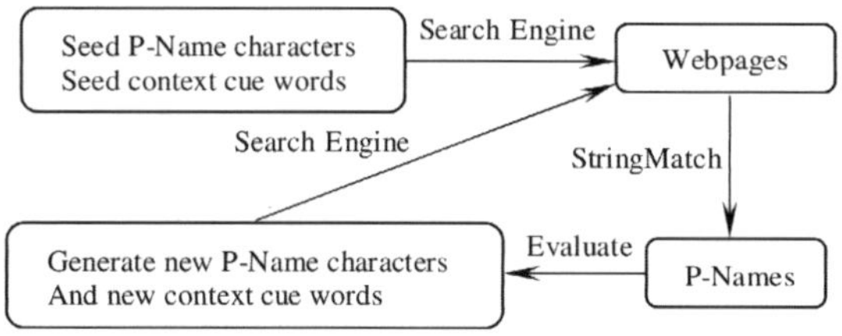

Figure 1: Main components of the bootstrapping

The inputs to the PN-Finder are:

a) A seed P-Name character set $\underline{C}_s^{(0)}$ consisting of 5 characters {"阿", "尔", "巴", "斯", "基"}.
b) A set of seed context cue words $\underline{CW}^{(0)}$ consisting of 60 context words, such as {"NULL", "记者", "说", "据", "在", "到"}. These are typical context words found around person, location and organization names in PKUC[1] (the PoS Corpus of Peking University), which contains one month of news from the People Daily.
c) A set of P-Name candidates $\underline{P}^{(0)}$, which is null at the beginning.
d) A common word dictionary extracted from PKUC by removing proper nouns, numbers and non-Chinese symbols. It contains about 37,000 words.

From the initial seeds, we perform the followings:

a) We use every two characters in $\underline{C}_s^{(i-1)}$ as query to retrieve relevant web pages from the Internet using a commercial search engine. We then extract possible P-Names from the returned web pages to update $\underline{P}^{(i)}$.
b) We find a most probable new P-Name character. Update $\underline{C}_s^{(i-1)}$ to $\underline{C}_s^{(i)}$ by adding the new character.
c) We bootstrap new context words around the new P-Names found to derive $\underline{CW}^{(i)}$. We then perform the lexical chaining to generalize these context words to generate semantic classes.
d) We repeat the process from step (a) until any of the following conditions is satisfied: (i) when no new P-Name is found; (ii) when the desired number of iterations is reached; or (iii) when the number of P-Names found exceeds a desired number.

The following subsections discuss the details of the bootstrapping process.

2.1 Querying and Extracting the P-Names from the Web

The first step of the algorithm is to derive good queries from the character set $\underline{C}_s^{(m-1)}$ to search the Internet to obtain new web pages. If we use all single characters from $\underline{C}_s^{(m-1)}$ to perform the search, we are likely to get too many pages containing irrelevant information. As a compromise, we use every two characters $c_i c_j$ in $\underline{C}_s^{(m-1)}$ (except those combinations that have been used in the previous iterations) to search the Internet using Google (by using its language tool[2]). We consider only up to 300 entries returned by Google. We divide the content of the web pages into text segments by using the non-alphanumeric characters as delimiters. We extract those text segments that contain the search characters c_i, c_j or both and store them in $\underline{R}^{(m)}$. For example, from the web page given in Figure 2, the text segments extracted include: strings "基斯洛夫斯基" and "基斯洛夫斯基的影片被认为" from the first entry; and strings "塔科夫斯基", "你是否知道当塔科夫斯基站立在街头巷尾的时候" and "请记住塔科夫斯基吧" from the second entry.

Given $\underline{R}^{(m)}$, we next extract the possible P-Names. Firstly, we segment those entries in $\underline{R}^{(m)}$ by performing the longest forward match using the common word dictionary. We then remove all

---

[1] http://icl.pku.edu.cn/Introduction/corpustagging.htm

[2] http://www.google.com/intl/zh-CN/

non-Chinese letters and common words containing more than one character. From the remaining string segments in $\underline{R}^{(m)}$, we locate all sub-strings with at least 2-character in length and contain the query terms c_i, c_j or c_ic_j. We extract those sub-strings that appear at least τ_n (we use 3) times as P-Name candidates by string matching. We store the new P-Name candidates found in $\underline{P}^{(m-1)}$ to obtain $\underline{P}^{(m)}$.

Figure 2: A web page returned by Google

For example, if we use “斯, 基” obtained from $\underline{C}_s^{(0)}$ as query to Google, among the returned entries, we will have:

“巴尔舍夫斯基(访问)(人民)(日报)...”
“(美国)(贸易)(代表)巴尔舍夫斯基说”
“就中美(WTO)(协议)(细节)巴尔舍夫斯基答(记者)问...”
“巴尔舍夫斯基说(中国)入世(谈判)...”
“巴尔舍夫斯基走出(使馆)...”

Here the bracketed words are common words or English letters and they are removed from string matching. The sub-string “巴尔舍夫斯基” appears 5 times and it is matched as a possible P-Name.

2.2 Deriving New P-Name Characters

Given the set of P-Name candidates in $\underline{P}^{(m)}$, we next use both the context words and corpus statistics to confirm the P-Name and extract new P-Name characters.

2.2.1 Classifying P-Names

From observation, context information is useful to comfirm a P-Name and determine its left and right boundary. Thus we use one-word context to confirm and classify P-Name candidates into person names or part of location or organization names. For each context word w_c in $\underline{CW}^{(m)}$, we first compute its probability vector of occurrences, $PV(w_c)$, around person, location and organization names in PKUC as follows:

$$PV(w_c) = < c_{-p}, c_{+p}, c_{-l}, c_{+l}, c_{-o}, c_{+o} > \qquad (1)$$

where: $$c_{+x}(w_c) = \frac{n_{+x}}{n_{+p} + n_{+l} + n_{+o}} \qquad (1.1)$$

$$c_{-x}(w_c) = \frac{n_{-x}}{n_{-p} + n_{-l} + n_{-o}} \qquad (1.2)$$

Here $x \in \{p, l, o\}$, and n_{-p} (or n_{+p}), n_{-l} (or n_{+l}), n_{-o} (or n_{+o}) respectively give the number of times w_c appears at the left (or right) boundary of person (p), location (l) and organization (o) names in PKUC. c_{-x} (or c_{+x}) gives the probability that the P-Name is of type x, if this cue-word is at the left (or right) boundary of the P-Name.

Given a P-Name candidate $p_k^{(m)}$ in $\underline{P}^{(m)}$, we extract the set of its left and right context words as $\underline{W}_c^{\,l}$ and $\underline{W}_c^{\,r}$. We then derive the average probability vectors of $\underline{W}_c^{\,l} = <c^l_{-p}, c^l_{+p}, c^l_{-l}, c^l_{+l}, c^l_{-o}, c^l_{+o}>$ and $\underline{W}_c^{\,r} = <c^r_{-p}, c^r_{+p}, c^r_{-l}, c^r_{+l}, c^r_{-o}, c^r_{+o}>$, and use these to compute the confidence vector of $p_k^{(m)}$ as:

$$CV(p_k^{(m)}) = < c_p, c_l, c_o > \qquad (2)$$

where $c_p = c^l_{-p} + c^r_{+p}$, $c_l = c^l_{-l} + c^r_{+l}$, $c_o = c^l_{-o} + c^r_{+o}$. Here we simply average the probabilities of the left and right context words to derive the final probability vector.

We assign $p_k^{(m)}$ to be part of a named entity of type x, if $c_x \geq \tau_p$ for $x \in \{p, l, o\}$. Here we set τ_p to be 0.8. In case that there are more than one value greater than τ_p, we select the one with the highest value in the type vector as the type of that P-Name.

2.2.2 Evaluating P-Names

We next derive an objective measure to evaluate how likely a candidate in $\underline{P}^{(m)}$ could be a P-Name. We observe that a string is likely to be a P-Name if: (a) it contains some sub-strings that frequently appear in typical P-Names such as “阿尔”, “斯基”, “洛夫”, etc; and (b) it has context words in $\underline{CW}^{(m-1)}$ set that indicates that it has high probability of being part of a named entity. Thus for each P-Name candidate $p_k^{(m)}$ ($p_k^{(m)} = c_1c_2 \ldots c_n$) in $\underline{P}^{(m)}$, we compute:

$$s(p_k^{(m)}) = s_1(p_k^{(m)})/M + \beta * s_2(p_k^{(m)}) \quad (3)$$

$$s_1(p_k^{(m)}) = \omega\sum_{i=1}^{n}\sum_{j=1}^{N} n_j(c_i) + \omega^2\sum_{i=1}^{n-1}\sum_{j=1}^{N} n_j(c_ic_{i+1}) + \omega^3\sum_{i=1}^{n-2}\sum_{j=1}^{N} n_j(c_ic_{i+1}c_{i+2}) \quad (3.1)$$

$$s_2(p_k^{(m)}) = \max(c_p, c_l, c_o) \quad (3.2)$$

where n is the number of characters in $p_k^{(m)}$, and N equals $|\underline{P}^{(m)}|$. $n_j(c_i)$, $n_j(c_ic_{i+1})$ and $n_j(c_ic_{i+1}c_{i+2})$ are respectively number of times the character strings c_i, c_ic_{i+1} and $c_ic_{i+1}c_{i+2}$ in $p_k^{(m)}$ also appear in other P-Name candidates in $\underline{P}^{(m)}$. β and ω are predefined constants (here we use β =0.5 and ω =1.5). Equation (3.1) gives higher weight to $p_k^{(m)}$ that has better match with longer string sequence of, say, $c_ic_{i+1}c_{i+2}$ with other known P-Names candidates. Equation (3.2) selects the highest confidence value of context words around $p_k^{(m)}$ as support for $p_k^{(m)}$. As s_1 and s_2 are of different scales, we normalize s_1 by dividing it by M, the maximum s_1 values found in the current iteration, before fusing the two values in Equation (3).

2.2.3 Generating New P-Name Characters

Since we would like to obtain more new P-Names during bootstrapping, in each iteration, we would like to expand the P-Name character set. In order to select the most likely P-Name characters, we derive a quasi-probability, $Conf(c_i^{(m)})$, to estimate how likely a character $c_i^{(m)}$ in the P-Name candidate set $\underline{P}^{(m)}$ could be used as a P-Name character. To do this, we make use of both the PKUC corpus and $\underline{P}^{(m)}$. We observe that most characters in $\underline{P}^{(m)}$ also appear in the PKUC corpus, sometimes as P-Name characters sometimes as common characters. Thus, intuitively we estimate $Conf(c_i^{(m)})$ by its occurrences in both PKUC and $\underline{P}^{(m)}$ as:

$$Conf(c_i^{(m)}) = \frac{\sum_{k=1}^{N_c} s(p_k^{(m)})}{\sum_{k=1}^{N_c} s(p_k^{(m)}) + N_{neg}} * \ln(\sum_{k=1}^{N_c} s(p_k^{(m)})) \quad (4)$$

Here we assume that there are N_c P-Name candidates in $\underline{P}^{(m)}$ that contain $c_i^{(m)}$; and N_{neg} is the number of times that $c_i^{(m)}$ is used as single-character word in PKUC. Equation (4) aims to identify characters that appear frequently as part of P-Names, but rarely as part of common words. It also favors characters that appear in more probable P-Names through the $s(p_k^{(m)})$ measures.

Although Equation (4) is effective in identifying individual P-Name characters, it is not good at locating the sequences of P-Name characters that form the P-Names. This is because there are many characters that have low $Conf(c_i^{(m)})$ values that are part of a P-Name. For example, in a P-Name "波列修克", the character "修" has low confidence to be a P-Name character as defined by Equation (4). However, it co-occurs with high confident P-Name characters such as "列" and "克". To overcome this problem, we modify the confidence value of each character by considering its neighbors (context) to derive a smoothed confidence measure in Equation (5).

$$SConf(c_i) = Conf(c_i) +$$
$$\alpha * \max\{e^{B^-(c_i)} * Conf(c_{i-1}), e^{B^+(c_i)} * Conf(c_{i+1})\} \quad (5)$$

where α is a predefined constant (we use α = 1), and $B^+(c_i) = \frac{C(c_ic_{i+1})}{C(c_i)}$; $B^-(c_i) = \frac{C(c_{i-1}c_i)}{C(c_i)}$.

$Conf(c_i)$ is defined in Equation (4); $C(c_i)$ and $C(c_ic_j)$ is respectively the co-occurrence of characters c_i and c_ic_j in the P-Name set. Equation (5) tries to supplement the confidence of c_i by its context, that is, it uses the higher of the bi-gram statistics with its preceding and succeeding word to enhance its confidence. We rank all the characters in $\underline{P}^{(m)}$ using Equation (5) and add the top new character into $\underline{C}_S^{(m-1)}$ to obtain $\underline{C}_S^{(m)}$.

2.3 Deriving New Context Words

In addition to finding new P-Name characters, there is also a need to expand the context word set $\underline{CW}^{(m-1)}$ in order to help identify more P-Names. As mentioned before, if at least one of c_p, c_l, c_o values of a P-Name candidate in Equation (2) is greater than a threshold τ_p, we regard it as part of a named entity. For these P-Names which could be possible part of named entities, the following steps are performed:

a) We retrieve all their context words in $\underline{R}^{(m)}$.
b) We add all new context words to form $\underline{CW}^{(m)}$.
c) We update probability vectors of the new context words using Equation (1).
d) We group these context words under the category of c_{-x} or c_{+x} (for x∈{p, l, o}) if their probabilities under that category is greater than a threshold τ_g (say, 0.5).
e) We then perform lexical chaining using HowNet to generalize the context words under each of the 6 categories separately. The general lexical chaining algorithm is given in detail in Chua and Liu (2002).

f) After lexical chaining, some semantically related words are grouped together. We update the confidence vectors of the semantic groups by averaging the confidence values of words in each of the semantic groups.

At the end of this process, we obtain a new set of context word $\underline{CW}^{(m)}$ which contains some generalized context word classes.

3 Identifying P-Names from New Texts

At the end of the bootstrapping process, we obtain expanded lists of likely P-Name characters $\underline{C}_s^{(m)}$, context cue words $\underline{CW}^{(m)}$ and P-Names $\underline{P}^{(m)}$. Given a new document, we want to use these resources to identify all P-Names. The process is carried out as follows:

a) We first use our common word dictionary to remove all common words.
b) Next we use knowledge of P-Name candidates and corpus statistics to identify a sequence of likely P-Name characters. Any sub-string in which the $Sconf(c_i)$ (see Equation (5)) of each consecutive character in that string is greater than a pre-specified threshold τ_c (we use 5) is considered as a P-Name.
c) A frequently occurring problem during testing is how to handle new characters not found in the $\underline{C}_s^{(m)}$ set that we do not know their confidence values. Such problem occurs as a same foreign name may be translated to different P-Names with similar Chinese PinYin. For these characters, we adopt the similar homophone approach to relate unknown characters to the known characters in $\underline{C}_s^{(m)}$ set with similar Chinese PinYin.

4 Evaluation

We devise several tests to evaluate our extraction scheme with bootstrapping. We use the MET-2 test corpus for two of the tests, and PKUC as basic language resource to support the process. We use PKUC to extract common word dictionary, which consists of about 37,000 words. We also use PKUC to extract and evaluate typical context cue words around person, location and organization names. Our experiments start from a "seed" P-Name character set:

$\underline{C}_s^{(0)}$ = {"阿", "尔", "巴", "斯", "基"};

and a set of 60 context cue words.

4.1 Obtaining P-Names from the Internet

We perform the bootstrapping process as discussed in Section 2 to extract P-Names from the Internet, and stopped after about 650 iterations. We manually count the number of correct P-Names obtained at the end of every 65-iterations. We also use the first 100,000 P-Names found at the end of the bootstrapping process as the ground truth to compute the accuracy of P-Name identification.

Figure 3 presents the results of the P-Name extraction process. From the figure, we can see that as we increased the number of iterations, the number of P-Names obtained also increased proportionally. This demonstrates that our bootstrapping process is consistent. We also observe that the system is able to maintain a high accuracy of over 85% even when the number of P-Names found approaches 100,000. This demonstrates that our method is effective.

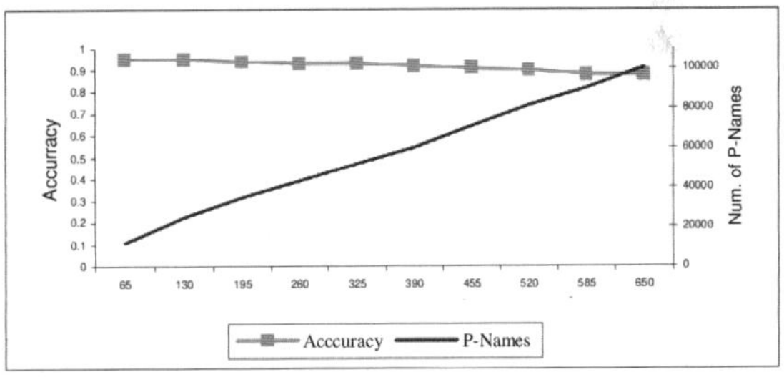

Figure 3: Obtaining P-Names with Bootstrapping

4.2 Extracting P-Names from MET-2 set

We use MET-2 test corpus to test the effectiveness of our approach to identify P-Names from new texts as discussed in Section 3. We consider a P-Name as correctly extracted only when every of its character are correctly identified. The results are presented in Table 1. The results show that we are able to achieve a recall of over 95% and precision of close to 90%. The results are encouraging as we did not use the training resource of MET-2 corpus to train the system, which is expected to lead to higher accuracy.

Table 1: Results of P-Name extraction from MET2

Actual #	System	N_c	N_p	N_m	N_s	Rc	Pr
457	491	437	20	0	34	95.6%	89%

N_c = number of P-Names correctly recognized.
N_p = number of P-Names partially recognized.
N_m = number of P-Names missed.
N_s = number of P-Names found but not in the annotated list.

Recall (Rc) = $N_c/(N_c + N_p + N_m)$;
Precision (Pr) = $N_c/(N_c + N_p + N_s)$.

As a by-product of the PN-Finder, we obtained a large set of context words. We found that we can use these context words to correctly classify about 25% of the extracted P-Names in MET-2 test set into person names or part of location or organization names using the method described in Section 2.2. The employing of context words to classify P-Names is mainly to confirm more P-Names and P-Name characters.

4.3 Contributions of PN-Finder to a Generic NE Recognition Module

The most important contribution of PN-Finder is that it can be used to improve the performance of a generic Chinese named entity recognizer as discussed in Chua and Liu (2002). Here, we conducted several trials by using the PN-Finder to extract a different number of P-Names. We use the first 100,000 P-Names found by the PN-Finder, together with the pattern rules in the general named entity recognizer, to conduct a baseline test. This test merely performs direct table look-up to locate all possible P-Names. Table 2 lists the performance of the general NE recognition system by using an increasing number of P-Names found by the PN-Finder, together with the use of the confidence statistics, context words obtained from the current sets of P-Names and pattern rules. The results indicate that as we increase the number of P-Names found by the PN-Finder, the performance of the general NE recognition system is improved steadily until it reaches over 92% in average F_1 value.

Table 2: Contributions to general NE recognition

# of P-Names used	Ave F_1
100,000 (baseline)	71.3
40,000	88.9
60,000	90.5
80,000	91.7
100,000	92.3

5 Conclusion and Future Work

The presence of P-Names brings more ambiguities to Chinese word segmentation and general Chinese named entity recognition. However, there is a dearth of annotated corpus for extracting and classifying P-Names. To cope with the problem of sparse training resources, this paper presents a bootstrapping module to identify P-Names and classify them into parts of named entitites if possible. The PN-Finder could also contribute to general Chinese named entity recognition and achieve promising performance on the MET-2 test corpus.

Currently, we use only a single word as the context, more context could be considered in the future research. We also aim to extend this method to extract organization names from Chinese documents obtained from the Internet.

References

Agichtein E. and Gravano L. (2000). *Snowball: Extracting Relations from Large Plain-Text Collections*. Proceedings of the 5th ACM International Conference on Digital Libraries.

Brin S. (1998). *Extracting Patterns and Relations from the World Wide Web.* WebDB Workshop at 6th International Conference on Extending Database Technology, EDBT' 98.

Chinchor A. Nancy (2001). *Overview of MUC7/MET-2*. available at:
http://www.itl.nist.gov/iaui/894.02/related_projects/muc/proceedings/muc_7_proceedings/overview.html

Chua T.S. and Liu J.M. (2002), *Learning Pattern Rules for Chinese Named Entity Extraction*. To Appear in AAAI'02.

Collins M. and Singer Y. (1999). *Unsupervised Models for Named Entity Classification.* In Proceedings of the Joint SIGDAT Conference on Empirical Methods in Natural Language Processing and Very Large Corpora.

Liu J.M. and Chua T.S. (2001), *Building semantic Perceptron net for topic spotting,* In Proceeding of Association for Computational Linguistics 39th Anniversary Meeting, 306-313

Mihalcea F. R. and Moldovan I. D. (2001) *A Highly Accurate Bootstrapping Algorithm for Word Sense Disambiguation.* International Journal on Artificial Intelligence Tools. Vol.10, No 1-2(2001). pp. 5-21

Riloff E. and Jones R. (1999) *Learning Dictionaries for Information Extraction by Multi-Level Bootstrapping.* In Proceedings of the Sixteenth National Conference on Artificial Intelligence, pp. 1044-1049.

Yu S. (1999), *The Specification and Manual of Chinese Word Segmentation and Part of Speech Tagging,* available at:
http://www.icl.pku.edu.cn/Introduction/corpustagging.htm

Combining Classifiers for Chinese Word Segmentation

Nianwen Xue

Institute for Research in Cognitive Science
University of Pennsylvania
Suite 400A, 3401 Walnut
Philadelphia, PA 19014
xueniwen@linc.cis.upenn.edu

Susan P. Converse

Dept. of Computer and Information Science
University of Pennsylvania
200 South 33rd Street,
Philadelphia, PA 19104-6389
spc@linc.cis.upenn.edu

Abstract

In this paper we report results of a supervised machine-learning approach to Chinese word segmentation. First, a maximum entropy tagger is trained on manually annotated data to automatically labels the characters with tags that indicate the position of character within a word. An error-driven transformation-based tagger is then trained to clean up the tagging inconsistencies of the first tagger. The tagged output is then converted into segmented text. The preliminary results show that this approach is competitive compared with other supervised machine-learning segmenters reported in previous studies.

1 Introduction

It is generally agreed among researchers that word segmentation is a necessary first step in Chinese language processing. Most of the previous work in this area views a good dictionary as the cornerstone of this task. Several word segmentation algorithms have been developed using a dictionary as an essential tool. Most notably, variants of the maximum matching algorithm have been applied to word segmentation with considerable success. The results that have been reported are generally in the upper 90 percentile range. However, the success of such algorithms is premised on a large, exhaustive dictionary. The accuracy of word segmentation degrades sharply as new words appear. Since Chinese word formation is a highly productive process, new words are bound to appear in substantial numbers in realistic scenarios (Wu and Jiang 1998, Xue 2001), and it is virtually impossible to list all the words in a dictionary. In recent years, as annotated Chinese corpora have become available, various machine-learning approaches have been applied to Chinese word segmentation, with different levels of success. Compared with dictionary-based approaches, machine-learning approaches have the advantage of not needing a dictionary and thus are more suitable for use on naturally occurring Chinese text. In this paper we report results of a supervised machine-learning approach towards Chinese word segmentation that combines two fairly standard machine learning models. We show that this approach is very promising compared with dictionary-based approaches as well as other machine-learning approaches that have been reported in the literature.

2 Combining Classifiers for Chinese word segmentation

The two machine-learning models we use in this work are the maximum entropy model (Ratnaparkhi 1996) and the error-driven transformation-based learning model (Brill 1994). We use the former as the main workhorse and the latter to correct some of the errors produced by the former.

2.1 Reformulating word segmentation as a tagging problem

Before we apply the machine-learning algorithms we first convert the manually segmented words in the corpus into a tagged sequence of Chinese characters. To do this, we tag each character with one of the four tags, LL, RR, MM and LR, depending on its position within a word. It is tagged LL if it occurs on the left boundary of a word, and forms a word with the character(s) on its right. It is tagged RR if it occurs on the right boundary of a word, and forms a word with the character(s) on its left. It is tagged MM if it occurs in the middle of a word. It is tagged LR if it forms a word by itself. We call such tags position-of-character (POC) tags to differentiate them from the more familiar part-of-speech (POS) tags. For example, the manually segmented string in (1)a will be tagged as shown in (1)b:

(1) a. 上海 计划 到 本 世纪 末 实现 人均 国内 生产 总值 五千 美元

b. 上/LL 海/RR 计/LL 划/RR 到/LR 本/LR 世/LL 纪/RR 末/LR 实/LL 现/RR 人/LL 均/RR 国/LL 内/RR 生/LL 产/RR 总/LL 值/RR 五/LL 千/RR 美/LL 元/RR

c. Shanghai plans to reach the goal of 5,000 dollars in per capita GDP by the end of the century.

Given a manually segmented corpus, a POC-tagged corpus can be derived trivially with perfect accuracy. The reason that we use such POC-tagged sequences of characters instead of applying n-gram rules to a segmented corpus directly (Hockenmaier and Brew 1998, Xue 2001) is that they are much easier to manipulate in the training process. Naturally, while some characters will have only one POC tag, most characters will receive multiple POC tags, in the same way that words can have multiple POS tags. The example in (2) shows how all four of the POC tags can be assigned to the character 产 ('produce'):

(2) 产 LL	产品 'product'
产 LR	产 'produce'
产 MM	生产力 'productivity'
产 RR	投产 'start production'

Also as in POS tags, the way the character is POC-tagged in naturally occurring text is affected by the context in which it occurs. For example, if the preceding character is tagged a LR or RR, then the next character can only be tagged LL or LR. How a character is tagged is also affected by the surrounding characters. For example, 关 ('close') should be tagged RR if the previous character is 开 ('open') and neither of them forms a word with other characters, while it should be tagged LL if the next character is 心 ('heart') and neither of them forms a word with other characters. This state of affairs closely resembles the familiar POS tagging problem and lends itself naturally to a solution similar to that of POS tagging. The task is one of ambiguity resolution in which the correct POC tag is determined among several possible POC tags in a specific context. Our next step is to train a maximum entropy model on the perfectly POC-tagged data derived from a manually segmented corpus and use the model to automatically POC-tag unseen text.

2.2 The maximum entropy tagger

The maximum entropy model used in POS-tagging is described in detail in Ratnaparkhi (1996) and the POC tagger here uses the same probability model. The probability model is defined over *H x T*, where *H* is the set of possible contexts or "histories" and *T* is the set of possible tags. The model's joint probability of a history *h* and a tag *t* is defined as

$$p(h,t) = \pi\mu\prod_{j=1}^{k}\alpha_j^{f_j(h,t)} \qquad \text{(i)}$$

where π is a normalization constant, $\{\mu, \alpha_1, ..., \alpha_k\}$ are the model parameters and $\{f_1, ..., f_k\}$ are known as features, where $f_j\ (h, t) \in \{0,1\}$. Each feature f_j has a corresponding parameter α_j, which effectively serves as a "weight" of this feature. In the training process, given a sequence *n* of characters $\{c_1,...,c_n\}$ and their POC tags $\{t_1,...,t_n\}$ as training data, the purpose is to determine the parameters $\{\mu, \alpha_1, ..., \alpha_k\}$ that maximize the likelihood *L* of the training data using *p*:

$$L(p) = \prod_{i=1}^{n} p(h_i,t_i) = \prod_{i=1}^{n}\ \pi\mu\prod_{j=1}^{k}\alpha_j^{f_j(h_i,t_i)} \qquad \text{(ii)}$$

The success of the model in tagging depends to a large extent on the selection of suitable features. Given *(h,t)*, a feature must encode information that helps to predict *t*. The features we used in this experiment are instantiations of the following feature templates:

(3) Feature templates used in this tagger:

a. The current character

b. The previous (next) character and the current character

c. The previous (next) two characters

d. The tag of the previous character

e. The tag of the character two before the current character

f. Whether the current character is a punctuation mark

g. Whether the current character is a numeral

h. Whether the current character is a Latin letter

In general, given *(h,t)*, these features are in the form of co-occurrence relations between *t* and some type of context. For example,

$$f_i(h_i, t_i) = \begin{cases} 1 & if\ t_{i-1} = LL \ \&\ t_i = RR \\ 0 & otherwise \end{cases}$$

This feature will map to 1 and contribute towards $p(h_i, t_i)$ if $c_{(i-1)}$ is tagged LL and c_i is tagged RR.

The feature templates in (3) encode three types of contexts. First, features based on the current and surrounding characters are extracted. Given a character in a sentence, this model will look at the current character, the previous two and next two characters. For example, if the current character is 化 ('-ize'), it is very likely that it will occur as a suffix in a word, thus receiving the tag RR. On the other hand, other characters might be equally likely to appear on the left, on the right or in the middle. In those cases, where a character occurs within a word depends on its surrounding characters. For example, if the current character is 爱 ('love'), it should perhaps be tagged LL if the next character is 护 ('protect'). However, if the previous character is 热 ('warm'), then it should perhaps be tagged RR.

In the second type of context, features based on the previous tags are extracted. Information like this is useful in predicting the POC tag for the current character just as the POS tags are useful in predicting the POS tag of the current word in a similar context. For example, if the previous character is tagged LR or RR, this means that the current character must start a word, and should be tagged either LL or LR. Finally, limited POS-tagging information can also be used to predict how the current character should be POC-tagged. For example, a punctuation mark is generally treated as one segment in the CTB corpus. Therefore, if a character is a punctuation mark, then it should be POC-tagged LR. This also means that the previous character should close a word and the following character should start a word. When the training is complete, the features and their corresponding parameters will be used to calculate the probability of the tag sequence of a sentence when the tagger tags unseen data. Given a sequence of characters $\{c_1, \ldots, c_n\}$, the tagger searches for the tag sequence $\{t_1, \ldots, t_n\}$ with the highest conditional probability

$$P(t_1, \ldots t_n \mid c_1, \ldots c_n) = \prod_{i=1}^{n} p(t_i \mid h_i) \qquad \text{(iii)}$$

in which the conditional probability for each POC tag *t* given its history *h* is calculated as

$$p(t \mid h) = \frac{p(h,t)}{\sum_{t' \in T} P(h,t')} \qquad \text{(iv)}$$

2.3 The transformation-based tagger

The error-driven transformation-based tagger we used in this paper is Brill's POS tagger (1994) with minimal modification. The way this tagger is set up makes it easy for it to work in conjunction with other taggers. When it is used for its original task of POS tagging, the model is trained in two phases. In the first phase lexical information, such as the affixes of a word, is learned to predict POS tags. The rules learned in this phase are then applied to the training corpus. In the second phase, contextual information is learned to correct the wrong tags produced in the first phase. In the segmentation task, since we are dealing with single characters, by definition there is no lexical information as such. Instead, the training data are first POC-tagged by the maximum entropy model and then used by the error-driven transformation-based model to learn the contextual rules. The error-driven transformation-based model learns a ranked set of rules by comparing the perfectly POC-tagged corpus (the reference corpus) with the same corpus tagged by the maximum entropy model (the maxent-tagged corpus). At each iteration, this model tries to find the rule that achieves the maximum gain if it is applied. The rule with the maximum gain is the one that makes the maxent-tagged corpus most like the reference corpus. The maximum gain is calculated with an evaluation function which quantifies the gain and takes the largest value. The rules are instantiations of a set of pre-defined rule templates. After the rule with the maximum gain is found, it is applied to the maxent-tagged corpus, which will better resemble the reference corpus as a result. This process is repeated until the maximum gain drops below a pre-defined threshold, which indicates improvement achieved through further training will no longer be significant. The training will then be terminated. The rule templates are the same as those used in Brill (1994), except that these rule templates are now defined over characters rather than words.

(4) Rule templates used to learn contextual information:

Change tag *a* to tag *b* when:

a. The preceding (following) character is tagged *z*.

b. The character two before (after) is tagged *z*.

c. One of the two preceding (following) characters is tagged *z*.

d. One of the three preceding (following) characters is tagged *z*.

e. The preceding character is tagged *z* and the following character is tagged *w*.

f. The preceding (following) character is tagged *z* and the character two before (after) was tagged *w*.

g. The preceding (following) character is *c*.

h. The character two before (after) is *c*.

i. One of the two preceding (following) characters is *c*.

j. The current character is *c* and the preceding (following) character is x.

k. The current character is *c* and the preceding (following) character is tagged *z*.

where *a*, *b*, *z* and *w* are variables over the set of four tags (LL, RR, LR, MM)

The ranked set of rules learned in this training process will be applied to the output of the maximum entropy tagger.

3 Experimental results

We conducted three experiments. In the first experiment, we used the maximum matching algorithm to establish a baseline, as comparing results across different data sources can be difficult. This experiment is also designed to demonstrate that even with a relatively small number of new words in the testing data, the segmentation accuracy drops sharply. In the second experiment, we applied the maximum entropy model to the problem of Chinese word segmentation. The results will show that this approach alone outperforms the state-of-the-art results reported in previous work in supervised machine-learning approaches. In the third experiment we combined the maximum entropy model with the error-driven transformation-based model. We used the error-driven transformation-based model to learn a set of rules to correct the errors produced by the maximum entropy model. The data we used are from the Penn Chinese Treebank (Xia *et al.* 2000, Xue *et al.* 2002) and they consist of Xinhua newswire articles. We took 250,389 words (426,292 characters or *hanzi*) worth of manually segmented data and divided them into two chunks. The first chunk has 237,791 words (404,680 Chinese characters) and is used as training data. The second chunk has 12,598 words (21,612 characters) and is used as testing data. These data are used in all three of our experiments.

3.1 Experiment One

In this experiment, we conducted two sub-experiments. In the first sub-experiment, we used a forward maximum matching algorithm to segment the testing data with a dictionary compiled from the training data. There are 497 (or 3.95%) new words (words that are not found in the training data) in the testing data. In the second sub-experiment, we used the same algorithm to segment the same testing data with a dictionary that was compiled from BOTH the training data and the testing data, so that there are no "new" words in the testing data.

3.2 Experiment Two

In this experiment, a maximum entropy model was trained on a POC-tagged corpus derived from the training data described above. In the testing phase, the sentences in the testing data were first split into sequences of characters and then tagged this maximum entropy tagger. The tagged testing data are then converted back into word segments for evaluation. Note that converting a POC-tagged corpus into a segmented corpus is not entirely straightforward when inconsistent tagging occurs. For example it is possible that the tagger assigns a LL-LR sequence to two adjacent characters. We made no effort to ensure the best possible conversion. The character that is POC-tagged LL is invariably combined with the following character, no matter how it is tagged.

3.3 Experiment Three

In this experiment, we used the maximum entropy model trained in experiment two to automatically tag the training data. The training accuracy of the maximum entropy model is 97.54% in terms of the number of characters tagged correctly and there are 9940 incorrectly tagged characters, out of 404,680 characters in total. We then used this output and the correctly tagged data derived from the manually segmented training data (as the reference corpus) to learn a set of transformation rules. 214 rules were learned in this phase. These 214 rules were then used to correct the errors of the testing data that was first tagged by maximum entropy model in experiment two. As a final step, the tagged and corrected testing data were converted into word segments. Again, no effort was made to optimize the segmentation accuracy during the conversion.

3.4 Evaluation

In evaluating our model, we calculated both the tagging accuracy and segmentation accuracy. The calculation of the tagging accuracy is straightforward. It is simply the total number of correctly POC-tagged characters divided by the total number of characters. In evaluating segmentation accuracy, we used three measures: precision, recall and balanced F-score. Precision (p) is defined as the number of correctly segmented words divided by the total number of words in the automatically segmented corpus. Recall (r) is defined as the number of correctly segmented words divided by the total number of words in the gold standard, which is the manually annotated corpus. F-score (f) is defined as follows:

$$f = \frac{p \times r \times 2}{p + r} \qquad \text{(v)}$$

The results of the three experiments are tabulated as follows:

tagger	tagging accuracy		segmentation accuracy		
	training	testing	testing		
			p(%)	r(%)	f(%)
1	n/a	n/a	87.34	92.34	89.77
2	n/a	n/a	94.51	95.80	95.15
3	97.55	95.95	94.90	94.88	94.89
4	97.81	96.07	95.21	95.13	95.17

Table 1

1 = maximum matching algorithm applied to testing data with new words
2 = maximum matching algorithm applied to testing data without new words
3 = maximum entropy tagger

4 = maximum entropy tagger combined with the transformation-based tagger

4 Discussion

The results from Experiment one show that the accuracy of the maximum matching algorithm degrades sharply when there are new words in the testing data, even when there is only a small proportion of them. Assuming an ideal scenario where there are no new words in the testing data, the maximum matching algorithm achieves an F-score of 95.15%. However, when there are new words (words not found in the training data), the accuracy drops to only 89.77% in F-score. In contrast, the maximum entropy tagger achieves an accuracy of 94.89% measured by the balanced F-score even when there are new words in the testing data. This result is only slightly lower than the 95.15% that the maximum matching algorithm achieved when there are no new words. The transformation-based tagger improves the tagging accuracy by 0.12% from 95.95% to 96.07%. The segmentation accuracy jumps to 95.17% (F-score) from 94.89%, an increase of 0.28%. That fact that the improvement in segmentation accuracy is higher than the improvement in tagging accuracy shows that the transformation-based tagger is able to correct some of the inconsistent tagging errors produced by the maximum entropy tagger. This is clearly demonstrated in the five highest-ranked transformation rules learned by this model:

(5) Top five transformation rules

RR MM NEXTTAG RR
LL LR NEXTTAG LL
LL LR NEXTTAG LR
MM RR NEXTBIGRAM LR LR
RR LR PREVBIGRAM RR LR

For example, the first rule says that if the next character is tagged RR, then change the current tag to MM from RR, since an RR RR sequence is inconsistent.

Incidentally, the combined segmentation accuracy is almost the same as that of the maximum matching method when there are no new words.

Evaluating this approach against previous results can be a tricky matter. There are several reasons for this. One is that the source of data can affect the segmentation accuracy. Since the results of machine-learning approaches are heavily dependent on the type of training data, comparison of segmenters trained on different data is not exactly valid. The second reason is that the amount of training data also affects the accuracy of segmenters. Still some preliminary observations can be made in this regard. Our accuracy is much higher that those reported in Hockenmaier and Brew (1998) and Xue (2001), who used error-driven transformation-based learning to learn a set of n-gram rules to do a series of merge and split operations on data from Xinhua news, the same data source as ours. The results they reported are 87.9% (trained on 100,000 words) and 90.2% (trained on 80,000 words) respectively, measured by the balanced F-score.

Using a statistical model called prediction by partial matching (PPM), Teahan *et al* (2000) reported a significantly better result. The model was trained on a million words from Guo Jin's Mandarin Chinese PH corpus and tested on five 500-segment files. The reported F-scores are in a range between 89.4% and 98.6%, averaging 94.4%. Since the data are also from Xinhua newswire, some comparison can be made between our results and this model. With less training data, our results are slightly higher (by 0.48%) when using just the maximum entropy model. When this model is combined with the error-driven transformation-based learning model, our accuracy is higher by 0.77%. Still, this comparison is just preliminary since different segmentation standards can also affect segmentation accuracy.

5 Conclusion

The preliminary results show that our approach is more robust than the dictionary-based approaches. They also show that the present approach outperforms other state-of-the-art machine-learning models. We can also conclude that the maximum entropy model is a promising supervised machine learning alternative that can be effectively applied to Chinese word segmentation.

6 Acknowledgement

This research was funded by DARPA N66001-00-1-8915. We gratefully acknowledge comments from two anonymous reviewers.

7 References

Eric Brill. 1995. Some Advances In Rule-Based Part of Speech Tagging, *AAAI* 1994

Julia Hockenmaier and Chris Brew. 1998. Error-driven segmentation of Chinese. *Communications of COLIPS*, 1:1:69-84.

Adwait Ratnaparkhi. 1996. A Maximum Entropy Part-of-Speech Tagger. In *Proceedings of the Empirical Methods in Natural Language Processing Conference*, May 17-18, 1996. University of Pennsylvania.

W. J. Teahan, Rodger McNab, Yingying Wen and Ian H. Witten. 2000. A Compression-based Algorithm for Chinese Word Segmentation. *Computational Linguistics*, 26:3:375-393

Andi Wu and Zixin Jiang. 1998. Word Segmentation in Sentence Analysis. In *Proceedings of the 1998 International Conference on Chinese Information Processing*. Nov. 1998, Beijing, pp. 167-180.

Fei Xia, Martha Palmer, Nianwen Xue, Mary Ellen Okurowski, John Kovarik, Shizhe Huang, Tony Kroch, Mitch Marcus. 2000. Developing Guidelines and Ensuring Consistency for Chinese Text Annotation. In *Proc. of the 2nd International Conference on Language Resources and Evaluation (LREC-2000)*, Athens, Greece.

Nianwen Xue. 2001. *Defining and Automatically Identifying Words in Chinese*. PhD Dissertation, University of Delaware.

Nianwen Xue, Fu-dong Chiou, Martha Palmer. 2002. Building a Large Annotated Chinese Corpus. To appear in *Proceedings of the 19th International Conference on Computational Linguistics*. August 14 - September 1, 2002. Taipei, Taiwan.

WSD and Closed Semantic Constraint

Jiangsheng Yu*
Institute of Computational Linguistics
Peking University, Beijing, China, 100871

Abstract *The application-driven construction of lexicon has been emphasized as a methodology of Computational Lexicology recently. We focus on the closed semantic constraint of the argument(s) of any verb concept by the noun concepts in a WordNet-like lexicon, which theoretically is related to Word Sense Disambiguation (WSD) at different levels. From the viewpoint of Dynamic Lexicon, WSD provides a way of automatic construction for the closed semantic constraints and also benefits from the semantic descriptions.*
Keywords *dynamic lexicon, evolution, WSD, WordNet-like lexicon, closed semantic constraint*

1 Introduction

As the underlying resource of semantic analysis, the most important descriptions in a semantic lexicon are the relationships between verbs and nouns, which usually comes down to the closed semantic constraint of each argument of any verb. Once the structure of the semantic lexicon is determined, the closed semantic constraint becomes a well-defined problem.

Example 1.1 The verb *dǎ* has many meanings in Chinese, which differ in *dǎ háizi* (punish the child), *dǎ máoyī* (weaver the sweater), *dǎ jiàngyóu* (buy the soy), etc. Actually, the semantics of *dǎ* is distinguished by the semantics of its arguments.

Different from the traditional lexicon, we advocate the conception of dynamic lexicon ([15]) and its evolution oriented to some particular application, which will be mentioned in Section 2. The WordNet-like lexicon is treated as a dynamic one, which means that the structures representing semantic knowledge could be changed according to some empirical standards. In the next section, we'll define the WSD based on the WordNet-like lexicon, and then discuss the training of concept TagSet and the statistical model of WSD. By the statistical WSD, in Section 4, we introduce an approach to the automatic construction of the closed semantic constraints in a WordNet-like lexicon. The last section is the conclusion.

*This paper is supported by National Foundation of Natural Science (Research on Chinese Information Extraction), No. 69483003 and Project 985 in Peking University.

2 Dynamic Lexicon and Its Structural Evolution

Definition 2.1 A *dynamic lexicon* is a triple $\mathsf{Lex} = \langle S, R, T\rangle$ in which

1. S is a well-structured set with a type[1] t,
2. R is the set of deductive rules on S, and
3. T is the set of all structural transformations of S, keeping the type t.

Definition 2.2 Lexicon $\langle S', R, T\rangle$ is called the *evolution result* of the lexicon $\langle S, R, T\rangle$ if $\exists t \in T^*$ such that $S \xrightarrow{t} S'$ (or briefly $S \rightsquigarrow S'$). The process of a dynamic lexicon to its evolution result is called an *evolution*. Obviously, T is a group with the operation of composition.

Definition 2.3 $\langle S, R, T\rangle$ is called *simple structured* if T is a commutative group, otherwise *complex structured*.

The more complex is the structure of S, the more difficult are the applications of R and T. Since some part of semantic knowledge is represented by the structure, the complexity balance between the structure and R (or T) is one of the serious problems in Computational Lexicology.

Definition 2.4 Let $\Omega(S)$ denote the least number of operations constructing S, and $\Omega(S \rightsquigarrow S')$ the least number of operations from S to S'. It's easy to verify that

Theorem 2.1 $\Omega(\cdot)$ is a distance, i.e., it satisfies that $\forall S, S', S''$,

1. $\Omega(S \rightsquigarrow S') \geq 0$
2. $\Omega(S \rightsquigarrow S') = 0 \Leftrightarrow S = S'$
3. $\Omega(S \rightsquigarrow S') = \Omega(S' \rightsquigarrow S)$
4. $\Omega(S \rightsquigarrow S'') \leq \Omega(S \rightsquigarrow S') + \Omega(S' \rightsquigarrow S'')$

[1] For instance, labeled tree or complete lattice.

Corollary 2.1 $\Omega(S') \leq \Omega(S) + \Omega(S \rightsquigarrow S')$

Definition 2.5 The *degree of structural destruction* from S to S', is defined by

$$\rho(S \rightsquigarrow S') = 1 - \frac{\Omega(S')}{\Omega(S) + \Omega(S \rightsquigarrow S')} \quad (1)$$

Property 2.1 $0 \leq \rho(S \rightsquigarrow S') \leq 1$

Definition 2.6 Let $S \rightsquigarrow S_1 \rightsquigarrow \cdots \rightsquigarrow S_n \rightsquigarrow \cdots$ be a sequence of evolution, the sequence is called *convergent* if there exists a constant A s.t. $0 \leq A \leq 1$ and $\lim_{n\to\infty} \rho(S \rightsquigarrow S_n) = A$.

It's easy to see that a local evolution of the lexicon may not be an optimization even for a specific application. The index ρ indicates the convergence of lexical structure, guaranteeing a stable machine learning of the dynamic lexicon. Actually, the structure of the so-called common knowledge is nothing but a statistical distribution, which is effected by the cultures and personal experiences. Oriented, to a particular application, such as IE, IR, MT, etc, the appropriate semantic descriptions in a WordNet-like lexicon seem necessary.

Example 2.1 C = {*earthquake, quake, temblor, seism*} is not only a kind of C' = {*geological phenomenon*}, but also a kind of C'' = {*natural disaster*}.

3 WSD based on WordNet-like Lexicon

What does it mean that a machine could **understand** a given sentence S or a text T? As we know, Turing Test of NLU includes at least the meaning of any word w in S or T. Thus, the prerequisite WSD is to tag the semantic information of w automatically. WordNet[2] in Princeton University, in despite of its disputed quality, provides an approach to the formalization of concepts in natural language, in which a concept is defined by a synonym set (SynSet). A more important work in WordNet is the construction of a well-structured concept network based on the hypernymy relation (the main framework) and other accessorial relations, such as, the opposite relation, the holonymy relation, entailment, cause, etc.

Definition 3.1 A *WordNet-like lexicon* is a dynamic lexicon with the type of WordNet:

1. restricted to each category, S is a labeled tree from the viewpoint of the hypernymy relation for both noun concepts and verb concepts,
2. some accessorial relations between the noun (or verb) concepts, and
3. closed semantic constraint of the argument(s) of each verb concept from the noun concepts.

The WordNet-like lexicon is complex structured, it may not have the same ontology of WordNet, neither the semantic knowledge representations. But the description method seems a general format for all languages from the fact of EuroWordNet (see [12]), Chinese Concept Dictionary (CCD, see [7], [13], [14] and [15]), Korean WordNet, Tamil WordNet, etc.

Definition 3.2 Let Σ be the set of all words, then Γ, the set of all concepts (or SynSets) in a WordNet-like lexicon, is a subset of 2^{Σ}. The set of all SynSets containing w is denoted by $\Delta(w)$, in which each element is called a *sense* of w.

Definition 3.3 Given a well-defined sentence $S = w_1 w_2 \cdots w_n$, WSD is the computable processing which tags w_i a unique sense $s_i = \{w_i, w_{i_1}, \cdots, w_{i_k}\}$ such that each derived combinatorial path is a well-defined sentence with the semantics of S. The Principle of Substitution provides a corpus-based empirical approach to test a SynSet well-defined or not. The SynSet is the smallest unit in a WordNet-like lexicon, which is the underlying of the structural descriptions between the concepts.

The training of concept TagSet and the statistical model of WSD are interactional, which is the main idea of our approach to WSD based on a WordNet-like lexicon.

3.1 The Training of TagSet

The traditional semantic tags are from some ontology, the apriority of which is often criticized by computational linguists. For us, the empirical method must impenetrate each step of WSD because of the complexity of language knowledge. The statistical approach to WSD needs a well concept-tagged corpus as the training set for the concept TagSet and the statistical data in the Hidden Markov Model (HMM). To avoid the sparse data problem, only a few real subsets of Γ could act as the TagSet in the statistical model (see [15] and [16]). The first step leads to a set of structured TagSets $\{\mathsf{T}_1, \mathsf{T}_2, \cdots, \mathsf{T}_m\}$, then the second step is to choose the most efficient one which makes the best accuracy of the statistical concept tagging. Different from those unframed tags, the deductive rule along the hypernymy trees works out the sense of w by the following property:

[2] The specification of WordNet could be found in [3], [4], [5], [9], [10], [11], etc.

Property 3.1 Suppose that the TagSet is $\mathsf{T} = \{C_1, C_2, \cdots, C_k\}$, and the word w in a given sentence is tagged by C_i, then the sense of w here is the SynSet C which satisfies that $C_i \preceq C$ and $w \in C$, where $\preceq$ is the partial ordering of the nodes in the hypernymy tree.

3.2 Statistical Model of WSD

In some sense, WSD is the kernel problem of both NLU and NLP ([1], [6], [8]). POS and concept tag are two random variables in the HMM of WSD. Sometimes POS of w determines its sense, sometimes not. But in most cases, a sense of w implies a unique POS. The distribution of w's senses with the POS, P, is important in the (POS, concept)-tagging. A Hidden Markov Model with two parameters will be adopted as the main statistical model for WSD, and the Statistical Decision Theory and Bayesian Analysis, which are good at analyzing the small samples, conducted as a comparison. The training corpus, T, is done by hand, where the cursor sensitive display of the senses provides the help information.

Definition 3.4 Consider the well-defined sentence $S = w_1 w_2 \cdots w_n$. By the lexicon, let $S = w_1/_{P_1^{(i)}}\ w_2/_{P_2^{(i)}} \cdots w_n/_{P_n^{(i)}}$ be a possible POS tagged result, where $i \in I$. Define

$$\begin{aligned} f(i) &= \underset{j\in J}{argmax}\, \mathsf{P}(C_1^{(i,j)} \cdots C_n^{(i,j)} | P_1^{(i)} \cdots P_n^{(i)}) \\ &= \underset{j\in J}{argmax}\, \mathsf{P}(C_1^{(i,j)} \cdots C_n^{(i,j)}, P_1^{(i)} \cdots P_n^{(i)}) \quad (2) \\ &= \underset{j\in J}{argmax}\, \mathsf{P}(C_1^{(i,j)} \cdots C_n^{(i,j)}) \end{aligned}$$

The HMM of concept can simulate the HMM with two parameters of (POS, concept). $f(i)$ in (2) is predigested to

$$f(i) = \underset{j\in J}{argmax}\, \mathsf{P}(C_1^{(i,j)}) \prod_{k=2}^{n} \mathsf{P}(C_k^{(i,j)} | C_{k-1}^{(i,j)}) \quad (3)$$

Property 3.2 There exists a unique map g from the set of $\{P_1^{(i)} P_2^{(i)} \cdots P_n^{(i)} | i \in I\}$ to the set of $\{C_1^{(i,j)} C_2^{(i,j)} \cdots C_n^{(i,j)} | (i,j) \in I \times J\}$, which satisfies that

$$g(P_1^{(i)} \cdots P_n^{(i)}) = C_1^{(i,f(i))} \cdots C_n^{(i,f(i))} \quad (4)$$

where $\forall i, k, \exists C \in \Delta(w_k)$ s.t. $C_k^{(i,f(i))} \preceq C$. If there is $C' \neq C$ satisfying $C' \in \Delta(w_k)$ and $C_k^{(i,f(i))} \preceq C'$, then the one with more distribution is the selected sense of w_k.

Property 3.3 Let $s = w_1 w_2 \cdots w_n$ be any possible segmented sequence of S, corresponding a set of probabilities of POS sequences $A_s = \{\mathsf{P}(P_1^{(i)} P_2^{(i)} \cdots P_n^{(i)}) | i \in I\}$. Each $P_1^{(i)} P_2^{(i)} \cdots P_n^{(i)}$ corresponds a set of probabilities of concept sequences $B_s^{(i)} = \{\mathsf{P}(C_1^{(i,j)} C_2^{(i,j)} \cdots C_n^{(i,j)}) | j \in J\}$, where $C_k^{(i,j)}$ has the POS of $P_k^{(i)}$, then

$$\underset{s}{argmax}(a \cdot \max_s(A_s) + b \cdot \max_{i,s}(B_s^{(i)})) \quad (5)$$

is the choice of segmentation, where $a > 0, b > 0$ and $a + b = 1$. More precisely, (5) is rewritten by

$$\underset{s}{argmax}\{\max_i\{a \cdot \mathsf{P}(P_s^{(i)}) + b \cdot \mathsf{P}(g(P_s^{(i)}))\}\} \quad (6)$$

where $P_s^{(i)} = P_1^{(i)} P_2^{(i)} \cdots P_n^{(i)}$.

4 WSD driven Closed Semantic Constraint

From the corpus and the statistical WSD, we can make an induction of the arguments along the hypernymy tree, which leads to the closed semantic constraints automatically. At the same time, the closed semantic constraints also provide a possible approach to the empirical optimization of Γ_N and Γ_V. While the total optimization of a WordNet-like lexicon is still an open problem.

4.1 Similarity between Concepts

Definition 4.1 A *labeled tree* is a 5-tuple $T = \langle N, Q, D, P, L \rangle$ satisfying that:

1. N is a finite set of nodes
2. Q is a finite set of labels
3. D is a partial ordering on N, called *dominance relation*
4. P is a strict partial ordering on N, called *precedence relation*
5. $(\exists x \in N)(\forall y \in N)[(x,y) \in D]$
6. $(\forall x, y \in N)[[(x,y) \in P \vee (y,x) \in P] \leftrightarrow [(x,y) \notin D \wedge (y,x) \notin D]]$
7. $(\forall x, y, z, w \in N)[[(w,x) \in P \wedge (w,y) \in D \wedge (x,z) \in D] \rightarrow (y,z) \in P]$
8. $L : N \rightarrow Q$ is a *label map*

Definition 4.2 A hypernymy tree is a labeled tree, in which the label map is one-to-one. Always, we presume that the hypernymy tree is not degenerative.

In a hypernymy tree of a WordNet-like lexicon, a node is a code and a label is a SynSet. Since the label map is injective, without generality, a SynSet is usually denoted by a node. We assume that the precedence relation between the brother nodes always implies an ordering of time, usage, frequency, mood, etc. For instance, $\{\text{spring}, \text{springtime}\} \prec \{\text{summer}, \text{summertime}\} \prec \{\text{fall}, \text{autumn}\} \prec \{\text{winter}, \text{wintertime}\}$ as the hyponyms of $\{\text{season}, \text{time of year}\}$.

Definition 4.3 Let f, b and B denote *father*, *the nearest younger-brother* and *the nearest elder-brother* respectively, satisfying that $f = fb, f = fB$ and $Bb = bB = \mathbf{1}$.

Definition 4.4 $\forall x, y \in N$, let $z \in N$ be their nearest ancestor satisfying $z = f^m(x)$ and $z = f^n(y), D(x, y) \overset{\text{def}}{=} m + n$. $k \in \mathbb{N}$ is called the *offset* of x from its eldest brother if $\exists B^k(x)$ and $\nexists B^{k+1}(x)$. Let the offset of y is l, the *similarity* between x and y is:

- If $mn = 1, S(x, y) \overset{\text{def}}{=} \langle 0, |k - l| \rangle$
- If $mn \neq 1, S(x, y) \overset{\text{def}}{=} \langle m + n, 0 \rangle$

Definition 4.5 Suppose that $S(x_1, y_1) = \langle a_1, b_1 \rangle$ and $S(x_2, y_2) = \langle a_2, b_2 \rangle$, the comparison of similarities is defined as follows:

1. $a_1 = a_2$
   - $S(x_1, y_1) \preceq S(x_2, y_2) \leftrightarrow b_1 \leq b_2$
2. $a_1 \neq a_2$
   - If $a_1 < a_2$, then $S(x_1, y_1) \prec S(x_2, y_2)$
   - If $a_1 > a_2$, then $S(x_2, y_2) \prec S(x_1, y_1)$

Theorem 4.1 $\langle \{S(x, y) | x, y \in N\}, \preceq \rangle$ is a totally ordered set.

The elementary structural transformations in a WordNet-like lexicon include:

1. *insert* a non-root brother-node;
2. *collapse* a non-root node to its father-node;
3. *root* is adding a new root;
4. *add* a link between two labeled trees;
5. *delete* a link between two labeled trees.

4.2 Induction of Constraints

Γ_N (or Γ_V) denotes the set of noun (or verb) concepts. Let $C \in \Gamma_V$ be a verb concept with one argument. Suppose that we have gotten the initial closed semantic constraint of its argument, $C' \in \Gamma_N$, from a concept-tagged sentence. A link from C' to C is added between Γ_N and Γ_V. If C'' from another sentence is also a close semantic constraint of C's argument, then the infimum of C' and $C'', \inf(C', C'')$, is the new C'. $\forall x \in \Gamma, C' \preceq x$, if the substitution from C to x still induces well-formed sentences, then the induction succeeds. Otherwise, the disjointed union $C' \oplus C''$ is the closed semantic constraint.

Definition 4.6 The induction of the closed semantic constraints of $C, D \in \Gamma$ is defined by

$$C \sqcap D = \begin{cases} \inf(C, D) & \text{if } \forall x[\inf(C, D) \preceq x] \\ & \text{succeeds in the substitution} \\ C \oplus D & \text{otherwise} \end{cases}$$

Definition 4.7 By **Theorem 4.1**, the induction between $C \oplus D$ and $E \in \Gamma$ is defined by

$$(C \oplus D) \sqcap E = \begin{cases} (C \sqcap E) \oplus D & \text{if } S(C, E) \preceq S(D, E) \\ C \oplus (D \sqcap E) & \text{otherwise} \end{cases}$$

Theoretically, if $C_1 \oplus C_2 \oplus \cdots \oplus C_n$ is the closed semantic constraint of the argument of $C \in \Gamma_V$, then $\forall i, \forall x[C_i \preceq x]$ succeeds in the substitution. Thus, in the WordNet-like lexicon, there are n links from Γ_N to Γ_V for C, where n is called the *length of the constraint*. The approach to the closed semantic constraints of the verb concepts with two arguments is similar.

4.3 Clustering of Constraints

Definition 4.8 Suppose that there are N arguments for all verb concepts and the length of the i-th constraint is l_i, then $\bar{l} = \sum_{i=1}^{N} l_i / N$ is called the *average length of the constraints*.

$\bar{l}$ indicates the rationality of the concept classification in a WordNet-like lexicon, which also acts as an index of the evolution. Our presupposition is that the optimization of the lexicon must have the least average length of the constraints. The clustering of noun concepts constrained by the arguments of the verb concepts should be a standard of the classification of Γ_N.

Definition 4.9 $S \rightsquigarrow S_1 \rightsquigarrow \cdots \rightsquigarrow S_n \rightsquigarrow \cdots$ is *Cauchy sequence of evolution* iff $\forall \epsilon > 0, \exists N \in \mathbb{N}, \forall i, j > N, \rho(S_i \rightsquigarrow S_j) < \epsilon$.

Theorem 4.2 The Cauchy sequence of evolution is convergent. And $\forall \epsilon > 0, \exists i, j \in \mathbb{N}$ s.t. $|\bar{l}(S_i) - \bar{l}(S_j)| < \epsilon$.

Γ_N is structured by not only the hypernymy relation but also the closed semantic constraints. Of course, the hypernymy relation in Γ_N is principal, but not necessarily unique. As described in **Example 2.1**, the distinct angles of view provide enough space for the evolution. By the hypernymy relation in Γ_V, we have

Property 4.1 $\forall C, C' \in \Gamma_V, C \preceq C'$, if the closed semantic constraint of C' is $C_1 \oplus C_2 \oplus \cdots \oplus C_n$, then $\exists C_{n+1}, \cdots, C_m \in \Gamma_N$ such that $(((C_1 \oplus C_2 \oplus \cdots \oplus C_n) \sqcap C_{n+1}) \sqcap \cdots \sqcap C_m)$ is the closed semantic constraint of C.

This property provides an approach to the empirical testing of the concept classification of Γ_V if Γ_N is fixed. Separately, Γ_N (or Γ_V) can be evaluated by some indexes and evolves to a satisfiable result. A little more complicated, the closed semantic constraints destroy the independent evolution of Γ_N and Γ_V. If Γ_V is fixed, then the optimization of Γ_N may be implemented (but not completely reliable) and vice versa. While it is still an open problem to define a numerical measure that could formalize the optimization of the total structures in a WordNet-like lexicon, especially Γ_N and Γ_V.

5 Conclusion

A scheme of the closed semantic constraint in a WordNet-like lexicon based on WSD has been described as an application driven construction of a dynamic lexicon. At the same time, the further topic leads to how the rule-based concept tagging benefits from the descriptions of semantic constraint. The empirical method is much emphasized in the WSD and the development of the dynamic lexicon, such as the TagSet training, the SynSet testing and the evolution of a WordNet-like lexicon (see [15], [16] and [17]). The author believes that the computable part in Computational Lexicology is nothing but the evolution of the dynamic lexicon oriented to a particular application, which is actually the optimization of the language knowledge base.

Acknowledgement

I appreciate all my colleagues participating in the CCD project, the blithesome collaboration with them is always memorable for me. Many thanks to my friends in the Second and the Third Workshop on Chinese Lexical Semantics for their kindly discussion with the author. Lastly, the most thankful words are given to my wife for her longtime tolerance to my weaselling from the housework under the false pretense of research.

References

[1] ALPAC 1966 *Language and Machine: Computers in Translation and Linguistics*, National Research Council Automatic Language Processing Advisory Committee, Washington, D.C.

[2] Aristotle 1941 *Categoriae*, in The Basic Works of Aristotle, R. McKeon (ed). Random House, New York.

[3] Beckwith R. 1998 *Design and Implementation of the WordNet Lexical Database and Searching Software*, in [5], pp105-127.

[4] Fellbaum C. 1998 *A Semantic Net of English Verbs*, in [5], pp69-104.

[5] Fellbaum C. (ed) 1999 *WordNet: An Electronic Lexical Database*, The MIT Press.

[6] Ide N. and Véronis J. 1998 *Introduction to Special Issue on Word Sense Disambiguation: The State of Art*, Computational Linguistics, Vol. 24, No. 1, pp1-40.

[7] Liu Y, Yu S.W. and Yu J.S. *Building a Bilingual WordNet: New Approaches and algorithms*, accepted by COLING2002.

[8] Manning C.D. and Schütze H. 1999, *Foundations of Statistical Natural Language Processing*, The MIT Press.

[9] Miller G.A. et al 1993 *Introduction to WordNet: An On-line Lexical Database*, in the attached specification of WordNet 1.6.

[10] Miller G.A. 1998 *Nouns in WordNet*, in [5], pp23-46.

[11] Priss U. 1999 *The Formalization of WordNet by Methods of Relational Concept Analysis*, in [5], pp179-196.

[12] Vossen P. (ed.) 1998 *EuroWordNet: A Multilingual Database with Lexical Semantic Networks*. Dordrecht: Kluwer.

[13] Yu J.S. and Yu S.W. et al 2001 *Introduction to Chinese Concept Dictionary*, in International Conference on Chinese Computing (ICCC2001), pp361-367.

[14] Yu J.S. 2001 *The Structure of Chinese Concept Dictionary*, accepted by Journal of Chinese Information Processing, 2001.

[15] Yu J.S. 2001 *Evolution of WordNet-like Lexicon*, in The First International Conference of Global WordNet, Mysore, India, 2002.

[16] Yu J.S. and Yu S.W. 2002 *Word Sense Disambiguation based on Integrated Language Knowledge Base*, in The 2nd International Conference on East-Asian Language Processing and Internet Information Technology (EALPIIT'2002).

[17] Yu J.S. 2002 *Statistical Methods in Word Sense Disambiguation*, draft (can be downloaded from http://icl.pku.edu.cn/yujs/) of seminar at the Institute of Computational Linguistics, Peking Univ..

Automatic Recognition of Chinese Unknown Words[1] Based on Roles Tagging[2]

Kevin Zhang (Hua-Ping ZHANG) Qun LIU Hao ZHANG Xue-Qi CHENG
Software Division, Institute of Computing Technology, Chinese Academy of Sciences
NO. 6, South Road, Kexueyuan, Zhongguancun, Haidian Dist. P.O. BOX 2704, Beijing, P.R. China, 100080
Email: {zhanghp,liuqun, zhanghao,cxq}@software.ict.ac.cn

Abstract

This paper presents a unified solution, which is based on the idea of "roles tagging", to the complicated problems of Chinese unknown words recognition. In our approach, an unknown word is identified according to its component tokens and context tokens. In order to capture the functions of tokens, we use the concept of roles. Roles are tagged through applying the Viterbi algorithm in the fashion of a POS tagger. In the resulted most probable roles sequence, all the eligible unknown words are recognized through a maximum patterns matching. We have got excellent precision and recalling rates, especially for person names and transliterations. The result and experiments in our system ICTCLAS shows that our approach based on roles tagging is simple yet effective.

Keywords: Chinese unknown words recognition, roles tagging, word segmentation, Viterbi algorithm.

Introduction

It is well known that word segmentation is a prerequisite to Chinese information processing. Previous research and work in word segmentation have made great progresses. However, cases with unknown words are not satisfactory. In general, any lexicon is limited and unable to cover all the words in real texts or speeches. According to our statistics on a 2,305,896-character news corpus from *the People's Daily*, there are about 1.19% unknown words. But they are difficult to be recalled and often greatly reduce the recognition rate of known words close to them. For example, the sentence "部长孙家正在工作。" (Pronunciation: "Bu Zhang Sun Jia Zheng Zai Gong Zuo.") has two valid segmentations: "部长/孙家正/在/工作" (The minister Sun Jiazheng is at work) and "部长/孙家/正在/工作" (The minister Sun Jia now is at work). "孙家正" is a person name in the first, while "孙家" is another name in the latter. Meanwhile, the string "孙家正在" will lead to overlapping ambiguity and bring a collision between the unknown word "孙家正" (Sun Jiazheng) and "正在"(zheng zai; now). What's more, the recognizing precision rates of person names, place names, and transliterations are 91.26%, 69.12%, and 82.83%, respectively, while the recalling rates of them are just 68.77%, 60.47%, and 78.29%, respectively. (Data from official testing in 1999) [Liu (1999)] In a word, unknown words recognition has become one of the biggest stumbling blocks on the way of Chinese lexical analysis. A proper solution is important and urgent.

Various approaches are taken in Chinese unknown words recognition. They can be broadly categorized into "one-for-one", "one-for-several" and "one-for-all" based on the number of categories of unknown words, which can be recognized. One-for-one solutions solve a particular problem, such as person name recognition [Song (1993); Ji (2001)], place name recognition [Tan (1999)] and transliteration recognition [Sun (1993)]. Similarly, one-for-several approaches provide one solution for several specific categories of unknown words [Lv (2001); Luo (2001)]. One-for-all solutions, as far as we know, have not been applicable yet [Chen (1999); He (2001)].

Although currently practicable methods could achieve great precision or recalling rates in some special cases, they have their inherent deficiencies. First of all, rules applied are mostly summarized by linguists through painful study of all kinds of huge "special name libraries" [Luo (2001)]. It's time-consuming, expensive and inflexible. The categories of unknown words are diverse and the amount of such words is huge. With the rapid development of the Internet, this situation is becoming more and more serious. Therefore, it's very difficult to summarize simple yet thorough rules about their compositions and contexts. Secondly, the recognition process cannot be activated until some "indicator" tokens are scanned in. For instance, possible surnames or titles often trigger person name recognition on the following 2 or more characters. In the case of place name recognition, the postfixes such as “县”(county), “市”(city) will activate the recognition on the previous characters. What's more, these methods tend to work only on the monosyllabic tokens, which are obvious fragments after tokenization [Luo (2001); Lv (2001)]. It takes the risk of losing lots of unknown words without any explicit features. Furthermore, this trigger mechanism cannot resolve the ambiguity. For example, unknown word “方林山” (Fang Lin Shan) maybe a person name “方/林山”(Fang Linshan) or a place name “方林/山”(Fanglin Mountain).

This paper presents a one-for-all approach based on roles tagging to avoid such problems. The process is: tagging tokens after word segmentation with the most probable roles and making unknown words recognition based on roles sequence. The mechanism of roles tagging is just like that of a small and simple Part-Of-Speech tagger.

The paper is organized as follows: In section 2, we will describe the approach in general. Following that, we will present the solution in practice. In the final part, we provide recognition experiments using roles-tagging methods. The result and possible problems are discussed as well.

1 Unknown words recognition based on roles tagging

1.1 Lexical roles of unknown words

Unknown words are often made up of distinctive components, most of which are monosyllabic characters or short words; in addition, there are some regular relations between unknown words and their locality, especially with their left and right context. As we often write or speak, a Chinese person name is usually comprised of a one-or-two-character surname and a following given name of one or two characters, like “肖建群”(Xiao Jianqun) and “诸葛亮”(Zhu-Ge Liang). The previous words are mostly titles, occupations or some conjunctive words, such as “经理”(Manager), “司机”(Driver) and “对”(To). The following words tend to be verbs such as “说” (to say) , “表示”(to express). Similar components, contexts and relations can be discovered in place name, transliteration, organization name, or other types of unknown words.

We define unknown word roles with respect to varied internal components, previous and succeeding contexts and other tokens in a particular sentence. Various roles are extracted according to their functions in the forming of different unknown words. Person names roles and transliterations roles set are shown in table 1a and 1b respectively. Using the roles set of person name, the tokens sequence “馆/内/陈列/周/恩/来/和/邓/颖/超生/前/使用/过/的/物品/” (What Zhou Enlai and Deng Yunchao used before death are presented in the museum) will be tagged as “馆/A 内/A 陈列/K 周/B 恩/C 来/D 和/M 邓/B 颖/C 超生/V 前/A 使用/A 过/A 的/A 物品/A”.

Role	Significance	Examples
B	Surname or family name.	*张*/华/平/先生；*欧阳*/修
C	First Chinese char in the 2-char given name	张/*华*/平/先生
D	Last Chinese char in the 2-char given name.	张/华/*平*/先生
E	Given name with a single Chinese char.	张/*浩*
F	Prefix in the name.	*老*/刘、*小*/李
G	Postfix in the name.	王/*总*、刘/*老*、肖/*氏*
K	Previous context before person name.	又/*来到*/于/洪/洋/的/家
L	Succeeding context following person name.	新华社/记者黄文/*摄*
M	Parts between two person names.	编剧/邵/钧/林/*和*/稽/道/青/说
U	Known words generated by previous context and the first component of name.	这里/*有关*/天/培/的/壮烈/; 现任/主席/*为何*/鲁/丽/。/
V	Known words generated by the last component and next context.	龚/学/*平等*/领导/, 邓/颖/*超生*/前
	.....	
A	Others tokens not mentioned above.	*全国*/*人民*/*深切*/缅怀/邓/小/平/

Table 1a: Roles set of Chinese person names

Role	Significance	Examples
B	The first component of transliteration	克/林/顿
C	Middle component	史/蒂/芬/·/斯/皮/尔/伯/格
D	Last component	克/林/顿
.....		

Table 1b: Roles set of transliterations

1.2 Roles tagging and unknown words recognition

On the one hand, the sentence include words with different roles for a particular category of unknown words, on the other hand, such words can be recognized after identifying their roles sequence. That is: tagging tokens after word segmentation with the most probable roles sequence, then recognizing unknown words by maximum patterns matching on the final roles sequence.

Roles tagging is similar to Part-Of-Speech tagging. Our tagging process is based on Viterbi Algorithm [Rabiner and Juang (1989)], which is to select the optimum with maximum probability from all possible tag sequences. The methodology and its deduction is given as below:

Suppose that T is the tokens sequence after word segmentation and R is the roles sequence for T. We take the role sequence $R^{\#}$ with the maximum probability as the best choice. That is:

$T=(t_1, t_2, \dots , t_m)$,

$R=(r_1, r_2, \dots , r_m)$, $m>0$,

$$R^{\#}=\arg\max_R P(R|T) \text{..............................E1}$$

According to the Bayes equation, we can get:

$$P(R|T)= P(R)P(T|R)/P(T) \text{..................E2}$$

For a particular token sequence, P(T) is a constant. So, We can get E3 based on E1 and E2:

$$R^{\#}=\arg\max_R P(R)P(T|R) \text{......................E3}$$

We may consider T as the observation value sequence while R as the state sequence hidden behind the observation. Now we introduce Hidden Markov Model [Rabiner and Juang (1986)] to resolve such a typical problem:

$$P(R)\,P(T|R)\approx \prod_{i=0}^{m} p(t_i \mid r_i)p(r_i \mid r_{i-1})$$

$$\therefore R^{\#}\approx \arg\max_R \prod_{i=0}^{m} p(t_i \mid r_i)p(r_i \mid r_{i-1}) \text{.......E4}$$

$$\Leftrightarrow R^{\#}\approx$$

$$-\arg\min_R \sum_{i=0}^{m}\{\ln p(t_i \mid r_i)+\ln p(r_i \mid r_{i-1})\} \text{......E5}$$

E5 is simpler for computation than E4.

Now, we can find the most possible token sequence with equation E5. It's a simple application of Viterbi Algorithm.

The final recognition through maximum pattern matching is not performed on the original texts but performed on roles sequence. The person patterns are {BBCD, BBE, BBZ, BCD, BE, BG, BXD, BZ, CD, FB, Y, XD}. Before matching, we should split the tokens whose roles are like "U" or "V"(which indicate that the related token is generated by internal components and the outside contexts of unknown words) into two proper parts. Such a processing can recall more unknown words and reduce the overlapping collision. As for the above sample sentence, the final roles sequence after splitting is "AAK*BCD*M*BCD*LAAAAAA". Therefore, we can identify the possible person names "周恩来" and "邓颖超" according to the recognition pattern "BCD".

1.3 Automatic acquisition of roles knowledge

As described in E5, the tag sequence $R^{\#}$ is decided by two kinds of factors: $p(t_i \mid r_i)$ and $p(r_i \mid r_{i-1})$. $p(t_i \mid r_i)$ is the probability of a token t_i given the condition of being tagged with role r_i, while $p(r_i \mid r_{i-1})$ is the transitive probability from role r_{i-1} to role r_i. Both factors are useful lexical knowledge for tagging and final recognition. According to laws of large numbers, if the training corpus is large enough, we can acquire the roles knowledge as following:

$$p(t_i \mid r_i) \approx C(t_i,r_i)/C(r_i) \text{.................................. E6}$$

Where $C(t_i, r_i)$ is the count of token t_i being role r_i; and $C(r_i)$ is the count of role r_i.

$$p(r_i \mid r_{i-1}) \approx C(r_{i-1},r_i)/C(r_{i-1}) \text{...........................E7}$$

Where $C(r_{i-1},r_i)$ is the count of role r_{i-1} followed by role r_i.

$C(t_i,r_i)$, $C(r_i)$ and $C(r_{i-1},r_i)$ are extracted from corpus through a training process. The training corpus came from one-month news from the *People's Daily* with 2,305,896 Chinese characters, which are manually checked after word segmentation and POS tagging (It can be downloaded at icl.pku.edu.cn, the homepage of the Institute of Computational Linguistics, Peking University).

However, the corpus is tagged with the Part-Of-Speech set. Before training, the original POS tags should be converted to the proper roles by analysing every token in the sentence.

2 Algorithm and implementation

The unknown words recognition based on roles tagging has three main steps: automatic acquisition of roles knowledge from the corpus; roles tagging with Viterbi algorithm and unknown words recognition through maximum pattern matching.

Viterbi algorithm is a classic approach in statistics. It aims to select the optimum roles sequence with maximum possibility from all possible results. Our evaluation function for decision-making is E5 given in sub-section 1.2. Considering the length limitation of this paper, we skip the details.

Therefore, we only provide algorithms for roles knowledge learning. In the last part, the entire process of unknown words recognition will be listed.

2.1 Roles knowledge learning

Input: Corpus which is segmented and POS tagged

T: the type of unknown words;

R: Roles set of T

Output: $C(t_i,r_i)$, $C(r_i)$ and $C(r_{i-1},r_i)$

Algorithm:

(1) Get one sentence S from corpus C;

(2) Extract all tokens and POS tags from S;

(3) Convert all POS tags to roles in T after role analysis.

(4) Store the tokens whose role is not 'A' into the recognition lexicons of unknown words T, where 'A' is not internal components nor context role.

(5) Calculate the total number $C(t_i,r_i)$ of token t_i being role r_i. At the same time, count $C(r_i)$, which is the number of role r_i appearances.

(6) Sum $C(r_{i-1},r_i)$ which is the times of role r_{i-1} followed by role r_i.

(7) If no more sentences in the corpus C, exit; else go to (1)

First of all, we must explain step (3). Our corpus is tagged with POS and person, place or organization name are tagged with 'nr', 'ns' or 'nt' respectively; Such POS are unique and different from noun. Transliterations can be extracted from words tagged with 'nr' or 'ns' and through analysing its component chars. So we can easily locate such kinds of words. Meanwhile, we can judge whether a word is unknown by looking it up in the core lexicon. Then we can identify roles of words according to their locality, which are before or following a particular unknown word.

Here we provide a sample sentence from our corpus like "本报/r 蚌埠/ns 1 月/t 1 日/t 电/n 记者/n 黄/nr 振中/nr 、/w 白/nr 剑峰/nr 报道/v". In step (2), we can extract tokens and tags like "本报"/ 'r'; "蚌埠"/ 'ns' and so on. When we train person recognition roles, firstly, we locate person name "黄/nr 振中/nr" and "白/nr 剑峰/nr" just by searching POS 'nr'; Secondly, judge whether they are unknown after looking them up in the core lexicon; At last we can tag unknown words component and their context near their locality. So the final roles after conversion are "本报/A 蚌埠/A 1 月/A 1 日/A 电/A 记者/K 黄/B 振/C 中/D 、/M 白/B 剑/C 峰/D 报道/L". Then we can train the parameters based on new segmentation and person recognition roles sequence.

In addition, we train every different kind of unknown word on the same corpus individually. That is: person roles, place roles and other roles are acquired respectively. Therefore, the unknown place recognition roles sequence of the above sentence may like "本报/K 蚌/B 埠/D 1 月/L 1 日/A 电/A 记者/K 黄/A 振中/A 、/A 白/A 剑峰/A 报道/A". Such a mechanism can greatly reduce the problem of sparse data.

2.2 The entire process of Unknown words recognition

Input: Original sentence S;

R: the roles set of unknown words;

P: pattern sets for recognition.

Output: Possible unknown words of type T.

Algorithm:

(1) Word segmentation (we segment words on sentence S with N-shortest paths method [Hua-Ping ZHANG, Qun LIU (2002)]);

(2) Tag tokens sequence with roles in set R using

Viterbi algorithm. Get the roles sequence $R^{\#}$ with maximum possibility.
(3) Split tokens whose role is like 'U' or 'V' in the person roles. These roles indicate that the internal components glue together with their context.
(4) Maximum match final roles sequence to the recognition patterns P and record their position.
(5) Generate the candidate unknown words according to the result of pattern matching.
(6) Exclude those candidates which are fit for the exclusive rules.(For example, Chinese person name can not include non-Chinese chars.)
(7) Output the possible unknown words.

Now, we take person recognition on the sentence "本报蚌埠 1 月 1 日电记者黄振中、白剑峰报道" as exemplification. In the first place, we can get the sequence "本报/蚌埠/ 1 月/ 1 日/电/记者/黄/振/中/、/白/剑/峰/报道/" after rough word segmentation; Then we tag it with Viterbi algorithm using person recognition roles lexicon and transitive array. So, the most probable roles sequence is "AAAAAK<u>*BCD*</u>M<u>*BCD*</u>L".Therefore, candidate perosn names "黄振中" and "白剑峰" can be recognized after maximum string matching.

3 Experiments and Discussions

Both close and open recognition test were conducted. In the close test, we tested our system within the training corpus, which is the knowledge base for recognition. Open test, however, is more realistic, because it is performed on arbitrary real texts outside the training corpus. The corpus in our experiments is from 2-months news in 1998 from *the People's Daily*.

In this paper, we only provide the recognition results of Chinese person and transliterations. The recognition of place names and other kind of unknown words can get similar performance.

3.1 Recognition experiment of Chinese person name

Test Type	Close	Open
Corpus (news date)	1.1-2.20	2.20-2.28
Corpus Size	14,446K	2,605K
Num of Chinese person names	21,256	3,149
Num of recognized person names	27,813	4,130
Num of correctly recognized names	20,865	2,886
Precision rate	75.02%	69.88%
Recalling rate	98.17%	91.65%
F-measurement	85.05%	79.30%

Table 2 Experiment results of Chinese person names recognition

In Tables 2, precision rate and recalling rate are defined as equations E6 and E7 respectively. In addition, F-measurement is a uniformly weighted harmonic mean of precision rate and recalling rate as shown in E8.

Precision rate=

$$\frac{\text{num of correctly recognized words}}{\text{num of recognized words}} \quad \text{........E6}$$

Recalling rate=

$$\frac{\text{num of correctly recognized words}}{\text{num of total unknown words}} \quad \text{........E7}$$

F-measurement =

$$\frac{\text{Recalling rate} \times \text{Precision rate} \times 2}{\text{Recalling rate} + \text{Precision rate}} \quad \text{........E8}$$

3.2 Recognition Experiments of transliterations

Test Type	Close	Open
Corpus (news date)	1.1-2.20	2.20-2.28
Corpus Size	14,446K	2,605K
Num of transliterations	9,059	1,592
Num of recognized transliterations	10,013	1,930
Num of correctly recognized transliterations	8,946	1,496
Precision rate	89.35%	77.52%
Recalling rate	98.75%	93.97%
F-measurement	93.85%	84.96%

Table 3 Results of transliterations recognition

3.3 Discussions

The traditional ways to test unknown words recognition is to collect sentences including unknown words and to make recognition experiments. Those sentences that haven't the type of unknown words will be excluded from experiments in the pre-processing. In our experiments, we just take the realistic corpus and make no filtering. Therefore, the precision rates may be lower but closer to the realistic linguistic environment than previous tests. We have made experiments in the traditional way and the precision rate can be improved by less than 15%. In a word, there is no comparable with precision rates of previous unknown words recognition experiment.

In addition, our experiments show that the unknown words recognition based on role tagging can achieve very high recalling rates. For such a problem, recalling is more essential than precision. Low recalling rate means that we have no chance to recognize many unknown words through any efforts in the following steps, although words recognized are mostly valid; However, precision rate can be greatly improved in other processes, such as POS tagging or sentence simple parsing. In our system ICTCLAS (Institute of Computing Technology, Chinese Lexical System), we can exclude most invalid unknown words during POS tagging. The precision rate of Chinese person names recognition can achieve over 95% after POS tagging while the recalling rate is not reduced.

Our approach is purely corpus-based. We all know that, in any usual corpus, unknown words are sparsely distributed. If we depend totally on the corpus, the problem of sparse data is inevitable. But in the fine-tuning of our system, we found some countermeasures and successfully solved the problem.

Lexical knowledge from linguists can be incorporated into the system. This does not mean that we fall back to the old ways. We just demand for those general rules about name formation to avoid apparent mistakes. As to person name recognition, there are several strict restrictions, such as the length of name, the order between surname and given name.

Except for enlarging the training corpus, we provide two more counteractions:

Firstly, a "best n" approach [Hua-Ping ZHANG, Qun LIU (2002)], which provides n (n>1) possible tag sequences with leading probabilities, is feasible. Usually the desired tag sequence could be re-targeted or constructed from the best n sequences. In this way, we improved the recalling rate at the cost of precision rate. But given a better recalling, we could remedy in latter stages of language processing. When 3 most probable sequences are employed, the recalling and precision of unknown words in ICTCLAS can be enhanced obviously.

The second resolution is training on a name library in addition to training on a corpus. As we all know, it's easier and cheaper to get a person name library or other special name libraries than to segment and tag a corpus. We could extract the inner components relations from the unknown words libraries, and then merge these data into the roles information from the original corpus. When the special name libraries were introduced, both precision and recalling rates can be improved.

Conclusion

The paper presents a one-for-all approach for Chinese unknown words recognition based on roles tagging. At first, we define roles set for every category of unknown words according to the function of tokens, such as internal component or contexts. Unknown words are recognized on roles sequence, tagged with the roles set using Viterbi algorithm. The knowledge about roles is extracted from the learning on corpus. Experiments on large size corpus verify that the approach based on role tagging is simple and applicable.

Acknowledgements

First of all, our thanks go to the Institute of Computational Linguistics, Peking University for providing the corpus. And we owe lots of thanks to our colleagues: Zougang, Li Jifeng, Li Sujian,Li Shengtao, Zhu Hailong, Zhao Hongchao, Wang Shuxi and Dr. Zhou Lixin. We would especially express gratitude to the chief scientist Bai Shuo.

References

K.Y. Liu (1999) *The Assessment to Automatic Word Segmentation and POS Tagging Software.* Proceedings of the 4th Conference on Chinese Computer Intelligent Interface and Application, Beijing.

Z. Luo and R. Song (2001) *Integrated and Fast Recognition of Proper Noun in Modern Chinese Word Segmentation.* Proceedings of International Conference on Chinese Computing 2001, Singapore, pp. 323-328.

H. Luo and Z. Ji (2001) *Inverse Name Frequency Model and Rules Based on Chinese Name Identifying.* In "Natural Language Understanding and Machine Translation", C. N. Huang & P. Zhang, ed., Tsinghua Univ. Press, Beijing, China, pp. 123-128.

R. Song (1993) *Person Name Recognition Method Based on Corpus and Rule.* In "Computational

Language Research and Development", L. W. Chen & Q. Yuan, ed., Beijing Institute of Linguistic Press.
H. Y. Tan *(1999) Chinese Place Automatic Recognition Research.* In "Proceedings of Computational Language ", C. N. Huang & Z.D. Dong, ed., Tsinghua Univ. Press, Beijing, China.
M.S. Sun *(1993) English Transliteration Automatic Recognition.* In "Computational Language Research and Development", L. W. Chen & Q. Yuan, ed., Beijing Institute of Linguistic Press.
Y.J. Lv, T. J. Zhao (2001) *Levelled Unknown Chinese Words Resolution by Dynamic Programming.* Journal of Chinese Information Processing. 15, 1, pp. 28-33.
X. H. Chen (1999) *One-for-all Solution for Unknown Word in Chinese Segmentation.* Application of Language and Character, 3.
Y. He (2001) *Identification of Unlisted Words on Transitive Probability of Monosyllabic Words.* In "Natural Language Understanding and Machine Translation", C. N. Huang & P. Zhang, ed., Tsinghua Univ. Press, Beijing, China, pp. 123-128.
Hua-Ping ZHANG, Qun LIU (2002) *Model of Chinese Words Rough Segmentation Based on N-Shortest-Paths Method.* Journal of Chinese Information Processing. 16, 5, pp. 77-83.
L. R.Rabiner (1989) *A Tutorial on Hidden Markov Models and Selected Applications in Speech Recognition.* Proceedings of IEEE 77(2): pp.257-286.
L.R. Rabiner and B.H. Juang, (Jun. 1986) *An Introduction to Hidden Markov Models.* IEEE ASSP Mag., Pp.4-166.

基于角色标注的中文未登录词自动识别研究[3]

张华平　刘 群　张 浩　程学旗
Email : zhanghp@software.ict.ac.cn
中国科学院计算技术研究所软件室
北京 2704 信箱海淀区中关村科学院南路 6 号，中国

摘要： 本文提出了一种基于角色标注的中文未登录词识别通用方法。角色指的是未登录词的内部组成成分、上下文以及句子中的其他部分。我们识别未登录词依据的是句子角色序列。首先，采取 Viterbi 算法对切分后的 Token 序列进行角色标注，这和词性标注类似。然后得到一个概率最大的角色序列，在此基础上，采取模式最大匹配识别未登录词。和角色相关的这些语言学知识可以从对语料库的训练学习当中抽取得到。作者做了几个识别实验，取得了较好的准确率和召回率，尤其是中国人名和音译名的识别。我们将基于角色标注识别未登录词的方法集成到了计算所汉语词法 ICTCLAS 系统，取得了较好的效果。实验结果表明：基于角色标注的未登录词识别方法是简单可行、令人满意的。

关键词:中文未登录词识别，角色标注，分词，Viterbi 算法

---

[1] We define unknown words to be those not included in the core lexicon and unable to be generated by FSA, such as person name, place name. But numeric or common time word is not unknown because they can generate by a simple FSA.

[2] Related research in this paper is supported by Foundation of National Key Basic Research Project (ID: G1998030507-4 and G1998030510).

[3] 本文有关研究得到国家重点基础研究项目(编号：G1998030507-4；G1998030510)资助。

Chinese Base-Phrases Chunking

Yuqi Zhang and Qiang Zhou

State Key Laboratory of Intelligent Technology and Systems
Department of Computer Science and Technology
Tsinghua University, Beijing, 100084, P.R.China

{zyq, zhouq}@s1000e.cs.Tsinghua.edu.cn

Abstract

This paper introduces new definitions of Chinese base phrases and presents a hybrid model to combine Memory-Based Learning method and disambiguation proposal based on lexical information and grammar rules populated from a large corpus for 9 types of Chinese base phrases chunking. Our experiment achieves an accuracy (F-measure) of 93.4%. The significance of the research lies in the fact that it provides a solid foundation for the Chinese parser.

1 Introduction

Recognizing simple and non-recursive base phrases is an important subtask for many natural language processing applications, such as information retrieval. Gee and Grosjean (Gee and Grosjean, 1983) showed psychological evidence that chunks like base phrases play an important role in human language understanding. CoNLL-2000's shared task identified many kinds of English base phrases, which are syntactically related non-overlapping groups of words (Tjong and Buchholz, 2000). The shared task has significantly heightened the progress in the techniques of English partial parsing. For Chinese processing, Zhao (1998) put forward a definition of Chinese baseNP that is a combination of determinative modifier and head noun (Zhao, 1998). Based on that research, Zhao et al. (2000) extended the concept of baseNP to seven types of Chinese base phrases. These base phrases may consist of words or other base phrases, but its constituents, in turn, should not contain any base phrases.

In this paper, we put forward the new definition of Chinese base phrases, which are simple and non-recursive, similar to the CoNLL-2000's shared task. The definition enables us to resolve most local ambiguities and is very useful for NLP tasks such as name entity recognition and information extraction.

We construct a hybrid model to recognize nine types of Chinese base phrases. Many researches in Chinese partial parsing (Zhou, 1996; Zhao, 1998; Sun, 2001) have shown that statistical learning is of great use for Chinese chunking, especially for large corpus. However, the lack of morphological hints in Chinese makes it necessary to use semantic and syntactic information such as context free grammar rules in Chinese processing. In our approach, viewing chunking as a tagging problem by encoding the chunk structure in new tags attached to each word, we use Memory-Based Learning (MBL) method to set a tag indicating type and position in a base phrase on each word. After which grammar rules are used to disambiguate the tags. Our test with a corpus of about 2 MB showed that the experiment achieves 94.4% in precision and 92.5% in recall.

2 Definitions of Chinese Base Phrases

The idea of parsing by chunks goes back to Abney (1991). In his definition of chunks in English, he assumed that a chunk has syntactic structure and he defined chunks in terms of major heads, which are all content words except those that appear between a function word f and the content word which f selects. A major head is the 'semantic' head (s-head) for the root of the chunk headed by it. However, s-heads can be defined in terms of syntactic heads. If the syntactic head h of a phrase P is a content word, h is also the s-head of P. If h is a function word, the s-head of P is the s-head of the phrase selected by h.

The research enlightens us about the definition of Chinese base phrases. In this paper, a Chinese base phrase consists of a single content word surrounded by a cluster of function words. The single content word is the semantic head of the base phrase. The forms of base phrases can be expressed as follows.

{Modifier} * + head + {complement}* or Coordinate structure

The components of 'modifier' and 'complement' are optional. A head could be a simple word as well as the structure of "modifier + head" or "head + complement", but not "modifier + head + complement". Coordinate structure could not consist of coordinate symbols such as comma and co-ordinating conjunction. The type of base phrases is congruent with its head's semantic information. In most cases, the type accords with the head's syntactical information, for example, when the head is a noun, the phrase is a noun phrase. However, when a head is a noun that denotes a place, the base phrase including that head is not a noun phrase, but a location phrase.

We consider 9 types of Chinese base phrases in our research: namely adjective phrase (ap), distinguisher phrase (bp), adverbial phrase (dp), noun phrase (np), temporal phrase (tp), location phrase (sp), verb phrase (vp), quantity phrase (mp), quasi quantity phrase (mbar). The inner grammar structures of every base phrase are very important too, but we will discuss that in another paper.

3 Overview

The frame of Chinese base phrase parsing is composed of two parts: one is the "Type and bracket tagging model", the other is the "Base phrases acquisition model" which consists of two modules which are "brackets matching "and "correct the types of base phrases". (See figure 1.) The input to the system is a sequence of POS. In the "Predict the phrase boundary" module, we predict the type, which each word belongs to, and the position of each word in a base phrase with Memory-Based Learning (MBL)(Using the software package provided by Tilburg University.). And the result is expressed as a pair formed by base phrase type and position information. Because our Chinese base phrases are non-recursive and non-overlapping, the left and right boundaries of base phrases must match with each other which means they should be a pair and alternative. However, the errors involving in the first part will lead to incorrect base phrases because the boundaries do not match, for example "[…[…]". In the second part, grammar rules that indicate the inner structures of base phrases are used to resolve the boundary ambiguities. Furthermore, it also takes lexical information into account to correct the type mistakes.

The corpus used in the experiment includes 7606 sentences. It comes from the Chinese Balance Corpus including about 2000 thousand words with four types: literature (44%), news (30%), academic article (20%) and spoken Chinese (6%). These 7606 sentences are split into 6846 training sentences and 760 held out for testing.

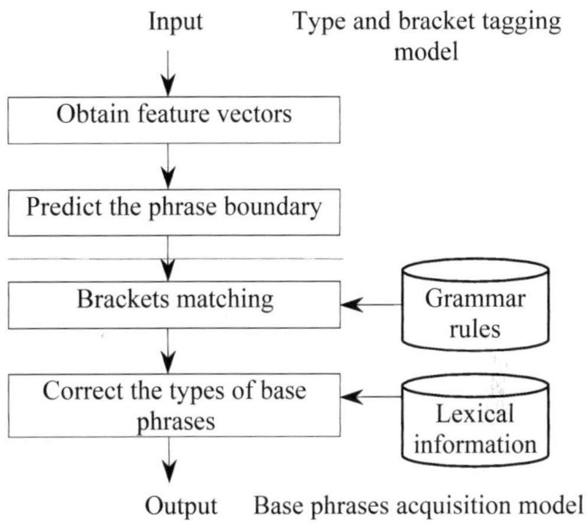

Figure 1: system overview

4 Predicting the phrase boundaries with MBL

Memory-Based Learning (MBL) is a classification based, supervised learning approach: a memory-based learning algorithm constructs a classifier for a task by storing a set of examples. Each example associates a finite number of classes. Given a new feature vector, the classifier extrapolates its class from those of the most similar feature vectors in memory (Daelemans et, al., 1999). The input to the "Predict the phrase boundary" module is some feature vectors, which compose of a sequence of POS. The solution of the module is to find $< r_i, c_i >$ (Wojciech and Thorsten, 1998), a duple formed by a type tag and a boundary tag for each word t_i. Here r_i indicates the boundary tag, while c_i denotes the type tag. $c_j \in \{np, vp, ap, dp, sp, tp, bp, mp, mbar, -\}$ ("-" denotes the word is not in any type of base phrases.) $r_i \in \{L, R, I, O, LR\}$ The r_i indicates the position of the word in a base phrase as shown below:

'L': the left boundary, 'R': the right boundary,

'I': the middle position, 'O': outside any base phrases, 'LR': the left and right boundary.

What information is used to represent data in feature vectors is an important aspect in MBL algorithms. We tried many feature vectors with various lengths. And it is interesting to note that the feature window is not the bigger the better. When the feature window is (-2, +2) in the context, the result is the best. So the feature vector in the experiment is: (POS-2, POS-1, POS0, POS+1, POS+2). The pattern describes the combination of feature vector and result duple $< r_n c_m >$ $0 \le n \le 4, 0 \le m \le 9$:

(POS-2, POS-1, POS0, POS+1, POS+2, $< r_n c_m >$).

For the experiment in the first step, we use [1]*TiMBL*, an MBL software package developed in the ILK-group (Daelemans et, al., 2001). The results of phrase boundary prediction with MBL shows in table 1.

Table1: The result of word boundary prediction

	Precision for$< r_n c_m >$	Recall For$< r_n c_m >$
np	92.27%	93.61%
vp	90.40%	89.65%
sp	75.15%	48.41%
tp	82.87%	71.62%
ap	93.52%	91.89%
bp	92.60%	76.38%
dp	97.56%	97.63%
mp	93.90%	92.38%
mbar	74.15%	72.26%
Total1	91.90%	91.65%
-	97.85%	98.41%
Total2	93.83%	93.83%

Table 1 shows that there is much difference between the results of various types of base phrases. The precisions and recalls of np, vp, mp, ap and dp are all almost over 90%. Comparatively, the results of sp, tp, bp and mbar are much lower, especially their recalls. This is due to some resemblances between sp, tp and np in Chinese syntactical grammars. Sp and tp may be considered as belong to NP, however, in the definition of Chinese base phrases, sp, tp and np are defined separately for the semantic difference. And the separation can also help in other tasks such as proper noun identification, information retrieval etc.

[1]*TiMBL* is a software bag about many MBL algorithms. It can be download free from http://ilk.kub.nl/

5 Obtaining Chinese base phrases

5.1 The errors in phrase boundary prediction

There are three types of errors in the results of first processing model.

(1) Boundary ambiguity: the r_i 's mistakes will cause the multiple choices regarding the boundaries. For example: "{np 这/rN } 一/m 创举/n }，/， 对/p {np 后世/t {np 针灸/n } 的/u {np 发展/vN 影响/vN } {ap 很/dD 大/a } 。/。". (Please pay attention to the '__' part.) There are altogether three modalities: "{ c_m …{ c_m …}", "{ c_m …}…}" and "{ c_m …{ c_m …}…}". These are caused by the redundancy and absence of boundaries.

(2) The type mistake of base phrases: For example: in the sentence of "{np 藏医/n } {dp 基本上/d } {vp 是/vC } {np 青藏高原/nS } 上/f {tp 藏族/nR 人民/n } 在/p…", the parser mistakes the type of "{ 藏族/nR 人民/n }" ,which is np, for tp. This error type commonly appears between sp, tp and np, as well as mbar and mp.

(3) Boundaries absence: For example, in the sentence of "{vp 包括/v } {np 内服/n } 、/、 {np 外用/n 药物/n } 以及/c {vp 放血/v }", "{np 外用/n 药物/n }" should be "{np 外用/n } {np 药物/n }". It is very difficult to correct this type of errors because the boundary distribution accords with the definition of Chinese base phrases. The left and right boundaries alternate with each other. Therefore, it is very difficult to find the errors in the sequence from the modalities.

5.2 Obtaining the whole base phrases with Grammar rules

With the bracket (boundary) representation, incorrect bracket will be generated but these will be eliminated in the bracket combination process. In the experiment, we attempt to apply grammar rules that represent the inner structures of Chinese base phrases to get rid of the boundary ambiguities. These grammar rules are derived from the corpus. On the other hand, boundary predictions can find many base phrases that do not accord with the limited grammar rules.

Figure 2 shows the main strategy of how to use the grammar rules. When if ()>1, there are more

Step 1: Finding the sequence where the errors appear. The sequences are three types: "{…{…}", "{…}…}", "{…{…}…}".

Step 2: if (the number of sequences of POS in a pair of matched boundaries according with the grammar rules) >1
then {Select the boundaries that make the sequence longest}

Step 3: if (the number of sequences of POS in a pair of combined boundaries according with the grammar rules) =1
if (Only the sequence with the shortest length accords with the grammar rules).
then { Find partitions such as conjunctions, localizers, punctuations and some prepositions between the ambiguous boundaries in sequences;
if (The partitions exist)
then {Add boundaries to generate whole base phrases according to the partitions}
}

Figure 2: The Algorithm of Matching Boundaries

than one pair of combined brackets in which the sequences accord with the grammar rules. We are apt to choose the longest possible because the shorter sequences appear more in the corpus. The longer the sequence, the more weight it should carry. When there is only the shorter sequence according with grammar rules, it is more possible to be the correct one. In this case, one or more boundaries will be left. They often need some other boundaries to match, so we try to retrieve some missing boundaries through the partitions in the sentences that should not belong to any base phrases. These partitions are the marks of base phrase boundaries. If we find these partitions between two ambiguous boundaries, we will know where to place the new boundary.

5.3 Correct the type mistake with lexical information

In the Chinese language, some POS sequences may belong to different types. For example, "{vN n}" could be np, sp or tp. These sequences often appear in np, sp, tp, mp and mbar. It is difficult to know its right type even with the grammar rules, as we have done in section 5.2. In order to resolve this problem, we attempt to use lexical information because it implies semantic information to some extent.

The lexical information is distinctive between mp and mbar. mbar is often composed of numbers such as "1200" and numbers in Chinese such as "四". The lexical information between tp and np is also obvious, such as "时候", "时代" and "世纪" etc. For sp and np, the words are "地区", "流域" etc.

5.4 Experimental results

The simplest bracket combination algorithm is very strict: it only uses adjacent brackets if they appear next to each other in the correct order (first open and then close) without any intervening brackets. The result of the algorithm is shown in table 2, as the baseline of the boundary combination experiment.

Table 2: The base-line result

	Precision	Recall	F_M
Np	93.9%	86.1%	89.8%
Vp	90.6%	86.2%	88.4%
Sp	75.5%	47.7%	58.4%
Tp	85.4%	70.2%	77.0%
Ap	93.4%	83.4%	88.1%
Bp	93.4%	71.3%	80.9%
dp	97.7%	94.0%	95.8%
mp	92.0%	85.3%	88.5%
mbar	-------	0	-------
Total	92.9%	85.7%	89.2%

Table 3: The result of disambiguation with grammar rules

	Precision	Recall	F_M
np	94.3%	91.9%	93.1%
vp	95.0%	94.2%	94.6%
sp	73.6%	50.9%	60.2%
tp	84.9%	73.8%	79.0%
ap	93.5%	89.7%	91.5%
bp	91.6%	79.4%	85.0%
dp	97.6%	98.1%	97.8%
mp	86.7%	90.9%	88.7%
mbar	63.6%	12.6%	21.1%
Total	93.9%	92.0%	92.9%

From the table 2, we could see the recalls are commonly low. We change another strategy to obtain the whole base phrases as described in section 5.2. The result of using the grammar rules is shown in table 3.

With the help of grammar rules, all kinds of base phrases improved their f-measures though the precisions or recalls of some types decrease slightly. Comparing with the baseline results in table 2, all the recalls increase significantly. However, the recalls of sp, tp and mp still do not satisfy us. There are more than twenty structures of np which also belong to tp or sp. Except in the case where mp and mbar have the same structure {m}, they are easily distinguished in other structures. (Mbar is always composed of numerals and mp always ends with a quantifier.) In order to distinguish tp from np, sp from np and mbar from mp, we use lexical information for the type disambiguation. The results are shown in table 4.

Table 4: The result after using lexical information

	Precision	Recall	F_M
np	95.0%	91.9%	93.5%
vp	95.0%	94.3%	94.6%
sp	69.2%	71.3%	70.2%
tp	79.8%	84.1%	81.9%
ap	93.1%	90.0%	91.5%
bp	91.6%	79.4%	85.0%
dp	97.6%	98.1%	97.8%
mp	93.4%	90.9%	92.1%
mbar	67.6%	54.1%	60.1%
Total	94.4%	92.5%	93.4%

From the table 4, we could see improvement in all the results (precisions and recalls) of mp and mbar. It shows that the lexical information is effective for distinguishing between them. On the contrary, although the f-measures of np and sp increase, their precisions decline. Thus, those words marking tp and sp are not appropriate for disambiguation. We could see the effect of lexical information is limited because it is difficult to find the words that could distinguish different types of base phrases.

6 Conclusions

The experiment on identifying Chinese base phrases shows that the definition of Chinese base phrases is suitable for parsing. It shows good results and the efficiency of the proposed approach in simplifying sentence structures. Many tasks such as chunking on high level could benefit from this.

With the system described here, we get 9 types of Chinese base phrases, and acquire high precisions and recalls on most types of base phrases. The results of the experiment also show that the use of grammar rules is necessary. Grammar rules have effects on boundary disambiguation particularly. The lexical information is effective in distinguishing between mbar and mp.

Acknowledgements

This work was supported by the National Science Foundation of China (Grant No. 69903007), National 973 Foundation (Grant No. 1998030507) and National 863 Plan (Grant No. 2001AA114040).

References

Abney, Steven. (1991) Parsing by chunks. In Berwick, Abney, and Tenny, editors, *Principle-Based Parsing.* Kluwer Academic Publishers.

Erik F. Tjong Kim Sang and Sabine Buchholz. (2000). "Introduction to CoNLL-200 Shared Task: Chunking". *Proceedings of CoNLL-2000 and LLL-2000.* Lisbon, Portugal. 127-132.

J. P. Gee and F. Grosjean (1983) Performance structures: A psycholinguistic and linguistic appraisal. *Cognitive Psychology*, 15:411-458

Sun Honglin (2001) A Content Chunk Parser for Unrestricted Chinese Text, Dissertation for the degree of Doctor of Science, Peking University.

Walter Daelemans, Jakub Zavrel, Ko van der Sloot (2001) TiMBL:Tilburg Memory-Based Learner version 4.0 Reference Guide. http://ilk.kub.nl/downloads/pub/papers/ilk0104.ps.pz.

Wojciech Skut and Thorsten Brants (1998) Chunk Tagger, Statistical Recognition of Noun Phrase, In *ESSLLI-98 Workshop on Automated Acquisition of Syntax and Parsing*, Saarbrvcken.

Zhao Jun (1998) The research on Chinese BaseNP Recognition and Structure Analysis, Dissertation for the degree of Doctor of Engineering, Tsinghua University.

Zhao et al., (2000) Tie-jun ZHAO, et al. "Statistics Based Hybrid Approach to Chinese Base Phrase Identification", In *Proceedings of the Second Chinese Language Processing Workshop, ACL 2000*, 73-77.

Zhou, Qiang (1996). Phrase Bracketing and Annotating on Chinese Language Corpus, Ph.D. dissertation, Peking University.

Learning Rules for Chinese Prosodic Phrase Prediction

†Zhao Sheng ‡Tao Jianhua §Cai Lianhong
Department of Computer Science and Technology
Tsinghua University, Beijing, 100084, China
†szhao00@mails.tsinghua.edu.cn {‡jhtao, §clh-dcs}@tsinghua.edu.cn

Abstract

This paper describes a rule-learning approach towards Chinese prosodic phrase prediction for TTS systems. Firstly, we prepared a speech corpus having about 3000 sentences and manually labelled the sentences with two-level prosodic structure. Secondly, candidate features related to prosodic phrasing and the corresponding prosodic boundary labels are extracted from the corpus text to establish an example database. A series of comparative experiments is conducted to figure out the most effective features from the candidates. Lastly, two typical rule learning algorithms (C4.5 and TBL) are applied on the example database to induce prediction rules. The paper also suggests general evaluation parameters for prosodic phrase prediction. With these parameters, our methods are compared with RNN and bigram based statistical methods on the same corpus. The experiments show that the automatic rule-learning approach can achieve better prediction accuracy than the non-rule based methods and yet retain the advantage of the simplicity and understandability of rule systems. Thus it is justified as an effective alternative to prosodic phrase prediction.

1 Introduction

Prosodic phrase prediction or prosodic phrasing plays an important role in improving the naturalness and intelligence of TTS systems. Linguistic research shows that the utterance produced by human is structured in a hierarchy of prosodic units, including phonological phrase, intonation phrase and utterance. (Abney, 1995) But the output of text analysis of TTS systems is often a structure of syntactic units, such as words or phrases, which are not equivalent to the prosodic ones. Therefore the object of prosodic phrasing is to map the syntactic structure into its prosodic counterpart.

A lot of methods have been introduced to predict prosodic phrase in English text such as Classification and Regression Tree (Wang and Hirschberg, 1992), Hidden Markov Model (Paul and Alan, 1998). For Chinese prosodic phrasing, the traditional method is based on handcrafted rules. Recurrent Neural Network (Ying and Shi, 2001) as well as POS bigram and CART based methods (Yao and Min, 2001) is also experimented recently. Due to the difference in training corpus and evaluation methods between researchers, these results are generally less comparable.

In this paper, a rule-learning approach is proposed to predict prosodic phrase in unrestricted Chinese text. Rule-based systems are simple and easy to understand. But handcrafted rules are usually difficult to construct, maintain and evaluate. Thus two typical rule-learning algorithms (C4.5 induction and transformation-based learning) are employed to automatically induce prediction rules from examples instead of human. Generally speaking, automatic rule-learning has two obvious advantages over the previous methods:

1) Statistical methods like bigram or HMM usually need large training corpus to avoid sparse data problem while rule-learning doesn't have the restriction. In the case of prosodic phrase prediction, the corpus with prosodic labelling is often relatively small. Rule-learning is just suitable for this task.
2) CART, RNN or other neural network methods have good learning ability but the learned knowledge is represented as trees or network weights, which are not so much understandable as rules.

Once rules are learned from examples, they can be analyzed by human to check if they agree with the common linguistic knowledge. We can add prediction rules converted from our linguistic knowledge to the rule set, which is especially useful when the training corpus doesn't cover wide enough phenomena of prosodic phrasing. Furthermore, we can try to interpret and understand rules learned by machine so as to enrich our linguistic knowledge. Hence rule-learning also helps us mine knowledge from examples.

Since features related to prosodic phrasing come from various linguistic sources, several comparative experiments are conducted to select the most effective features from the candidates. The paper also suggests general evaluation parameters for prosodic phrase prediction. With these parameters, our methods are compared with RNN and bigram based statistical methods on the same corpus. The experiments show that the automatic rule-learning approach can achieve better prediction accuracy than the non-rule based methods and yet retain the advantage of the simplicity and understandability of rule systems. The paper proceeds as follows. Section 2 introduces the rule-learning algorithms we used. Section 3 describes prosodic phrase prediction and its evaluation parameters. Section 4 discusses the feature selection and rule-learning experiments in detail. Section 5 reports the evaluation results of rule based and none-rule based methods. Section 6 presents the conclusion and the view of future work.

2 Rule Learning Algorithms

Research on machine learning has concentrated in the main on inducing rules from unordered set of examples. And knowledge represented in a collection of rules is understandable and effective way to realize some kind of intelligence. C4.5 (Quinlan, 1986) and transformation-based learning (Brill, 1995) are typical rule-learning algorithms that have been applied to various NLP tasks such as part-of-speech tagging and named entity extraction etc.

Both algorithms are supervised learning and can be used to induce rules from examples. But they also have difference from each other. Firstly the C4.5 rule induction is a completely automatic process. What we need to do is to extract appropriate features for our problem. As to transformation-based learning (henceforth TBL), transformation rule templates, which determine the effectiveness of the acquired rules, have to be designed manually before learning. Thus TBL can only be viewed as a semi-automatic method. Secondly the induction of C4.5 rules using a divide-and-conquer strategy is much faster than the greedy searching for TBL ones. In view of the above facts, C4.5 rules are induced from examples first in our experiments. And then the rules are used to guide the design of rule templates for TBL. See section 4.8 for detail.

3 Prosodic Phrase Prediction

3.1 The Methodology

Linguistic research has suggested that Chinese utterance is also structured in a prosodic hierarchy, in which there are mainly three levels of prosodic units: prosodic word, prosodic phrase and intonation phrase (Li and Lin, 2000).. Figure 1 shows the prosodic structure of a Chinese sentence. In the tree structure, the non-leaf nodes are prosodic units and the leaves are syntactic words. A prosodic phrase is composed of several prosodic words, each of which in turn consists of several syntactic words. Since intonation phrase is usually indicated by punctuation marks, we only need to consider the prediction of prosodic word and phrase.

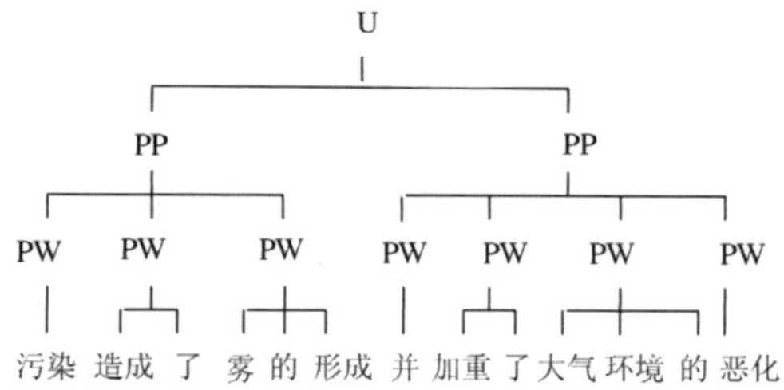

Figure 1: Two-level prosodic structure tree (U for intonation phrase, PP for prosodic phrase, PW for prosodic word)

Suppose we have a string of syntactic words i.e. $w_1, w_2, \ldots w_n$, the boundary between two neighbouring words is represented as $< w_i - w_{i+1} >$. There are total three types of boundaries labelled as B_0 (w_i, w_{i+1} are in the same prosodic word), B_1 (the words are in the same prosodic phrase, but not the same prosodic word), or B_2 (the words are in different prosodic phrases) respectively. Thus prosodic phrase prediction is to predict such boundary labels, which can be viewed as a classification task. We believe these labels are determined by the contextual linguistic information around the boundary. If we have a speech corpus with prosodic labelling, features related to prosodic phrasing can be extracted at each boundary and combined with the corresponding boundary labels to establish an example database. Then rule-learning algorithms are executed on the database to induce rules for predicting boundary labels.

3.2 Evaluation Parameters

As a classification task, prosodic phrase prediction should be evaluated with consideration on all the classes. The rules induced from examples are applied on a test corpus to predict the label of each boundary. The predicted labels are compared with labels given by human, which are thought to be true, to get a confusion matrix as follows:

True labels	Predicted labels		
	B_0	B_1	B_2
B_0	C_{00}	C_{01}	C_{02}
B_1	C_{10}	C_{11}	C_{12}
B_2	C_{20}	C_{21}	C_{22}

Table 1: Confusion matrix

C_{ij}s are the counts of boundaries whose true label are B_i but predicted as B_j. From these counts, we can deduce the evaluation parameters for prosodic phrasing.

$$\mathrm{Re}\,c_i = C_{ii} / \sum_{j=0}^{2} C_{ij} \qquad (i = 0,1,2) \tag{1}$$

$$\mathrm{Pr}\,e_i = C_{ii} / \sum_{j=0}^{2} C_{ji} \qquad (i = 0,1,2) \tag{2}$$

$$F_i = 2 * \mathrm{Re}\,c_i * \mathrm{Pr}\,e_i / (\mathrm{Re}\,c_i + \mathrm{Pr}\,e_i)(i = 0,1,2) \tag{3}$$

$$Acc_1 = \sum_{i=0}^{2} C_{ii} / \sum_{j=0}^{2} \sum_{i=0}^{2} C_{ij} \tag{4}$$

$$Acc_2 = (\sum_{j=1}^{2} \sum_{i=1}^{2} C_{ij} + C_{00}) / \sum_{j=0}^{2} \sum_{i=0}^{2} C_{ij} \tag{5}$$

$\mathrm{Re}c_i$ defines the recall rate of boundary label B_i. $\mathrm{Pr}\,e_i$ defines the precision rate of B_i. F_i is a combination of recall and precision rate, suggested by (Rijsbergen, 1979). Acc_1 is the overall accuracy of all the labels. If we merge B_1 and B_2 into one label, which can be viewed as the prediction of prosodic word boundary, Acc_2 defines the overall accuracy of this case.

4 Experiments

4.1 The Corpus

In our experiments, the speech corpus of our TTS system is used for training and testing. The corpus has 3167 sentences, which are randomly selected from newspaper and read by a radiobroadcaster. We manually labelled the sentences with two-level prosodic structure by listening to the record speech. For example, the sentence in Figure 1 is labelled as "污染/B_1 造成/B_0 了/B_1 雾/B_0 的/B_0 形成/B_2 并/B_1 加重/B_0 了/B_1 大气/B_0 环境/B_0 的/B_1 恶化/B_2". Preliminary tests show that manually labelling can achieve a high consistency rate among human. Therefore it is reasonable to make the manually labelled results as the target of learning algorithms.

The sentences of the corpus are also processed with a text analyzer, where Chinese word segmentation and part-of-speech tagging are accomplished in one step using a statistical language model. The segmentation and tagging yields a gross accuracy rate over 94%. The output of the text analyzer is directly used as the training data of learning algorithms without correcting segmentation or tagging errors because we want to train classifiers with noisy data in the real situation.

Here are some statistical figures about the corpus. There are 56446 Chinese characters in the corpus, which constitute 37669 words. The number of prosodic word boundaries is 16194 and that of prosodic phrase ones is only 7231. The average length of syntactic word, prosodic word, prosodic phrase and sentence are 1.5, 2.4, 7.8 and 17.0 in character, respectively.

4.2 Candidate Features

Feature selection is crucial to the classification of prosodic boundary labels. Linguistic information around the word boundary is the main source of features. The features may come from different levels including syllable, word, phrase, sentence level. And the type of features may be phonetic, lexical, syntactic, semantic or pragmatic. Which features have most close relation with prosodic phrasing and how to represent them are still open research problems. In our approach, we decide to list all the possible features first and figure out the most effective ones by experiments. The features we currently consider are presented in the following.

4.2.1 Phonetic information

Chinese is well known as a monosyllabic, tonal language. And phonetic study shows sound will change in continuous speech because of context or prosodic structure. Retroflex, neutral tone and tone sandhi are important phonetic phenomena that cause sound variation. (Li and Lin, 2000). Thus phonetic information about phone and syllable is related to prosodic phasing. There are too many tonal syllables (about 1300) in Chinese to consider. Instead, the initials and finals of the syllables (total about 60) near a word boundary are taken into accounts, which are represented as *SYIF* in the following text.

Similarly the tones of the syllables, denoted by *TONE*, are also included as phonetic features.

4.2.2 Lexical information

Words in natural language have different occurrence frequency. And words that have high occurrence frequency may be especially important to prosodic phrasing (e.g. some functional words in Chinese, "的", "和" etc). Therefore lexical word is treated as a candidate feature, represented as *WORD*.

4.2.3 Syntactic information

Syntactic information has close relation with prosodic structure. *POS*, which denotes part-of-speech of words, is a basic syntactic feature much easier to obtain with automatic POS taggers. And it has been widely adopted in previous researches. Since POS tag sets varies with taggers, we try to determine the best one for predicting prosodic phrase by experiments.

4.2.4 Other information

From the statistical figures of the corpus, both prosodic word and phrase have limitation in length. The length of syntactic word (*WLEN*), the length of the sentence in character (*SLENC*) and word (*SLENW*) are considered as length features. In HMM-based methods, the chain of boundary labels in a sentence is supposed to conform to Markov assumption. And according to experience, it is less possible for two boundaries with label B_2 to locate very close to each other. Thus the label of previous boundaries (*BTYPE*) and the distances from them to current position are also possible features.

4.3 Example Database

All of the possible features are extracted from the corpus at each boundary to establish an example database. Table 2 shows parts of the example entries of two word boundaries in Figure 1. Each row is a type of feature. The row name has a format of feature name plus a number. The number indicates which word the feature comes from. And the range of the number is limited by a window size. For example, *POS_0* denotes part-of-speech of the word just before the word boundary, *POS_-1* denotes that of the second word previous to the boundary and *POS_1* denotes that of the word just after the boundary. The rest may be deduced by analogy. *BTYPE_0* is the label of current boundary and also the target to be predicted.

Boundaries / Features	<污染—造成>	<形成—并>
SYIF_0	an	eng
SYIF_1	z	b
TONE_0	3	2
TONE_1	4	4
WORD_0	污染	形成
WORD_1	造成	并
POS_0	vn	v
POS_1	v	c
POS_-1	w	u
WLEN_0	2	2
WLEN_1	2	1
BTYPE_0	B_1	B_2

Table 2: Example database entries

4.4 Feature Selection Experiments

Once the example database is established, we can begin to induce rules from it with rule learners. If all the features were used in one experiment, the feature space would get too large to learn rules quickly. Moreover we want to eliminate less significant features from the database. A series of comparative experiments is carried out to figure out the effective features. C4.5 learner is used to perform the learning task in the following experiments.

4.4.1 Baseline experiment (No.1)

Since *POS* features are widely used, a baseline experiment is performed with only two *POS* features that are *POS_0* and *POS_1*. The *POS* tag set has total 30 tags from the tagger.

4.4.2 POS window-size (No.2-9)

The window size determines the number of words whose features are considered. Suppose the window size is *L+R*, which means the features of *L* words left to the boundary and *R* words right to it are used. We design experiments with the combination of different value of *L* and *R* to find the best window of *POS* features. The features in the window are denoted by *POS{-L+1, R}* in a range form.

4.4.3 POS set (No.10-11)

Experiments are conducted on three *POS* sets, which are *BSET*, *LSET* and *CSET*. *BSET* is the basic *POS* set from the tagger. *LSET* is an enlarged version of *BSET*, which includes the most frequent 100 words as independent tags. *CSET* is built with clustering technique. Each *POS* in the *BSET* is represented as a 6-dimension vector, whose components are the probabilities of the boundary labels after and before that *POS*. Then these vectors are clustered into 10 groups. The window size used is 1+1.

4.4.4 Other experiments (No.12-17)

WORDLEN and *SLEN* are added into the baseline system to investigate the importance of length features in No.12 and 13. *SYIF*, *TONE* features of syllables around the boundary are considered in No.14. Previous boundary labels (*BTYPE_-1*, *BTYPE_-2*) are tested in the experiments No.15 and 16. *WORD* features are used in No.17 to find if there exist some words that have special prosodic effects.

No.	Features	POS tag set	F_0	F_1	F_2	Acc_1	Acc_2
1	*POS{0,1}*	*BSET*	0.69	0.72	0.76	0.72	0.79
2	*POS{0,0}*	*BSET*	0.57	0.53	0.14	0.50	0.64
3	*POS{-1,0}*	*BSET*	0.55	0.59	0.37	0.54	0.68
4	*POS{0,2}*	*BSET*	0.70	0.72	0.76	0.72	0.79
5	*POS{-1,1}*	*BSET*	0.71	0.71	0.76	0.72	0.79
6	*POS{-1,2}*	*BSET*	0.71	0.70	0.75	0.71	0.79
7	*POS{-2,1}*	*BSET*	0.71	0.70	0.75	0.71	0.79
8	*POS{-2,2}*	*BSET*	0.70	0.70	0.75	0.71	0.79
9	*POS{-3,3}*	*BSET*	0.71	0.70	0.74	0.71	0.79
10	*POS{0,1}*	*LSET*	0.72	0.74	0.77	0.74	0.81
11	*POS{0,1}*	*CSET*	0.67	0.67	0.73	0.68	0.75
12	*POS{0,1},WLEN{0,1}*	*BSET*	0.81	0.77	0.76	0.79	0.86
13	*POS{0,1},WLEN{0,1},SLEN*	*BSET*	0.82	0.76	0.74	0.78	0.87
14	*POS{0,1},TONE,SYIF*	*BSET*	0.71	0.72	0.75	0.72	0.79
15	*POS{0,1},BTYPE_-1*	*BSET*	0.75	0.74	0.76	0.75	0.82
16	*POS{0,1},BTYPE_{-1,-2}*	*BSET*	0.75	0.73	0.76	0.74	0.82
17	*POS{0,1},WORD{0,1}*	*BSET*	0.64	0.72	0.72	0.70	0.78

Table 3: Results of feature selection (F_0, F_1, F_2, Acc_1, Acc_2 are defined in section 3.2)

4.5 Feature selection results

The results of these experiments are listed in Table 3. From the evaluation figures in the table, we can draw the following conclusions on the effect of the features on prosodic phrase prediction:

1) Part-of-speech is a basic and useful feature. A window size of 2+1 is already enough. Larger window size will greatly lengthen the time of training but make no significant improvement on the accuracy rate.
2) The largest POS set *LSET* performs better than smaller ones like *BSET* and *CSET*. That's because small POS sets lead to small feature space, which may be not big enough to distinguish the training examples.
3) Length features are beneficial to prosodic phrase prediction.
4) Phonetic features are less useful than what we think before.
5) Former boundary information is also useful. When training, the former and latter boundary labels are both known, but when testing, exact former boundary labels do not exist. We can use the boundary labels that are already predicted to help make decision on current label. Although the error prediction of former labels may lead to error of current prediction, the result shows the accuracy rate is improved.
6) *WORD* feature is not appropriate to use, since the using of it greatly enlarges the feature space and needs more training examples.

4.6 C4.5 Experiments

According to the feature selection results, we know some features are effective to prosodic phrase prediction but some are not. And the solely using of effective features doesn't result in a high enough accuracy rate. In order to improve the prediction accuracy, we combine the effective features such as *WLEN{-1, 1}*, *BTYPE{-1}*, *SLEN* and *POS{-1,1}* in *LSET* tag set together to induce C4.5 rules.

4.7 Examples of C4.5 Rules

As mentioned above, rule systems have the advantage of simplicity and understandability. We examine the rules learned by C4.5 and find they certainly reflect the usage of prosodic structure in some sense. Here are some rules followed by example sentences with the current boundary labels in bold:

1) if POS_1 == 了 then BTYPE_0 = B_0
   我/B_0 去/B_1 **参观/B_0** 了/B_1 动物园/B_2
2) if POS_1 == 的 then BTYPE_0 = B_0
   学校/B_0 的/B_1 环境/B_1 不错/B_2

3) if POS_0 == 不 then BTYPE_0 = B_0
肚子/B_1 **不/B_0** 饿/B_2
4) if POS_0 == v && POS_1 == 于 then BTYPE_0 = B_0
他/B_1 **生/B_0** 于/$B_1$1998 年/B_2
5) if POS_1 == c && WLEN_0 > 2 then BTYPE_0 = B_2
游击队/B_2 并/B_1 没有/B_1 解散/B_2
她/ B_1 并/B_0 不/B_1 想/B_0 来/B_2
6) if POS_-1 == n && POS_0 == 是 && BTYPE_-1 == B_0 then BTYPE_0 = B_2
中国/B_0 **是/B_2** 伟大/B_0 的/B_0 国家/B_2

Rule 1, 2 and 3 shows the special prosodic effect of functional words such as "了", "的", "不", which tends to adhere to prosodic words in the sentences. Rule 4 exemplifies that the syntactic structure "Verb+于" usually acts as a prosodic word. Rule 5 concerns the conjunction word, the boundary before which would be B_2 (prosodic phrase boundary) if the previous word had a length above 2. The B_2 boundary is thought to accentuate the word before the conjunction. Rule 6 deals with the structure "Noun+是". We can see that these rules coincide with the experience of prosodic phrasing by human.

4.8 TBL Experiments

A general TBL toolkit (Grace and Radu, 2001) is used in our TBL experiments. The analysis on C4.5 rules casts lights on the design of the transformation rule templates of TBL. Since the same features as C4.5 learning are used in the rule templates, linguistic knowledge, which has been embodied by C4.5 rules, should also be captured by transformation rule templates. Suppose a C4.5 rule, "if (*POS_0* == n && *POS_1* == u) then *BTYPE_0* = B_0", has a high prediction accuracy, it is reasonable to make this rule as an instantiation of TBL rule templates. Table 4 lists some of the rule templates used in TBL experiments.

POS_0 POS_1 => BTYPE_0
POS_-1 POS_0 POS_1 => BTYPE_0
BTYPE _0 POS_0 POS_1 => BTYPE_0
BTYPE _0 POS_-1 POS_0 POS_1 => BTYPE_0
POS_0 POS_1 WLEN_0 WLEN_1=> BTYPE_0
WORD_0 POS_0 POS_1 => BTYPE_0
WORD_0 POS_-1 POS_0 POS_1 => BTYPE_0
BTYPE_0 WORD_0 POS_0 POS_1=>BTYPE_0
……

Table 4: Rule templates for TBL

The left part of a rule template is a list of features, and the right is the target, *BTYPE_0*. For example, "*POS_0 POS_1 => BTYPE_0*", which is a short form of "if (*POS_0* == *X* && *POS_1* == *Y*) then *BTYPE_0* = *Z*", means if current *POS* were *X* and the next *POS* were *Y*, the boundary label would be *Z*. *X, Y, Z* are template variables. Let *X*=n *Y*=u *Z*=B_0, the template is instantiated into the C4.5 rule above.

Due to the mechanism of TBL rules, there exist rule templates like "*BTYPE_0 POS_0 POS_1 => BTYPE_0*", in which the former *BTYPE_0* is the label before applying the rule and the latter is after applying it. That's actually what transformation means. When training, the initial boundary labels are all set to B_1. At each step, the algorithm tries all the possible values for template variables to find an instantiated rule that can achieve the best score. When testing, the initial boundary labels are set the same way, and then transformation rules are applied one by one.

5 Evaluation Results

To evaluate the generalization ability of the acquired rules, 5-fold cross validation tests are executed on the corpus for both C4.5 and TBL. We reimplemented the RNN algorithm and POS bigram statistical model to predict prosodic word boundary on the same corpus for comparison. Since our corpus is not large enough for HMM training and the CART method is also decision-tree based as C4.5, we didn't realize them in our experiments. The evaluation results are shown in Table 5.

Both the C4.5 rules and the TBL rules outperform the RNN algorithm and POS bigram method because the overall accuracy rates Acc_2 of the rule based methods are higher. TBL achieves comparable accuracy with C4.5 induction, which demonstrates that the design of transformation rule templates is successful.

Comparing Acc_1 and Acc_2 in Table 5, we discover that prosodic word boundaries can be more accurately predicted than prosodic phrase ones. It can be explained as follows. Prosodic word is the smallest prosodic unit in the prosodic hierarchy, which has more relation with the word level features such as POS, word length etc. Prosodic phrase is a larger prosodic unit less related to word level features, thus it cannot be predicted accurately using these features.

Tests	Rec_0	Pre_0	F_0	Rec_1	Pre_1	F_1	Rec_2	Pre_2	F_2	Acc_1	Acc_2
C4.5	0.914	0.837	0.874	0.814	0.822	0.818	0.712	0.829	0.766	0.829	0.904
TBL	0.849	0.884	0.866	0.782	0.848	0.814	0.851	0.613	0.713	0.818	0.895
bigram	0.653	0.746	0.696	0.874	0.816	0.844	N/A	N/A	N/A	N/A	0.793
RNN	0.764	0.803	0.783	0.883	0.857	0.870	N/A	N/A	N/A	N/A	0.837

Table 5: Evaluation results

6 Conclusion and Future Work

In this paper, we describe an effective approach to generate rules for Chinese prosodic phrase prediction. The main idea is to extract appropriate features from the linguistic information and to apply rule-learning algorithms to automatically induce rules for predicting prosodic boundary labels. C4.5 and TBL algorithms are experimented in our research. In order to find the most effective features, a series of feature selection experiments is conducted. The acquired rules achieve a best accuracy rate above 90% on test data and outperform the RNN and bigram based methods, which justifies rule-learning as an effective alternative to prosodic phrase prediction.

But the problem of prosodic phrase prediction is far from solved. The best accuracy rate got by machine is still much lower than that by human. In our future work, the study on this problem will go more deep and wide. Other machine learning methods will be experimented and compared with C4.5 and TBL. Features from deep syntactic, semantic or discourse information will be paid more attention to (Julia and Owen, 2001). And the speech corpus will be enlarged to cover more types of text and speaking styles.

Acknowledgements

Our work is sponsored by 863 Hi-Tech Research and Development Program of China (No: 2001AA114072). We also would like to thank the anonymous reviewers of the First SigHAN Workshop for their comments.

References

Abney Steven. (1995) Chunks and dependencies: bringing processing evidence to bear on syntax. Computational Linguistics and Foundations of Linguistic Theory, CSLI.

Eric Brill. (1995) Transformation-Based Error –Driven Learning and Natural Language Processing: A Case Study in Part-of-Speech Tagging. Computational Linguistics 21(4):543- 565.

C.J. van Rijsbergen. (1979) Information Retrieval. Butterworths, London.

Grace Ngai and Radu Florian. (2001) Transformation-Based Learning in the Fast Lane. Proceedings of the 39th ACL Conference.

Julia Hirschberg, Owen Rambow. (2001) Learning Prosodic Features using a Tree Representation. Eruospeech2001.

Li Aijun, Lin Maocan. (2000) Speech corpus of Chinese discourse and the phonetic research. ICSLP2000.

Michelle Wang and Julia Hirschberg. (1992) Automatic classication of intonational phrase boundaries. Computer Speech and Language 6:175–196.

Paul Taylor and Alan W Black. (1998) Assigning phrase breaks from part-of-speech sequences. Computer Speech and Language v12.

Quinlan,J.R. (1986) Induction of decision trees. Machine Learning, 1(1):81-106.

Yao Qian, Min Chu, Hu Peng. (2001) Segmenting unrestricted chinese text into prosodic words instead of lexical words. ICASSP2001.

Zhiwei Ying and Xiaohua Shi. (2001) An RNN-based algorithm to detect prosodic phrase for Chinese TTS. ICASSP2001.

A Knowledge-based Approach to Text Classification

Zhu Jingbo
Institute of Computer Software & Theory
Northeastern University, Shenyang Liaoning,
P.R.China 110006
zhujingbo@yahoo.com

Yao Tianshun
Institute of Computer Software & Theory
Northeastern University, Shenyang Liaoning,
P.R.China 110006
tsyao@china.com

Abstract

The paper presents a simple and effective knowledge-based approach for the task of text classification. The approach uses topic identification algorithm named FIFA to text classification. In this paper the basic process of text classification task and FIFA algorithm are described in detail. At last some results of experiment and evaluations are discussed.

Keywords: FIFA algorithm, topic identification, text classification, natural language processing

Introduction

The text automatic classification method is based on the content analysis automatically to allocate the text into pre-determined catalogue. The methods of text automatic classification mainly use information retrieval techniques. Traditional information retrieval mainly retrieves relevant documents by using keyword-based or statistic-based techniques (Salton.G1989). Generally, three famous models are used: vector space model, Boolean model and probability model, based on the three models, some researchers brought forward extended models such as John M.Picrrc(2001), Thomas Bayer, Ingrid Renz,Michael Stein(1996), Antal van den Bosch, Walter Daelemans, Ton Weijters(1996), Manuel de Buenaga Rodriguez, Jose Maria Gomez-llidalgo, Belen Diaz-agudo(1997), Ellen Riloff and Wendy Lehnert(1994).

One central step in automatic text classification is to identify the major topics of the texts. We present a simple and effective knowledge-based approach to text automatic classification. The approach uses topic identification algorithm named FIFA to text classification. In this paper the basic process of text classification task and FIFA algorithm are described in detail. At last some results of experiment and evaluations are discussed.

1 Knowledge-based text classification

The principal process for the Knowledge -based text classification is illustrated as following:

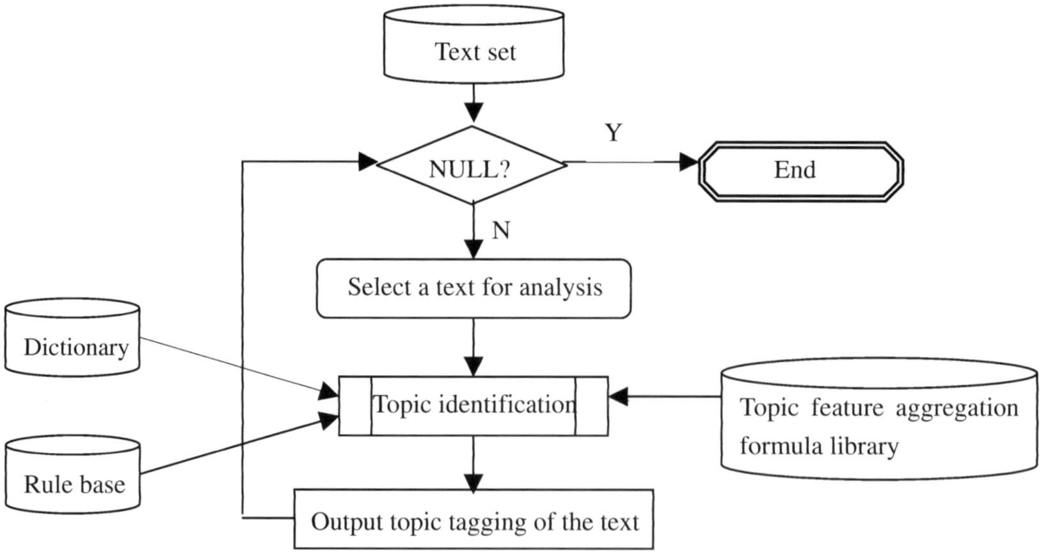

Figure 1 The principal process for the knowledge-based text classification

From the figure 1 we can know that the crucial technique of the text classification is the topic identification parser. The topic tagging of the text is identified as its catalogue.

2 Automatic Topic Identification

2.1 Feature Dictionary

The feature dictionary is mainly used to store some terms that can illustrate the topic feature concept, and we call these terms as "feature terms". The data structure of the feature dictionary is consist of word, POS, semantic, location and field attribute. Some examples of feature dictionary are described as following:

Feature terms	Attributes
会同县 HuiTong County	S(),,地名,地区(会同县),,国名(中国)省市(湖南)地区(怀化),领域(地理) S(),,LOCATION,LOCATION(HuitongCounty),,COUNTRY(China)PROVINCE (HuNan)CITY(HuaiHua),FIELD(geography)
中国银行 Bank of China	N(),,银行,机构(工商银行),,国名(中国),领域(银行)领域(金融) N(),,BANK,ORGANIZATION(bank),,COUNTRY(China),FIELD(bank) FIELD(finance)
作战情报中心 battle information center	N(),,情报中心,机构(作战情报中心),,,领域(情报)领域(军事) N(),,INFORMATION-CENTER,ORGANIZATION(battle information ceter),,,FIELD(information)FIELD(military)
三峡工程 Sanxia Project	N(),,工程,工程(三峡工程),,国名(中国),领域(水利) N(),,PROJECT,PROJECT(Sanxia Project),,COUNTRY(China), FIELD (irrigation)

Table 1: Some examples in the feature dictionary

Since 1996 we employed a semi-automatic method to acquire feature terms from pre-categorized corpus, and developed a feature dictionary including about 300,000 feature terms. There are about 1,500 kinds of semantic features, and about 1,000 kinds of field attributes to tag feature terms in this dictionary.

2.2 Topic Feature Distribution Computing Formula

According to the field attributes, frequencies and positions of feature terms, we could compute topic feature distribution. The computing steps are described as following:

1) According to the frequency and position of a feature term ft_i, we could compute the weight of the term ft_i. The computing formula is described as following:

$$p(ft_i) = \frac{freq(ft_i) + N_{title} + 0.5 \times N_{begin} + 0.5 \times N_{end}}{\sum freq(ft_i)} \qquad (1)$$

Where $p(ft_i)$ is the weight of the feature term ft_i. $freq(ft_i)$ is frequency of the feature term ft_i. N_{title} is times of the feature term ft_i occurring in the title. N_{begin} is times of the feature term ft_i occurring in the first sentence of a paragraph. N_{end} is times of the feature term ft_i occurring in the end sentence of a paragraph. $\sum freq(ft_i)$ is total frequency of the all feature terms in the text.

In the experiment we discovered that the feature terms in different position of a text have the different influence abilities on the topic features. So we take into account of this factor and use different experience coefficient in the weight computing formula of feature terms. In the formula (1), the coefficient of N_{title} is 1.0, the coefficient of N_{begin} is 0.5, and the coefficient of N_{end} is 0.5.

2) From the attribute of a feature term in the dictionary we could acquire its field attribute, in fact this field attribute is the topic feature illustrated by the feature term. The weight of a topic feature could be gotten by adding all weights of feature terms that illustrate the same topic feature. The more the feature terms illustrates the same topic feature, the higher the weight of the topic feature. The weight of a topic feature expresses its abilities illustrating the topic of the text. The weight $p(f_i)$ computing formula of a topic feature f_i is described as following:

$$p(f_i) = \sum_{ft_j \in f_i} p(ft_j) \qquad (2)$$

Where $p(f_i)$ is the weight of the topic feature f_i. $p(ft_j)$ is the weight of the feature term ft_j. $ft_j \in f_i$ shows feature term set illustrating the same topic feature f_i.

2.3 Topic Feature Aggregation Formula

The topic feature aggregation formula is described as following:

$$\xi_i : \beta(t_i) = \sum_{j=1}^{n} p(f_j) \times \mu(f_j) \qquad (3)$$

Where $\beta(t_i)$ is the weight of the topic t_i. f_j is the topic feature illustrating the topic t_i. $p(f_j)$ is the weight of the topic feature f_j. $\mu(f_j)$ is the coefficient of the topic feature f_j.

In the application system, we used automatic construction technique to construct a library, which called topic feature aggregation formula library that includes 105 topic feature aggregation formulas.

2.4 FIFA algorithm

Most of automatic text processing techniques uses topic identification as part of a specific task. The approaches to topic identification taken in these techniques can be summarized in three group: statistical, knowledge-based, and hybrid. The statistical approach (H.P.Luhn 1957, H.P.Edmundson 1969, Gerard Salton, James Allan, Chris Buckley, and Amit Singhal 1994) infers topics of texts from term frequency, term location, term co-occurrence, etc, without using external knowledge bases such as machine readable dictionaries. The knowledge-based approach (Wendy Lehnert and C. Loiselle 1989, Lin Hongfei 2000) relies on a syntactic or semantic parser, knowledge bases such as scripts or machine readable dictionaries, etc., without using any corpus statistics. The hybrid approach (Elizabeth D. Liddy and Sung H. Myaeng 1992, Marti A. Hearst 1994) combines the statistical and knowledge-based approaches to take advantage of the strengths of both approaches and thereby to improve the overall system performance.

This paper presents a simple and effective approach named FIFA (feature identification and feature aggregation) to text automatic topic identification. The core of algorithm FIFA is based on the equation:

Topic Identification = Topic Feature Identification + Topic Feature Aggregation.

Topic identification (TI) can be divided into two phases: topic feature identification (FI) and topic feature aggregation (FA).

1) Topic Feature Identification (FI): We use the term 'topic feature' to name the sub-topic in a text. In this phase algorithm FIFA identifies feature terms[1] in a text by dictionary-based and rule-based methods. The distribution of a topic feature is computed by attributes, frequencies and positions of topic feature terms.

2) Topic Feature Aggregation (FA): According to distribution of topic features, in this phase we use topic feature aggregation formulas to compute the weights of topics of a text, then the topic of a text could be determined by the weights computed. Topic feature aggregation formula will be introduced detailedly in the following chapters. Using machine-learning method, the topic feature aggregation formulas could be acquired automatically from pre-classified training corpus.

The topic identification algorithm FIFA could be described as following:

Step1: Text segmentation and POS tagging

Input: a raw text

1. Preprocessing phase: One major function is to recognize sentence boundaries, paragraph breaks, abbreviations, numbers, and other special tokens.
2. Segmentation phase: Employing maximal matching algorithm to segment a sentences into some words, and setting a word's POS set in machine readable dictionary as its POS tagging.
3. Disambiguation phase: Employing a technology based on ambiguous segmentation dictionary[2] to resolve the problem of word ambiguous segmentation, and base on rules to recognize the unknown words, such as name, location, company, organization noun etc.
4. POS tagging phase: Employing tri-gram based technology to POS tagging.

Output: a text with formats, segmentation and POS tagging

Step2: Topic feature identification

Input: a text with formats, segmentation and POS tagging

1. Feature-dictionary-based feature terms identification and tagging
   The core of the method is to use feature dictionary to realize the feature terms identification and tagging. If a term in the text is found in the dictionary, then we call this term as a feature term of the text and its

[1] Perhaps is a word, phrase, string, etc. According to need of the application system to determine the type of the feature term.

[2] Is a machine readable man-made dictionary which includes examples of ambiguous segmentation and its correct segmentation

field attribute in the dictionary is tagged as the topic attribute of the feature term.

2. Rule-based feature terms identification and tagging

   Because of the limitation of the feature dictionary, we could not identify all feature terms by feature-dictionary-based technique. To resolve the problem of the unknown feature terms, we use the technique of rule-based feature terms identification and tagging. There are two steps for the identification and tagging:

   1) We employ statistics-based approach to acquire some high-frequency terms from the text as analysis objects which length is composed of two or more words, and the frequency in the text should exceed two times.

   2) We employ rule-based technique to analyze the grammatical structure of the high frequency terms, and according to the grammatical structure of the terms and the attribute of the central word to estimate the field attribute of the term, which is tagged as the topic feature attribute of the term.

3. According to attributes, frequencies and positions of the feature terms to calculate the distribution of the topic feature of the text.

   Output: topic feature set ψ $(=\{(f_i,\beta_i)\})$ of the text. Where f_i is the ith text topic feature; β_i is the weight of the ith text topic feature f_i subjected to $\beta_i \in (0,1)$.

Step3: Topic feature aggregation

Input: The topic feature set ψ of the text.

1. Reading a formula ξ_i from the topic feature aggregation formula library, where the formula ξ_i is the aggregation formula of the topic t_i.
2. According to parameters in the topic feature set ψ, the weight of the topic t_i could be computed by the formula ξ_i.
3. If there are some other aggregation formulas in the library, then go to Step1, otherwise go to the next step.
4. Supposing the topic feature f_i in the set ψ $(=\{(f_i,\beta_i)\})$ as a topic, and β_i is the weight of the topic f_i. We sort the topic t_i and f_i by weight.

Output: Selecting the topic with maximal weight as topic tagging of the text.

Algorithm1: Topic identification algorithm FIFA

3. Experiment

To test the efficiency of the FIFA-based text automatic classification, and according to the pre-determined 10 topics we constructed a test corpus, which includes 1000 articles downloaded from the Internet. The composing of the test corpus is described as following:

Topic (abbreviation)	Number of articles
Sex (SEX)	100
Sex Healthy (SHE)	100
Fa Lun Gong (FLG)	100
Critical of Fa Lun Gong (CFLG)	100
Physical (PHY)	100
Military affairs (MIA)	100
Finance and economics (FAE)	100
Education (EDU)	100
Entertainment (ENT)	100
Computer (COM)	100
Total	1000

Table 2 The composing of the test corpus

Experiment 1: By classifying the test corpus, we could value the effect of the FIFA-based text automatic classification. The following figure 2 shows the results of text classification. Line ◆ represents precision percent while line ■ represents recall percent.

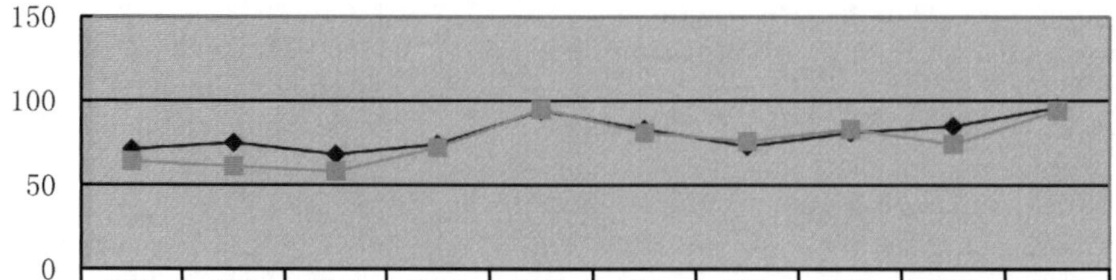

	SEX	SHE	FLG	CFLG	PHY	MIA	FAE	EDU	ENT	COM
precision%	71	75	68	74	94	83	73	81	85	96
recall%	64	61	58	72	95	81	76	83	74	94

Figure 2 The results of FIFA-based text classification

4. Conclusion

This paper presented a simple and effective approach to topic automatic identification. We use the topic identification approach for the task of text classification. The results of experiment show that a good precise and recall percent are achieved. In fact the topic identification approach called FIFA could be used not only as a stand-alone topic identification unit, but also in other text processing tasks such as text summarization, information retrieval, information routing etc.

References

Salton.G(1989), *Automatic Text Processing : The Transformation : Analysis and Retrieval of Information by Computer*, Addison-Wesley, Reading, Mass

John M.Picrrc(2001), *On the automated classification of web sites*, Linkoping Electronic Articles in Computer and Information Science, Vol.6, 2001, Sweden,

Thomas Bayer, Ingrid Renz,Michael Stein, Ulrich Kressel(1996), *Domain and language independent feature extraction for statistical text categorization*, proceedings of workshop on language engineering for document analysis and recognition - ed. by L. Evett and T. Rose, part of the AISB 1996 Workshop Series, April 96, Sussex University, England, 21-32 (ISBN 0 905 488628)

Antal van den Bosch, Walter Daelemans, Ton Weijters(1996), *Morphological analysis as classification: an inductive-learning approach*, Proceedings of NEMLAP-2, 2, July, 1996

Manuel de Buenaga Rodriguez, Jose Maria Gomez-llidalgo, Belen Diaz-agudo(1997), *Using WORDNET to complement training information in text categorization*, Second International Conference on Recent Advances in Natural Language Processing, 1997

Ellen Riloff and Wendy Lehnert(1994), *Information Extraction as Basis for High-precision Text Classification*, ACM Transactions on Information System, Vol12, No.3, July 1994

H.P.Luhn(1957). *A statistical approach to mechanized encoding and searching of literary information*. IBM Journal, p309-17, October 1957

H.P.Edmundson(1969). *New methods in automatic extracting*. Journal of the ACM, 16(2):264-85,1969

Gerard Salton, James Allan, Chris Buckley, and Amit Singhal(1994). *Automatic analysis, theme generation, and summarization of machine-readable texts*. Science, 264:1421-26, June 1994

Wendy Lehnert and C. Loiselle(1989). *An introduction to plot unit*. In David Waltz, editor, Semantic Structures-Advances in Natural Language Processing, p88-111, Lawrence Erlbaum Associates, Hillsdale, New Jersey, 1989

Lin Hongfei(2000), *Logic Model for Chinese Text Filtering*, Ph.D dissertation, Northeastern University, 2000.3

Elizabeth D. Liddy and Sung H. Myaeng(1992). *DR-LINK's linguistic- conceptual approach to document detection*. In Proceedings of the First Text Retrieval Conferece (TREC-1), p113-29, 1992

Marti A. Hearst(1994). *Context and Structure in Automated Full-Text Information Access*. PhD thesis, Computer Science Division, University of California at Berkeley, California, April 1994

AUTHOR INDEX

Association for Computational Linguistics
209 N. Eighth Street
Stroudsburg, Pennsylvania 18360

CURRAN ASSOCIATES INC
proceedings
.com

Workshop on Machine Translation and Parsing in Indian Languages

(MTPIL-2012)

Held at the 24th International Conference on Computational Linguistics (COLING 2012)

Mumbai, India
15 December 2012

ISBN: 978-1-62748-356-8